Discovering Africa's past

Basil Davidson

To the memory of Ken Forge and in gratitude for his inspiration.

LONGMAN GROUP LIMITED
Longman House, Burnt Mill, Harlow, Essex CM20 2JE, England and Associated Companies throughout the World.

First published 1978
Third impression 1984

ISBN 0 582 22048 3 Cased
0 582 22049 1 Paper

Printed in Hong Kong
by Sing Cheong Printing Co. Ltd.

ACKNOWLEDGEMENTS

We are grateful to the following for permission to reproduce photographs: A.A.A. Photo. Photo: Fievet, page 40; The American Numismatic Society, New York, page 67 *above and centre*; The Anglo American Corporation of South Africa Limited © page 19; Biblioteca Estense, Modena, page 106; British Library Board, page 72; Trustees of the British Museum, pages 48, 50, 58, 67 *below*, 85, 117, 121, 122, 128, 130, 133 and 158; Centro de Estudos Politicos & Sociais, page 34; The Commission for the Preservation of Historical Monuments and Relics, Rhodesia © page 143; Coptic Museum, Cairo, page 31; Photo: Basil Davidson, pages 12, 20, 23, 70, 170 and 208 *below*; Department of Information, Pretoria, South Africa, page 195; Edinburgh University Gazette, page 199; Fotomas, Barcelona, page 63; Gamma Diffusion, page 208 *above*; Ghana Information Services Department, Accra, page 202 *above*; illustrations on pages 45 and 46 from: *Discovering our African Heritage* by Basil Davidson. Publ. © Ginn & Co 1971 Boston, Mass; Robert Harding Associates. Photo: A. L. Durand, page 52; Historical Picture Service, pages 171 and 189; Photo: HOA-QUI, page 5; Hull Museum, Hull, page 177; 'T'oung Pao Archives', vol 34. Leiden, 1938, page 93; Mansell Collection, pages 83, 126, 173 and 179; *Nigeria*, No 90, 1966, page 200; Rhodesian Department of Information, page 3; Rex Features Limited, page 202 *below* and 203; Ronald Sheridan, pages 10 and 17; Rhodesia National Tourist Board, page 37; Photo: Science Museum, London, page 95; Staatliche Museen Preussischer Kulturbesitz, Berlin (West) Museum für Ägyptische Kunst, page 14; United Africa Co. Ltd. Photo: Jack Barker, pages 135 and 154; J. Vercoutter, page 24; Werner Forman Archive, pages 7, 22, 27, 29, 32, 61, 80, 97, 107, 137 and 146; Weidenfeld & Nicolson: *Africa History of a Continent* by Basil Davidson, page 109.

Contents

Introduction

The world is easier to move around in than it used to be. Crossing the Atlantic once meant a long sea voyage; today it can be a morning's flight. A hundred years ago the explorer Henry Stanley had to walk or canoe for nearly three years to traverse Africa from the Indian Ocean to the Atlantic Ocean. Now you can do that in several weeks by car, or in a day by air.

With better communications, distant peoples have begun to know each other, share each other's ideas, even help to solve each other's problems. For all these reasons they have also begun to see through the fears and fairy-stories of the past, when 'distant peoples' so often seemed to be 'savage peoples'. They have begun to find the truth of their common humanity. It turns out that this truth is more interesting and exciting than any of the old fairy-stories ever were.

The truth about the Africans, about the 'black peoples' (though few of them are any more black than western people are white), is now seen to be a large part of the history of the world. Historical discoveries made during the last fifty years, but especially during the last twenty, prove that the black peoples of today are the product of a long development of their own. This black development began in the very remote past. As the centuries went by it was marked by much that was original, and sometimes brilliant. Like the development of all other peoples, it passed through 'good periods' and 'bad periods', was the source of sorrow as well as joy, rose to peaks of achievement and fell now and then to valleys of defeat. But whether in joy or sorrow, triumph or setback, this story of the Africans' conquest of their vast and difficult continent now takes its place as a central chapter in the whole human story.

This book is an introduction to the history of the Africans. Because their history is very old and very rich in social texture, only some parts of it can be told here; but these pages try to tell the most important parts. They begin with the contribution of the Africans to the progress of the Ancient World during the enormously long periods of the Stone Age; during the rise and splendour of famous civilisations in the valley of the Nile, one of Africa's mightiest of many mighty rivers; and during other centuries when the modern world was still undreamed of. These are the subjects of Chapter 1.

Chapter 2 moves to the south of the Sahara Desert, whose wide wilderness began to appear some 4,000 years ago, and looks at all that great adventure of African peoples who spread across the lands to the south of the Desert, and who gradually tamed them for human settlement. Chapters 3, 4 and 5 show how Africans developed new forms of political and social and economic life long before the conquests by Europe in their countries. Here is the record of kingdoms large or small, or empires that became renowned for their power and wealth, of busy trading cities, of centuries of steady growth.

History is much more than what was done by kings and queens, rulers and other 'strong men'. Its essence lies in the way that ordinary people passed their lives and earned their living and worked out patterns of community agreement. The history of the black peoples is also rich in these 'ordinary things'. They form the subject of Chapter 6.

Modern Africa has long been involved in the affairs of the world, and especially of the western world. Its sons and daughters have peopled vast regions of the Americas; they and their descendants, the black peoples of the Americas and the Caribbean, have made a vital contribution to the development of the New World across the Atlantic. How did this come about? What were the effects on Africa of that long process of forced emigration which took place during the Atlantic slave trade? These are the kind of questions tackled in Chapter 7.

After the slave trade there came Europe's invasion of Africa and domination of most of Africa's peoples. And after that, beginning some twenty years ago, there came an end to that colonial period, and the beginning of a new period of African independence. Now it was that Africa's spokesmen were heard in the councils of the world, and Africa's importance received a new recognition. All this is the concern of Chapter 8.

It remains to say that this book rests on the work of many scholars of many lands and disciplines, including those of archaeology, economics, geography, linguistics, environmental research, as well as history itself. Serious books about Africa's development in the past already number many hundreds, and more are coming every year. My hope is that this brief introduction to black history will inspire readers to look further and probe deeper. To that end, I have added a short list of books for further reading.

Basil Davidson

1 Africa's share in the ancient world

A JOURNEY OF DISCOVERY

History is a journey of discovery. Exploring back into the past, historians look for the reasons why the world has come to be what it is now. They trace the wide roads and the narrow roads, or even the footpaths when they can, along which mankind has travelled. They examine how our distant forefathers solved the problems of the past, or failed to solve those problems, and what the consequences were for the making of the world of our own times. So history is a journey of self-discovery. In finding out about *them*, we find out about *us*.

It is a journey full of surprises. Those who have made it with success are the great historians who were also the modest historians, the ones who found the road to truth because they never stopped asking questions, the ones who put their prejudice behind them and went along with an open mind, weighing the evidence in a spirit of humility.

The truth about African history was hidden for a long time because those in Europe who explained it had not put their prejudice behind them, but had gone along with closed minds, convinced of their natural superiority. Often they were explorers with no gift for historical discovery. Yet many believed what they came back and told.

'Golden bracelets by the dozen'

In the year 1888 a lone white hunter called Posselt rode northward out of South Africa. He was one of the first white men ever to enter the land of the Shona and Ndebele peoples, the land of Zimbabwe which afterwards became the British settler-colony of Rhodesia. He found a pleasant country of upland plains, rich in the cattle of African stock-raisers, as well as in antelope and zebra, lion, elephant, and other big game. Day after day he travelled from village to village. At night he camped beneath a cloud of stars, and built blazing fires to keep the lions from his tent.

This explorer of a hundred years ago was looking for treasure. Exciting tales had reached South Africa of tall ruins in this inland country where gold ornaments could be found, made by some ancient folk who had long since disappeared.

Posselt found these ruins at a place called Zimbabwe. Strong grey walls of granite loomed among trees and bush. The main entrance was blocked by fallen

BC 35000	Evolution of Homo Sapiens – of our own most distant ancestors – from early types of mankind whose earliest types probably evolved in Africa		Evolution of Homo Sapiens from early types of mankind whose earliest types had probably come from Africa	
8000		Late Stone Age; origins of human (African) settlement of Nile Delta region, the cradle of Egyptian civilization		Late Stone Age; early development of farming in Middle East
7000				
6000				
5000				
4000	Africans of Sahara begin raising cattle	Egyptians begin using ploughs; further development of foundations of Egyptian civilization with emergence of States of Lower and Upper Egypt	Sumerian civilization in Mesopotamia	
3000	Early period of Pharaonic power			
2000	Late period of Pharaonic power			Minoan civilization in Crete Hittite empire Late Stone Age cultures in Britain; Stonehenge Babylonian Empire
1000		Early Berber Bronze Age in North Africa		
900	Decline of Pharaonic power			
800		Rise of Kushite power	Assyrian Empire	
700				
600		Foundation of city of Meroe		
500				
400		Phoenician city of Carthage now a major Mediterranean power		
300	332 BC. Alexander of Macedon invades Egypt		Rise of Roman power in Italy and western Mediterranean	
200				Romans war with Carthaginians for supremacy in Mediterranean region. Romans win
100	Rise of Axum in Northern Ethiopia	Romans greatly extend their settlements in North Africa		
		Final decline of Egypt	Romans in Britain	
AD 100				
200				
300		End of the city of Meroe	Rise of Eastern Roman Empire (Byzantium)	
400				
500				
600		Conversion of Nubians to Christianity; Nubian kingdoms in area of old Kushite empire		622. Muhammed founds Islam in Arabia. His followers soon embark on conquest of neighbouring countries. In 641 they drive the Byzantines (Greeks) out of Egypt, which becomes Muslim state under Arab government
700	Decline of Axum; origins of medieval Ethiopian state			
800			Rise of Caliphate of Cordoba under Arab and Berber rulers in Spain (al-Andalus)	
900				
1000	Fatimid line of rulers established 969 in Egypt. Foundation of city of Cairo (al-Kahira)		Establishment of Norman kingdom in France	
1100			1066. Normans invade Anglo-Saxon England. Origins of modern English state	
1200	1171. Ayubbid line of (Saracen) rulers established in Egypt	Wars with Christian Nubia		1189–92. Third Crusade of Western Christians against the Saracens in the Holy Land (Palestine)
1300	Decline and gradual disappearance of Christian Nubia	Mamluk line of rulers established in Egypt	Christian European slave trade in non-Christian Europeans, mainly to Egypt and North Africa	
1400				

Part of the ruins of the great stone buildings at Zimbabwe. On the right is the cone-shaped tower where Posselt slid down creepers to get into the ruins

stones, so he climbed the surrounding wall, about ten metres high, and walked along the top of it. After a while he reached a spot that was opposite a strange cone-shaped tower inside the wall. Here he reached out and took hold of creepers hanging from trees and slid down them into the interior. But 'I could not find', Posselt afterwards reported, 'any trace of human remains or of any implements, nor was the hope of discovering any treasure rewarded with success. Profound silence brooded over the scene.'

Other treasure-seekers followed Posselt. They found many ruins in this rolling inland country, and they also found treasure. In 1895 a man called Neal wrote to his eager backers in South Africa that he had picked up 'bracelets of pure gold by the dozen' as well as things in silver. He was sure that he would find more. 'Old George dropped on to two of their hiding places,' he wrote of one of his companions, 'and got about 6 pounds weight (of ornaments) in one, and 3 pounds in the other'.

Who were the people who had built these great stone walls and known how to make handsome bracelets of beaten gold? The first investigators who followed men like Neal had no doubt about the answer. No black people, they said, could ever have built such a civilisation. This must have been built by a vanished white people, perhaps by the subjects of King Solomon or the Queen of Sheba. For black peoples, they said, had no history of their own, and had never created any civilisation of their own.

Great Zimbabwe

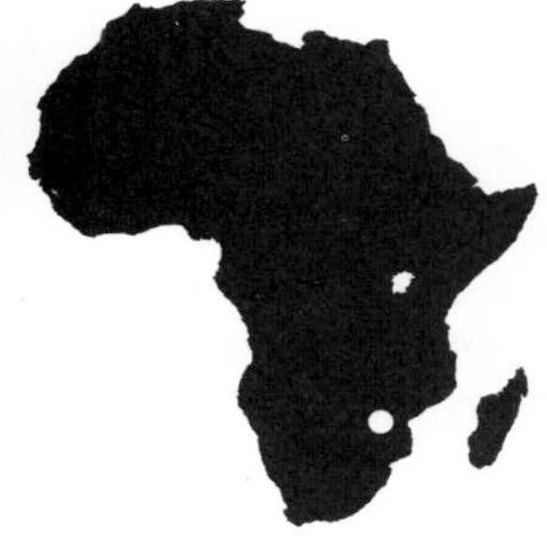

The drums of Kagurukute

Today we know that these investigators had got it wrong. The discovery of Africa's history has shown that the walls of Zimbabwe were first started nearly a thousand years ago. Later they were rebuilt to encircle the dwelling of a line of powerful kings. They were built by Africans who were the ancestors of the Africans who live in the Zimbabwe (Rhodesia) of today. One of the first of these kings was Mutota, who reigned about five centuries ago. He began the building of an empire over the lands between the Zambezi and Limpopo rivers. Mutota's people were skilled metal-workers and renowned traders in gold and ivory.

The Africans who live in Mutota's country today still remember him and his exploits. These Africans think of the heart of their land as being a hill by the Dande River where King Mutota was buried in about 1450. As one of them recently told a European scientist who wished to learn their history, 'there are old folk who say that, if you listen carefully, you can hear the roll of Kagurukute, the great drum of Mutota, at the time of the new moon, as you stand there looking down on the Dande, beside the lofty grave'.

Rescued by historical research, the story of Mutota and his people is part of the historical truth we can recognise today. Even if we cannot hear 'the roll of Kagurukute' while the new moon shines in the ripples of the Dande River, we can catch the clear echo of an African history that is long and various and exciting. By putting all the evidence together, we can build a picture of the Africans that shows growth and development in many different fields. We can see that this growth and development were valuable not only for the Africans but also for the rest of mankind. We can understand that black history and white history are inseparable parts of the same great human story, and belong together in our heritage today.

LEADERS IN STONE AGE PROGRESS

Our own world is the result of great advances in the knowledge and use of materials and machines, especially during the last seventy years or so. Ancient man faced altogether different problems of invention and organisation.

For long a very rare creature, ancient man had to learn how to get wild food and protect himself from the many natural dangers that he faced. Unlike you and me, he inherited no knowledge. He had to develop techniques such as the use of his hands for the chipping of stone tools or for the shaving of wooden spears and digging-sticks. He had to teach himself how to live in a community with his fellows, how to work together in groups, how to solve the problems of law and order.

Pioneering peoples

Scientists who have worked in Africa believe that the first populations of ancient Africa solved such problems, long ago, in a period of outstanding development. This was during the Stone Age, so named after the stone tools and weapons which were then invented, and which scientists have found in many places. During this immensely long period, which lasted more than two *million* years, the earliest Africans were few in number but evolved and developed their natural gifts. In several important aspects of their development, these lonely Africans were in advance of their neighbours in Europe and western Asia. For a long time they were among the leaders of human progress.

Charles Darwin, who had one of the most original minds of the nineteenth century, suggested this a hundred years ago at a time when most scientists thought that Central Asia had been the 'first cradle of mankind'. Darwin was sure that evidence would come to light which would show man's 'cradle' to have been in Africa. And this is what has happened during the last thirty years or so. Working in East Africa, archaeologists have found fossil bones at Olduvai in Tanzania, and at other sites, which bear out Darwin's forecast. These signals from the past indicate that Africa was indeed the birthplace of the earliest type of man, and the scene of some of man's first and most crucial stages of evolution.

Yet those most distant times are still wrapped in scientific disagreement on the details. It is not until about 12,000 years ago that the story of the Africans begins to reach fairly sure ground. By that time the early human inhabitants of Africa had become less rare. They had evolved ways of family and community life and had increased their numbers, perhaps to a total in all Africa of a few millions. These had spread across the vast continent and were living in most parts of it. They now possessed many helpful skills, were able to make excellent stone tools and weapons, and knew how to use a variety of wild plants for food. They had opened the way for Africans to become a major branch of the human family.

The people who lived in the Sahara plains during the Stone Age, before the Sahara became a desert, had artists who were very skilled in engraving and painting pictures on rock. This one is in the southern Sahara and was found by modern explorers in 1954

This map shows you some of the places where signs of early human existence have been found in Africa

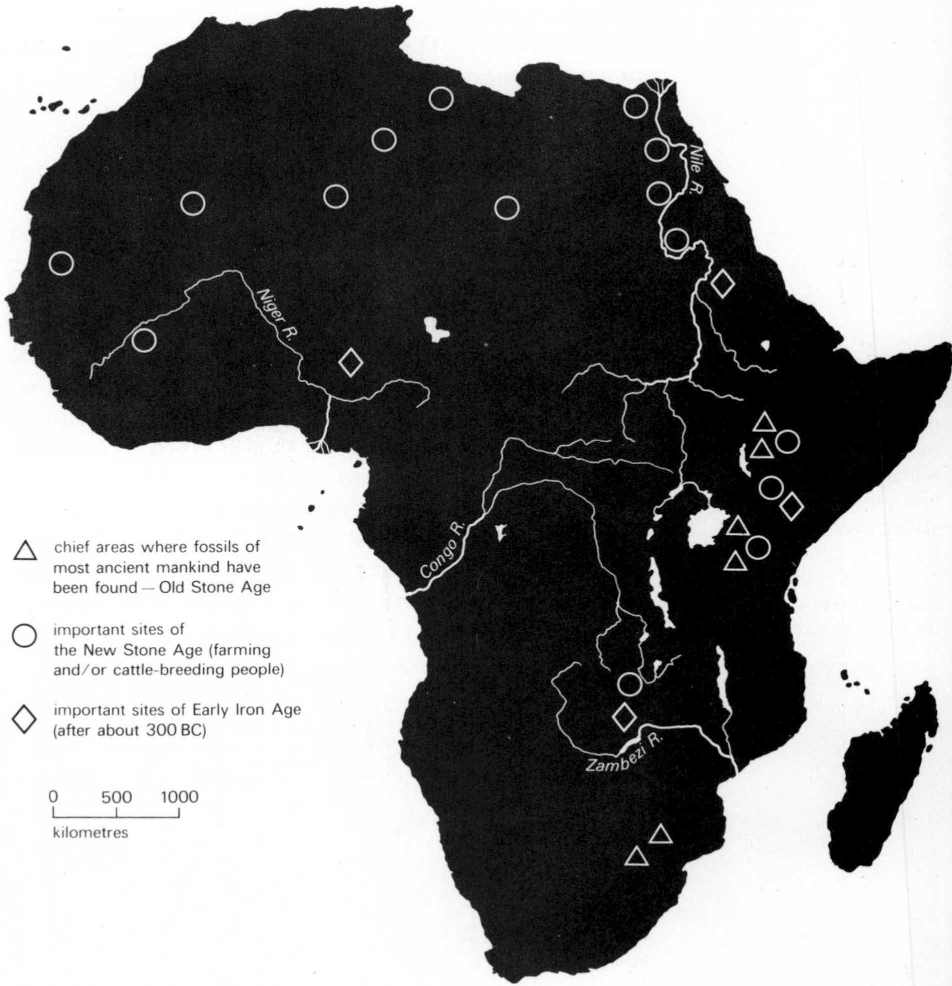

These African pioneering peoples of the last period of the Stone Age, of the time between about twelve thousand and two thousand years ago, were the forefathers of modern Africans. What did they look like?

Scientists believe they were of several different types. Of these the least rare, or few in numbers, were the ancestors of the black Africans of today, of the people whom the whites have called 'Negroes'. A second type were the ancestors of the Bushmen and the Pygmies, small folk never much more than about a metre and a half high with light-coloured skins.

Also there were other peoples, still fewer in numbers. In the north-eastern regions were Africans who had some Asian ancestors. Others along the shores of the Mediterranean Sea had ancestors who had come from Europe – just as there were people in Western Asia and Europe who had ancestors who had come from Africa. But these two groups did not penetrate deeply into Africa.

All these peoples, but especially the ancestors of the blacks or 'Negroes', continued to grow in number as they improved their mastery of nature and its problems, and moved out across the plains and through the forests of their vast continent. Gradually they multiplied and spread, found new homelands, developed new ways of life and new languages. At the same time they mingled together in marriage. But it was the descendants of the blacks or 'Negroes' who became the most numerous of Africa's peoples. From about two thousand years ago they have made most of the history of Africa.

Spreading and multiplying, from a few millions to many millions, they mastered one of the world's largest areas of land.

Crops and cattle

This mastering of a huge and difficult continent, so that men could live and prosper in most of its regions, was made possible by important advances in the understanding and use of nature. The most useful of these was the discovery of how to grow food, whether as meat or as yearly crops. Once men had learned how to do this they could enlarge their supplies of food, and, in so doing, increase their own numbers.

Although Africa had stood in the forefront of early Stone Age progress, the discovery of how to *produce* food was made in western Asia. This vital advance in knowledge spread into nearby northern Africa about six or seven thousand years ago. It spread not only into the fertile grasslands along the banks of the river Nile, but also farther westward into what is now the Sahara Desert. For in those times,

Stone Age rock-picture of a bull with long branching horns found in the Sahara

and onwards until about 2000 BC, the Sahara had many broad regions covered with grass and trees. Valleys that afterwards became uninhabitable wilderness were then watered by rivers and were rich in fish and game.

In this green Sahara, reaching from the Atlantic Ocean on the west to the Red Sea on the east, there lived many groups of Stone Age people. Having learned how to domesticate cattle, they raised big herds and grazed them through the fertile grasslands where they lived. As time went by, other Africans to the south also learned the skills of cattle raising, and this became a chief way of life for many peoples from the far north of the continent to the far south.

EGYPT OF THE PHARAOHS

The ancient Egyptian empire

None of the early Africans who learned the skills of farming and stock raising were as successful as those who lived along the banks of the river Nile in the land which afterwards became Egypt. These early Egyptians took advantage of the floods of the Nile that rose once a year and then went down again, as they still do, leaving wide fields where men could easily grow crops and feed their cattle. This regular yearly flooding by the Nile provided the basis for great improvements in food production, such as the use of ploughs. The Greek historian Herodotus, who wrote in about 450 BC, rightly called Egypt 'the gift of the Nile'.

Thanks to the water of the Nile and their developing skills in using it to irrigate land for crops and pasture, the Africans of ancient Egypt created a civilisation which for many centuries remained the most splendid triumph of man's early progress. It forms the great opening chapter in the history of the Africa we know today.

European civilisation built, in several important ways, on the brilliant achievements of the ancient Greeks. But the Greeks, in their turn, owed much to the ancient Egyptians, whether in the field of ideas or in that of practical skills. So it is to the delta and valley of the Nile that we must chiefly look for the deepest roots of our modern civilisation. It was here along the Nile that the arts of peace became an example to every people who had contact with them.

Earliest beginnings

The story of how and why this happened begins about ten thousand years ago. Today the map of Africa shows a narrow green line of fertile land winding northward from the mountains of East Africa, along the Nile, between deserts of rock and sand until it widens to the bulge of the Nile delta on the coast of the Mediterranean Sea. But ten thousand years ago the picture was different. Then the Nile was much wider, and covered the whole region of the delta all the year round.

After about 8000 BC there came a very gradual change of climate. There was less rainfall and the rivers began to shrink in size. As the waters of the Nile also shrank, bands of rich soil appeared on either bank. Nearby Stone Age Africans who lived by hunting game and gathering wild plants came to live here. Adapting new skills from their neighbours in western Asia, they cleared the land for farming. By about 4000 BC they were ploughing their fields and raising good crops of grain. The most important of these were wheat and barley. They had also begun the regular pasturing of cattle in the Nile Valley. With a bigger and better food supply their little settlements grew larger.

As more and more African farming people settled in the broad and fertile delta, and their population grew in number, they faced new problems of living together. Earlier peoples who were nomads, moving around in search of wild food, with each group very small in number, had needed little or no government beyond that of the heads of families. Larger and settled groups found this was not enough. They had to work out new ways of keeping peace among themselves, of making common decisions about ploughing and sowing and dividing up pastureland, of combining against rival peoples who might want their land or their town. They had to learn new methods of trading and of protecting trade routes from nomad raiders. These problems called for new laws and new ways of making sure they were obeyed. As different social groups gradually developed from early forms of the division of labour, there emerged the solution of government by a few people over many people.

This need for power 'at the centre' was continually increased by the process of change which created these settled communities. As soon as men could produce regular supplies of food, they could also produce more than they needed at any one time. They could produce, that is, a *surplus* of food over and beyond what they ate themselves. This food surplus was small at the beginning, hardly enough to carry over from one harvest to the next, but it made possible another big advance. It enabled farmers to support groups of people who did not produce food, but who specialized in producing other useful things, such as tools of stone or metal. This division of *labour* tended to break down the equality of the old nomadic ways of life, and so made the divisions in society. And power in society went to those who gained control of labour.

At one end of the scale, most Egyptians continued to be food-producers; at the other, kings emerged with political power and wealth, gathering much of the surplus for their own use; while in between there appeared a whole range of specialised groups such as metalsmiths, weavers, priests, government officials, each with varying amounts of wealth or power. With all this, there began in Egypt the history of social classes, and of strong central governments based either on personal or on group-owned property.

Unity and new power

Once launched on this pattern of growth, Egyptian civilisation developed with accelerating speed and astonishing results. As their settlements went on growing in size, and in complexity of production and trade, the early Egyptians gradually created new forms of government. By about 3500 BC they had formed themselves into two states, each with a king whose title was Pharaoh. Each state had a growing system of governors, soldiers and officials. In about 3200 BC these two states, one of them in the delta (lower or northern) and the other immediately to the south of the delta (upper or southern) fused into one.

At the same time progress was made in many fields. Such was the pace and success of these early developments that all the main achievements of Egyptian civilisation, at least in their first stages, were brought into existence during those few centuries before 3000 BC.

The kings who ruled over this united kingdom of Lower and Upper Egypt grew

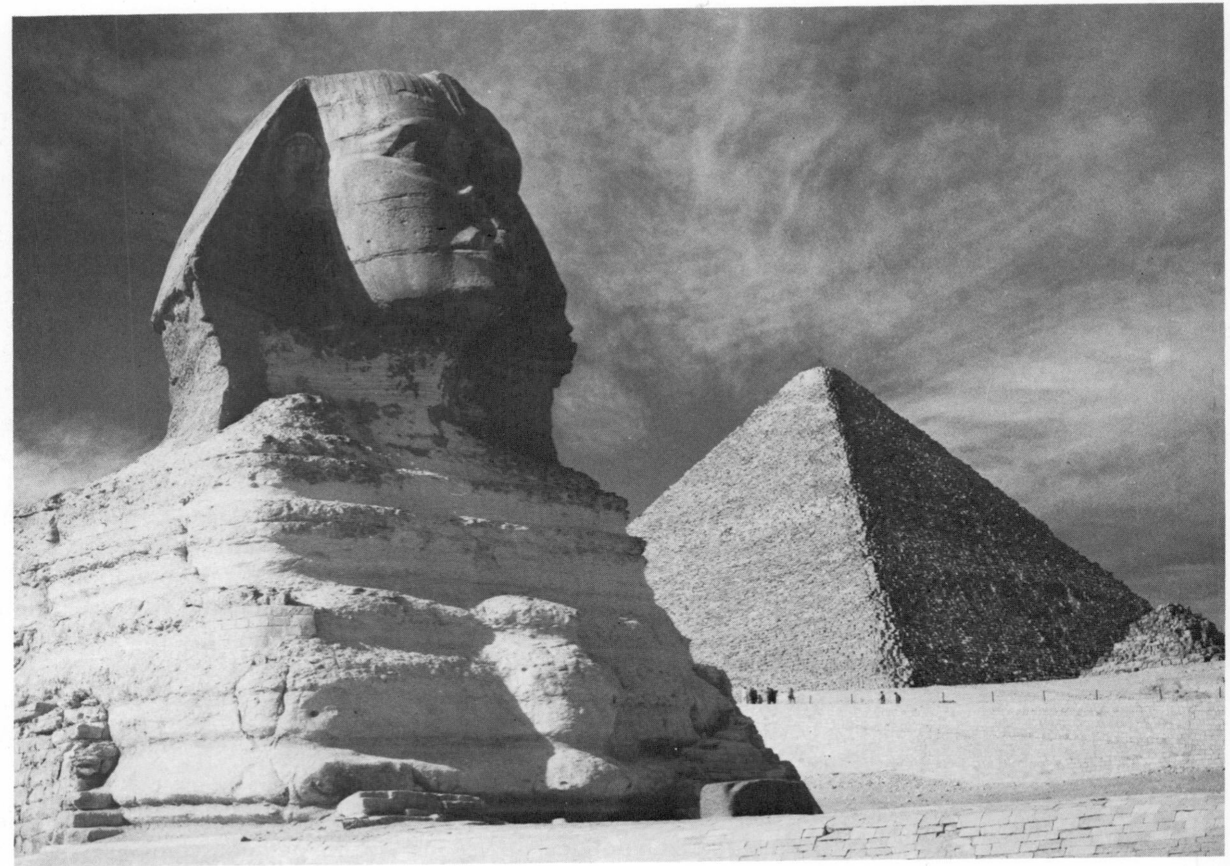

The mysterious Sphinx, and beyond it the Great Pyramid of Pharaoh Cheops, near Cairo, still tell of the majesty and power of ancient Egypt

rich and powerful. They were able to command the labour of large numbers of men and women. Part of this labour they used to build great monuments, either as tombs for themselves or as temples to their gods. Only six centuries after the unification of the two early kingdoms, Pharaoh Cheops was able to have built, as a tomb for himself, the largest stone monument the world has yet seen.

This Great Pyramid, near modern Cairo, was a development of earlier and smaller structures of the same type. Some idea of its size may be had from the estimate of its containing 2,300,000 blocks of stone whose average weight is two and a half tons. Another estimate reckons that all these stones, if cut into cubes 30 centimetres square and laid end to end, would form a line as long as two-thirds of the Equator.

The power to build monuments like this, and to exploit Egypt's wealth, lay in the 'gift of the Nile': in its regular floods and fertile soil, and in the surplus of food and other things that these made possible. But good use of the 'gift' depended on peace and order in the land. It was the Pharaoh's task to make sure of these. To do this he used governors and soldiers. He also used the power of Egyptian religion. The ancient Egyptians thought of their Pharaoh as the chief spokesman of the gods on Earth: he was the one, they believed, to whom the gods had given their wisdom, so that he could rule well. As such, the Pharaoh was a figure of towering prestige and influence. The Pharaohs and their priests had an obvious interest in encouraging this belief in their importance. They worked at doing this in a great many different ways. There came a time when the Pharaohs were themselves declared to be gods.

Like many other peoples, the Egyptians also believed that the spirits of men and women could never die. Out of this belief there arose, even in early times when the Pharaohs and their noblemen were less all-powerful than they afterwards became, the practice of embalming the bodies of the dead so that the spirits could journey in their bodies to the land of the gods. Along with this there came the practice of building great tombs for rulers and governors, and of filling the inmost part of these tombs with useful everyday things so that the spirits and the bodies would have food and comfort on their dark journey. All this was far too expensive for most ordinary people; but everyone who could manage it arranged for his or her 'journey' after death.

For reasons such as these, and others like them, Egypt became and remained a state with a strongly centralised power commanded by the Pharaohs and their governors and officials and priests. Men's needs for everyday life had given rise to a religion which promised to take care of them in this life and afterwards.

Sources for Egyptian history

This strongly unified civilisation lasted for nearly three thousand years after 3200 BC, though with a slow decline after about 1000 BC. Only in the period around AD 1 did it finally perish, its monuments engulfed in sand, and its brilliance forgotten. Yet its triumphs had influenced and moulded the ancient world. So important are they for the understanding of later history that the study of ancient Egypt has become a special branch of research. This is called Egyptology.

Egyptology began when the French under their Emperor Napoleon invaded Egypt at the end of the eighteenth century, almost two thousand years after the power of the Pharaohs had vanished from the scene. Then for the first time Europeans began to understand something of the greatness of the African past in Egypt. A Frenchman called Jean-François Champollion (1790–1832) discovered how to read the hieroglyphs, or picture-writing, of the ancient Egyptians. When this became possible historians could begin to read the many thousands of inscriptions on stone, and records written on reed-paper, which the ancient Egyptians had left behind them.

Champollion's discovery was a remarkable feat of historical detective work. It was possible mostly because of the finding of a large stone, near Rosetta in the delta of the Nile, which had on it an inscription in Greek as well as in Egyptian hieroglyphs. Being able to read the Greek inscription, Champollion was eventually able to work out the meaning of the hieroglyphs written alongside it. Champollion only made a start in this direction, but others have gone on to complete his work.

Another useful source of historical knowledge about the Pharaohs was provided much earlier, in about 300 BC, by an Egyptian priest called Manetho. He wrote down in Greek a long list of all the rulers whom people then remembered as having reigned in Egypt from the earliest times. Unfortunately, the complete list that Manetho made was lost after his death; we have only the parts of it which were copied by the Jewish historian Josephus, who lived in the first century AD,

The 'picture writing' of ancient Egypt, called hieroglyphics, that Champollion deciphered. This example is from a big temple at Karnak on the middle Nile

and by other early scholars. Yet Manetho's list still has value. Using it with knowledge gained from inscriptions and monuments, historians have been able to name nearly all the Pharaohs, and decide more or less the years of their reigns.

Five main periods

No short account could do justice to the long and splendid history of ancient Egypt. But it will be useful to have at least an outline of its development. This outline consists of five main periods of growth and change.

1. The first was the profoundly inventive period of early development about which we still know very little. Then it was that the Kingdoms of Upper and Lower Egypt were formed and fused into a single kingdom. This took place under a king called Narmer, who seems to have been the first to have had the right of wearing both the white crown of Upper Egypt and the red crown of Lower Egypt. The two crowns were afterwards united in a single design. Thus combined, the Egyptian state consisted of the lands of the Nile Delta, or Lower Egypt, and the lands on either side of the river for some way south of the Delta, or Upper Egypt. The Pharaohs of this kingdom ruled from about 3200 BC until about 2680 BC. They laid the foundations of Egyptian civilisation.

2. Next comes what is called the Old Kingdom. Among its Pharaohs were Cheops, Chephren and Mycerinus who built the great pyramids at Gizeh near the (much later) city of Cairo. These pyramids stand there to this day, huge monuments to their builders' majesty and power to command the labour of ordinary people. They and other Pharaohs of this period ruled over a country of growing prosperity. They sent out trading expeditions by land and water to neighbours near and far. Some of these expeditions went south along the Red Sea. Others were the earliest explorers of inner Africa. Among the latter were four big expeditions under a governor called Harkuf. He travelled far to the south into African lands of which the Egyptians then knew nothing.

On his third expedition, sometime around 2300 BC, Harkuf tells in one of his inscriptions how he went with three hundred donkeys laden with trading goods, and how he came to those distant lands and did business with their peoples. On his fourth expedition, again far to the south, he brought back a present which greatly pleased the Pharaoh of that time. This was a Pygmy. Pygmies were deeply respected in ancient Egypt because they were believed to live in 'the land of the spirits', the unknown country of inner Africa. The Pharaoh sent a message to Harkuf:

> Come back north to our court at once and bring this dwarf with you, and bring him prosperous and healthy from the land of the spirits. Appoint your best men to take care of him. Put them on each side of him in the boat [for the journey on the Nile], so that he runs no risk of falling in the water. Make them sleep next to him in his tent, and inspect them ten times every night.

Such trading expeditions led to military expansion. The Pharaohs of the Old Kingdom pushed their frontiers steadily to the west and east and south. They improved the organisation of their kingdom. They built grand monuments. By the end of this period, some time after 2300 BC, all the most important features of Egyptian civilisation were well developed.

But a price had to be paid for these successes. They deepened the divisions within Egyptian society, so that the Pharaohs began to face many troubles at home. There followed two centuries of breakdown in the power of central government. Civil strife broke out, and wars between princes. The inscriptions of that time tell the story from the standpoint of the rich and powerful, whose positions were threatened by the poor and oppressed.

'The bowman is ready', complains one of these inscriptions, 'the wrongdoer is everywhere. Men sit in the bushes until the unwary traveller comes by, so as to plunder his load.' Another inscription suggests that there were many poor men in this land of wealth who rebelled against their poverty and lack of power:

> The man who possessed no property has become a man of wealth. The poor man is full of joy. Every town says: Let us suppress the powerful among us. Those who had rich garments are now in rags.

3. Yet the time came when powerful Pharaohs were once more able to dominate the scene, and the remarkable development of Egyptian society could move on again, this time at the expense of foreign peoples. There followed the third main period of ancient Egyptian history, that of the empire-building Middle Kingdom whose ambitious Pharaohs ruled between about 2100 and 1790 BC. With them the centre of power shifted far south from the delta. They made their capital at a place called Thebes on the middle Egyptian

Nefertiti, a queen of ancient Egypt. She was the wife of Pharoah Akhnaton, who ruled in about 1372–1354 BC

part of the Nile. Here they raised temples and palaces whose great pillared ruins still stand today.

Like their predecessors, the Middle Kingdom Pharaohs sent military and trading expeditions into the lands of their neighbours. To the south they pushed their troops a great distance up the Nile into the land of the Nubians, exploiting gold mines there. They built strong forts on the southern frontier of Egypt so as to control the trade of the south, and repel any attempt the Nubians might make to invade the Egyptians in return. They filled the land of Egypt with splendid temples and tombs. The most successful of these Pharaohs were Inyotef, Menthotpe I, and Ammenemes.

Many men prospered in these times of expansion, but once again there was a price. The rule of the Pharaohs had to be harsh, if only to put down rivals and quell revolts, and sometimes it was cruel. An inscription of one of the Middle Kingdom Pharaohs, addressed as good advice to his son, shows that these great men did not always sit easily upon their thrones:

Hearken to what I say to you!
So that you may be King of the Earth.

Harden yourself against all lesser men.
The people obey the man who makes them fear him.

Guard your heart against your brothers.
Have no friends.
Make no companion . . .

Being human, not all the Pharaohs and their many governors and officials ruled wisely, or with skill.

After some 350 years of Middle Kingdom expansion there came another breakdown, caused this time by an invasion from western Asia. A nomad people called Hyksos, strong in cavalry and chariots, broke into Egypt and carried all before them. They were defeated and driven out only by the leaders of another great recovery in the sixteenth century BC.

4. The leaders who defeated the Hyksos invaders opened the fourth great period of Egyptian history, another long phase of conquest and prosperity known as the New Kingdom. This lasted roughly from 1580 to 1150 BC. Its Pharaohs revived and improved upon the successes of the Middle Kingdom, just as those of the Middle Kingdom had expanded the distant triumphs of the Old Kingdom. Once again Egypt stood at the peak of power in the ancient world. The wealth of many lands was added to the 'gift of the Nile'. The brilliant splendour of royal Egypt in those times was revealed for the modern world when archaeologists of the twentieth century discovered the intact tomb of one of the less important Pharaohs of the New Kingdom, Tutankhamun, who ruled from about 1347 BC to 1339 BC.

Other peoples were meanwhile growing strong in western Asia, and now several of the New Kingdom Pharaohs had to wage big and costly wars along their wide frontiers. Then towards 1400 BC, new rivals appeared from the plains of northern Africa. These were Berber nomads driven by the growing difficulty of living in their Libyan homelands as the deserts of the Sahara took shape. Some of the Pharaohs of the fourteenth century BC, notably Rameses I and Sethos I, had to fight great battles against these invading nomads. The Libyan Berbers were thrown back by these Pharaohs of the New Kingdom, but again and again returned, as an inscription tells us, 'to seek food for their mouths'.

5. Little by little these Libyans pushed their way in along the Nile and settled there. After 950 BC, with the Pharaoh's government weakened by defeats in western Asia, Libyan princes were able to seize power in Thebes and to reign over much of Egypt until about 722 BC. Then came another great change described in the next chapter: the invasion of Egypt by a strong people from the south. All this belongs to the fifth and last period of Egypt's ancient history, when the power of the Pharaohs steadily declined.

The rest of the story is largely one of Greek and then of Roman conquest. The Greeks came in 332 BC when their conquering emperor, Alexander of Macedon, set up a Greek line of kings and queens of whom the famous Cleopatra was the last, ruling Egypt from about 44 to 30 BC. This Ptolemaic line of Greek rulers, so named after the first of them, Ptolemy, adopted Egyptian customs and beliefs. They ruled as Pharaohs, and everyday life in most of Egypt was little different from before. Yet another great power was now rising in the Mediterranean region, that of Rome; and it was not long before the Romans, in their turn, embarked on campaigns of foreign conquest. So it was, in Egypt, that after Queen Cleopatra there came the Romans. They reduced Egypt to a Roman colony, and took all the wealth they could find.

The 'gift of the Nile' became a gift to the great city of Rome, capital of the Roman empire, feeding the Roman population with its harvests of corn; and every Egyptian protest was put down by force of arms. Then gradually the power of Rome in the eastern Mediterranean passed to Greek rulers, the emperors of Byzantium; and Egypt remained a province of Byzantium until AD 640. In that year the Arab warriors who followed the faith of the Prophet Muhammad, the religion of Islam, rode out of their desert lands and seized power in Egypt. In so doing, they launched the modern history of the Egyptians.

Inside the outline – 'It is people that matter'

The record of kings and queens, of governments and empires, is only one part of history. This record is useful, and needs to be known, because only by knowing it can we find our way through the tangled story of the past. Many of the kings and queens who will be mentioned in this book were bold and wise leaders who led their people through danger and difficulty. Yet without their peoples they were nothing; and it is the story of their peoples which gives history its true value. Behind the questions that have to do with kings and queens lie other questions which call for an answer. The modern German poet Bertolt Brecht has posed them in this way:

Who built Thebes of the seven gates?
In the books there stand the names of kings.
Was it the kings who hauled and heaved those lumps of stone?
And in Babylon so many times destroyed,
Who was it raised those walls again?
Which were the houses of gold-gleaming Lima
Where the masons dwelt? And where,
When the Chinese Wall was finished,
Did the builders go at the evening bell?

It is often hard to answer such questions, and sometimes impossible, since the records do not say much about 'ordinary people'. Yet we have to try, because it was 'ordinary people' who were the real makers of history, the creators of wealth, the food-providers, and the masons and the soldiers. This was just as true of ancient Egypt as of later kingdoms. The Pharaohs stood at the summit of a brilliant civilisation and a powerful government, supplied by the gold and cloth and other products of conquered lands and of their own land; but they still depended on their subjects. Putting Brecht's questions in another way, a saying of the Akan people of Ghana in West Africa makes this point very well:

I call Gold,
Gold is silent.
I call Cloth,
Cloth is silent.
It is people that matter.

People in ancient Egypt lived in a civilisation that is difficult for us to imagine today. It was a civilisation which had lasted so long without any big change in belief, or in organisation, or in general methods of production, that no change seemed necessary or even possible. It was a civilisation which had succeeded so well that any major change could only seem a threat to prosperity and peace.

The tomb-temple of Queen Hatshepsut, who ruled ancient Egypt in about 1490–1468 BC, at Deir al-Bahri near Thebes, on the middle Nile

This unwillingness to change meant that there were few pressures to improve the way of life. But this stagnation took place at what was for most of the people a relatively good standard of living, even if the taxes demanded by the rich and powerful were a constant and sometimes a heavy burden. The records of ancient Egypt say little about what ordinary people thought about their lives, because the records were written by rich and powerful people, and mostly about themselves. Even so, the glimpses that we can get, whether from tomb pictures or the writings of scribes, suggest a picture of everyday life that was often kindly and easy going.

Perhaps the villages of Egypt then were not so very different in appearance from those one can see today, little clusters of mud-and-thatch huts along the irrigation canals that help to make their fields so fertile. Such villages may seem poor and comfortless today, but in those times of long ago they were the scene of a security and self-respect that came from a civilisation at the forefront of technological and intellectual progress. Within the limits open to them, the Egyptians had achieved a point of everyday development that drew admiration from all other peoples who lived near them or could learn anything about them.

A little-changing world

In this civilisation every man and woman knew their place, and generally accepted it, even if, as we have seen, there were times of revolt and widespread discontent. Religion taught that the blessings of life flowed from obedience to the laws of the Pharaoh, who spoke for the gods. All this reinforced the conservatism of a civilisation in which change could occur only in moments of great upheaval. 'Otherwise', wrote Herodotus in about 450 BC, 'the Egyptians keep to their own customs and never adopt any from abroad.'

This conservatism helps to explain the long history of ancient Egypt: people followed the way of life of their parents and grandparents. Great strides in knowledge and invention were made in early Egyptian times. Yet these advances were developed very little in the many centuries that followed. For example, the early Egyptians developed hieroglyphic writing to a high point of efficiency, but, to the very end, only the priests and scribes could write or read it. Also, they were among the world's earliest mathematicians, and their architects were able to calculate to fine accuracy the size of the great pyramids and temples they designed and built. They were keenly interested in the stars, discovered much about their movement through the clear skies of Egypt, and invented a precise annual calendar. Yet it was only the priests and rulers who had this knowledge; and it was not developed further in later times. Early Egyptian metalworkers were highly skilled in the working of copper, gold, and some other metals; but not until after the invasion of the iron-using Assyrians, as late in Egyptian history as the seventh century BC, did the use of iron, a far more practical metal, begin to spread from western Asia and become common in Egypt.

In this little-changing world the ordinary people of Egypt were luckier than their neighbours because of all the food they could produce. The records of kings and queens may tell of many wars and times of trouble; yet most of the people were little affected by such disasters. They sometimes had to fight in wars, and they always had to pay taxes and to work for powerful masters. But only occasionally, so far as the records show, did these burdens prove so unbearable that men rose in anger against them. Otherwise, living in fertile lands with barren hills or fearful deserts on either side, they counted their blessings and probably were well enough content.

The way they liked to see their lives, at least in ideal terms, is shown by delightful wall paintings in the tombs of farmers and craftsmen. These display the many different crops that could be grown, the variety of birds and animals that could be raised or hunted, and the festivals for song and dance in which everyone could join.

Even in this well-provided land, real life was of course an uncertain affair. There was competition for jobs, rivalry for privileges, trouble with the authorities. Except for rulers and governors, the most favoured group were the priests and record-keepers of the temples of Egypt's many gods. Clever young men looked for safe careers in that direction. One of them wrote to a friend, warning him:

> I am told that you have given up the record-keeper's life and gone into farming, but have you forgotten the troubles of the farmer who has to pay his harvest-tax when snakes have carried off half the corn, and the hippopotamus has eaten up the rest? Then the mice abound, the locusts come, the cattle devour, the sparrows bring disaster; and what may still remain on the threshing floor is stolen by thieves. Yes, and that's when the clerk lands on the river bank to collect the tax. With him come guards with staves and Nubians with rods of palm, and they say, 'Hand over the corn,' but there is no corn. And then the farmer is beaten, bound, ducked in his well . . .

Understandably, the priests and record-keepers grew in number as time went by. By the reign of Rameses III, in the twelfth century BC, the records show that the priests of temples owned nearly a third of Egypt, and numbered about a fifth of the population. Towards the end of the New Kingdom, ambitious priests were even able to challenge the Pharaoh's power and set up governments of their own.

Such were the people whom the Greeks under Alexander the Great conquered in 332 BC. Yet even then, with its political and military organisation far in decline, Egypt remained a rich and comfortable land that was generally good to live in. Herodotus, who went to Egypt about a hundred years before the Greek conquest, had no doubt of this. He was a shrewd and witty observer of people and their ways. He praised the calm and dignity of Egyptian daily life, and admired the many festivals to which the people crowded with flutes and drums, wearing their best clothes. He extolled the virtues of Egyptian law and custom, and wrote glowingly of the hospitality and scholarship of priests and scribes.

Egypt and the rest of Africa

This splendid civilisation, towering above the achievements of other lands, was primarily African. Most Egyptians, and most aspects of their culture, owed their origins to the African peoples who had lived in the green Sahara, and who had first settled in the land of the Nile. The descendants of those early settlers borrowed some ideas from western Asia, and sometimes mingled in marriage with migrants from western Asia, but the civilisation which they built was certainly not Asian.

The African quality of ancient Egyptian life can be glimpsed even today, if faintly, in the many ideas, beliefs and customs which other Africans shared with ancient Egypt. Many religions of Africa share some of the beliefs of the people of the Pharaohs. Certain political ideas are also similar. At a more humble level, so are a number of everyday habits. Wooden head-rests such as the Egyptians used at night are still used by many African peoples.

Does this mean that other Africans learned such beliefs and habits from the ancient Egyptians? We do not know. It may mean that. More probably it means that all these Africans of long ago, whether in Egypt or not, drew beliefs and customs from a common source among the early populations of the green Sahara. The only certain thing is that the history of ancient Egypt and that of much of the rest of Africa are woven and bound closely together.

There is no doubt about the great influence Egypt had on peoples living not far away, whether in southern Europe, western Asia, or neighbouring regions of Africa. It was in the country south of Egypt that this influence proved strongest and again revealed, with many-sided brilliance, the creativeness of African life.

The Sudan: West(W), Central(C) and Eastern(E)

This country south of Egypt lay in the eastern region of what became known long afterwards as the Sudan, a broad belt of flat plains covered with grass which flow right across Africa, from the Nile to the Atlantic Ocean, along the southern flank of the Sahara Desert. The peoples of all the regions of these Sudanese grasslands were to play, as we shall see, a large part in African history. Under Egyptian stimulus, those of the eastern Sudan began early. Already in the seventeenth century BC, a people of this region, later called Nubia, built an important civilisation of their own. Then some of their descendants, growing strong in the same region after 1000 BC, carried this inner African progress to a new peak of achievement. These people were the Kushites, who built the memorable kingdom of Meroë (pronounced Merro-ay).

THE MAJESTY OF MEROË

The ever-inquiring Herodotus, asking useful questions wherever he went, was among the first to bring news of Meroë to Europe. He did that shortly before 400 BC. Unfortunately for us, he was unable to go to Meroë himself. 'I went as far as Elphantine Island [at Aswan near the southern frontier of modern Egypt] to see what I could with my own eyes. But for the country still farther south I had to be content with what I was told in answer to my questions.' It was a moment of bad relations between the governor of southern Egypt and the Kushites, and the roads were closed.

But the priests of Elphantine, an island in the Nile that is still crowded with the ruins of temples and houses, told Herodotus interesting things about the distant land of the Kushites. Fifty-seven days' journey to the south (nowadays you can do it in three days by boat and train) there lay the Kushite capital of Meroë, a strong and beautiful city. Outside the walls in a grassy plain, the priests told Herodotus, stood a famous temple dedicated to the sun. There the Meroites had the custom of putting 'a plentiful supply of boiled meat of all kinds; it is the duty of the magistrates to put the meat there at night, and during the day anybody who wishes may come there and eat it'.

This is what remains today of the great temple of the Kushites at Musawarat as-Safra, near Meroë. It dates from about 500 BC but was enlarged in later centuries until, around 250 BC, it reached its greatest size

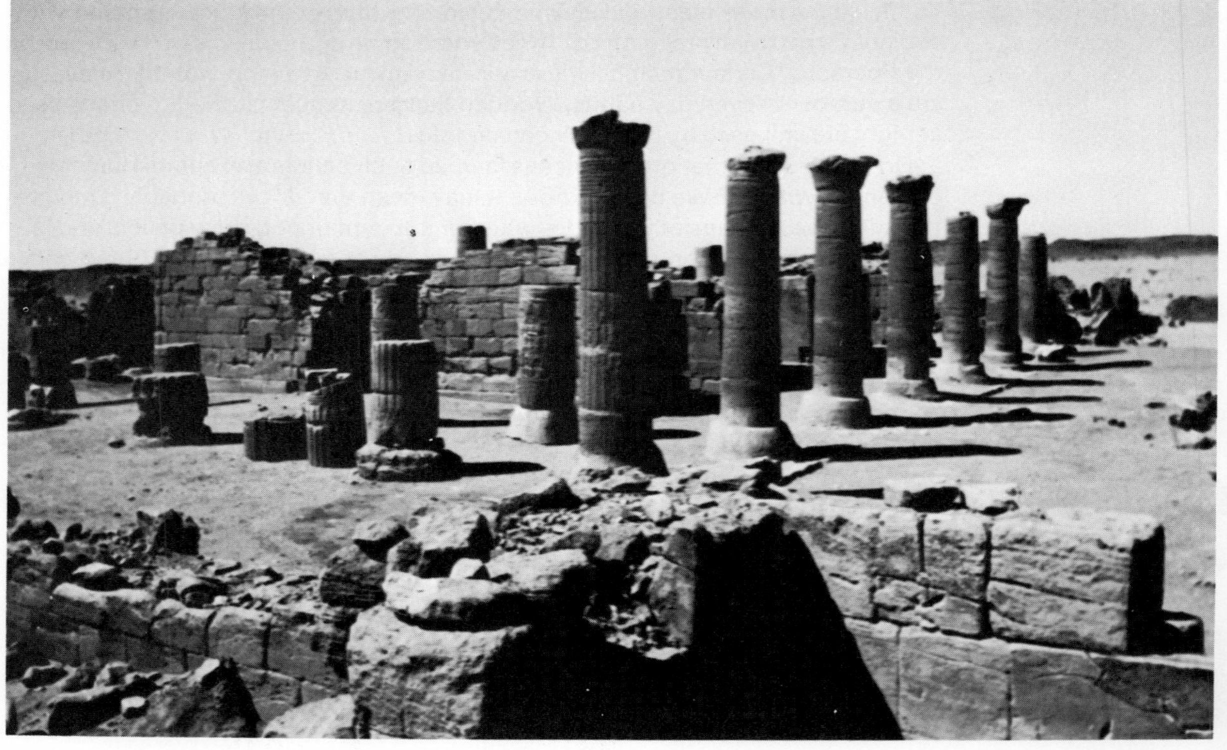

A vanished splendour

Whether or not the magistrates of Meroë really did this, there is no doubt about the existence of Meroë's Temple of the Sun. Today it is only a roofless ruin of walls and pillars where snakes bask in the heat, waiting to pounce on desert mice. Yet as recently as sixty years ago a British scientist reported that its inner chambers were still decorated with fine glazed tiles of pale blue and red, while black and white tiles paved the floor in gleams of vanished splendour.

And there is no doubt about the strength and beauty of the city of Meroë, capital of the kingdom of Kush. Visitors can still admire its skyline, tall with the ruins of temples and a majestic palace encircled by a massive wall. Meroë was the centre of a large trading community living in suburbs beside the Nile. Here the greatest of the ancient civilisations of inner Africa flourished. The people were proud of their own strength and culture, borrowing much from others but inventing much of their own. Trading as far afield as Rome and India, and through Indian middlemen even perhaps as far as China, the people of the kingdom of Kush spread their influence over their neighbours.

Kush as a world power

The kingdom of Kush

Kush was a kingdom built in two main stages. The first was under Egyptian influence. While Libyan princes were ruling southern Egypt, during the ninth century BC, the Kushites to the south of them were able to grow strong in their country of the eastern Sudan. Centuries of Egyptian imperial rule had left them with many Egyptian beliefs and customs. They worshipped the gods of the Egyptians, especially the god Amun whose chief temples were at Thebes.

After the collapse of the New Kingdom and its empire, the princes of the Kushites turned their thoughts to conquering Egypt. Their king, Kashta, began this conquest in about 750 BC. He and his successors, Piankhy and Shabaka, completed it. They established Kushite rule as far as the delta and the Mediterranean. With this the Kushites became a world power. Only a century later, around 650 BC, were they driven back by the invading armies of the emperor of Assyria in western Asia.

Tremendous battles were fought in Egypt between the Assyrians and the Kushites. The story of some of these is told in the *Bible*, in the *Second Book of Kings* (Chapter 19, verses 8–35), for the people of Israel stood right in the path of the invading Assyrians. We are told there how Taharqa (or Tirhaqa) one of the Kushite Pharaohs of Egypt, came out to fight against the Assyrian hosts, and how Jehovah, for the sake of Israel, caused 185,000 Assyrian soldiers to die of a mysterious sickness. All the same, the Assyrians were victorious in the end. Better armed and organised, they defeated the Kushite armies in one battle after another.

Pushed south by the iron-equipped armies of Assyria, the Kushites returned to their old capital of Kush itself, Napata. Here their kings continued to rule early in the sixth century BC. Then they transferred their capital to Meroë about 400 kilometres to the southward (or 140 kilometres north of modern Khartum). The ruler who made this change, for economic and political reasons, was probably King Aspelta, ruling from about 593 to 568 BC.

There now opened the second and greater stage of the Kushite kingdom, centred on the city of Meroë. The power and influence of Meroë lasted for about eight centuries. Study of royal tombs shows that about fifty-six kings or queens

Notice the following things on these carvings from Meroë:
1. the alphabetical writing invented by the Kushites around 200 BC. You can see this on the inside edges of the two stones;
2. the lion-god of the Kushites, Apedemak, on the right-hand stone and a Kushite king on the left-hand stone

followed Aspelta until Meroë was at last destroyed in about AD 320. This destruction was due to social and political decline which scientists cannot yet explain, but its end was completed by an invasion from neighbouring Axum in Ethiopia. Most of the names of these Kushite kings and queens of Meroë are known from inscriptions at Meroë and elsewhere, and scientists have worked ou a list of the probable dates of their reigns. Although they continued to build pyramids and temples like the Egyptians before them, their ways of life and their beliefs were no longer Egyptian but Kushite.

The culture of Meroë: local inventions, ideas from abroad

Much historical research is needed to understand the Kushite civilisation, and th work is still going on. Only in the last twenty years or so have historians begun to have some idea of its variety and power. But today we do know something about its general outline of history.

These Kushites were great travellers and traders, skilled in many useful arts, including that of writing. In their first stage, while their capital was still at Napata in the north, they wrote in Egyptian with Egyptian hieroglyphs. But in their second and more important stage, based at Meroë in the south, they developed new ways of writing. At first they were content to use Egyptian-type hieroglyphs to write their own language. Then, growing increasingly sure of themselves and of the value of their own culture, they made a remarkable advance of a kind that was rare in the ancient world. This people of inner Africa invented a new and efficient alphabet. It had signs for twenty-three letters.

In doing this, they may have been influenced by the Greeks who ruled Egypt and had an alphabet for writing Greek. But the Meroitic system of writing was no like the Greek. It was also superior to Greek in at least one respect: the Meroites used a sign for dividing words from one another while the Greeks did not. The earliest known use of Meroitic writing is that of an inscription, dated to about 180–170 BC, found in a small temple built near Meroë by Queen Shanak-dakete. But this important invention was probably developed about a hundred years before that.

Scientists are still working on the deciphering of the Meroitic writing system. They find this difficult because the language of the Kushites is long since dead. Nobody knows just what it was, although it was certainly an African language. Fortunately there are several good inscriptions in Egyptian and Meroitic alongside each other. These have enabled scientists, working as Champollion did with the Rosetta Stone, to give sounds to the letters of the Meroitic alphabet. This is partly how we know the names of the kings and queens of Meroë, although the way these names were pronounced by the Meroites is still a matter of guesswork. Progress is being made in deciphering the whole writing system. When this work is completed it will solve another of the mysteries of ancient Africa.

Even so, we do know some things about the everyday life of the Kushites of Meroë. They were mainly a people of skilful farmers like the Egyptians, and produced a large surplus of food which provided money for the building of fine cities built of stone. Here governors and scholars ruled and taught, craftsmen worked with fine painted pottery and various metals, and traders bargained for the goods of many lands. Near the palaces of kings they built the pillared temples to their gods, to Arens-Nuphis and to Sebiumeker, and to the lion-headed god of war, Apedemak.

Two developments helped to make the Kushites strong in war. One was their love of horses. This meant that they could use cavalry, which most neighbouring peoples could not. The other was their skill in taming the African elephant, a beast more difficult to control and use than its Indian cousin. In one ruined Kushite temple, not far from Meroë, there stands to this day the stone statue of a young elephant. Nearby, along the wall of another temple dedicated to the lion-god Apedemak, there is still a picture of a file of war elephants carved in the stones.

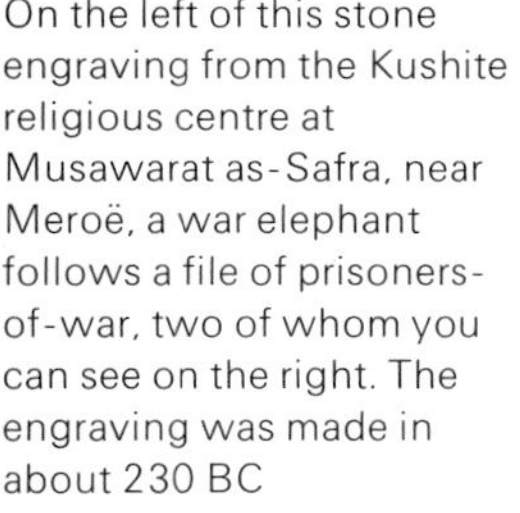

On the left of this stone engraving from the Kushite religious centre at Musawarat as-Safra, near Meroë, a war elephant follows a file of prisoners-of-war, two of whom you can see on the right. The engraving was made in about 230 BC

At the height of their power, through five centuries between about 300 BC an AD 200, the Kushites controlled most of the northern and central parts of the eastern Sudan, and ruled as far to the south as the swamps of the Upper Nile. Roads led to busy ports on the Red Sea where ships came and went between th land of the Kushites and many foreign countries. In the north they had generally good relations with the Greek Pharaohs of Egypt; and, by way of Egypt, they traded with countries round the Mediterranean. Their ambassadors travelled an lived in many lands.

This long-distance trade brought ideas to Meroë that the Kushites made their own. Like the people of most great cultures, they welcomed foreigners and foreign ideas while remaining careful to protect their independence and their ow ideas. For example, they began to carve pictures of Apedemak with two heads and four arms in a manner they may have borrowed from the temple pictures of India. They began to make pottery in styles they may have taken from China, whose goods came to their Red Sea ports in Indian or Arabian ships. Some of their temples were modelled on those of Egypt under its Greek, and later Roman rulers.

It is likely that they also gave much to the ancient world, and especially to Africa. They were skilled in iron-working. One of the reasons why they transferr their capital from Napata in the north to Meroë in the south may have been the iron ore and timber for smelting found near their new capital. All around the ruin of Meroë you can still see piles of slag where the iron-smelters worked. Some historians think that it was from Meroë that the skills of iron-working first spread to the rest of inner Africa, perhaps by way of trade routes leading from Meroë to the lands of the Niger and beyond.

A famous woman ruler

One feature of the political system of the Meroites was that they gave great importance to the mothers of kings, as did some other African peoples. Queens queen-mothers often ruled at Meroë. They were called by a word which the Greeks wrote down as *Candace*. One famous Candace was Queen Amani-

A portrait of Queen Amani-Shakete of Kush, found by archaeologists in the ruins of her palace on the Nile, near Meroë

Shakete, who ruled between about 41 and 12 BC. Her palace at an old Kushite port on the Nile, a few miles upstream from the city of Meroë, was excavated several years ago. This showed that it had been a fine two-storey building, richly decorated in painted plaster and with fittings of gold and other metals.

The end of this memorable kingdom of the Kushites came in the fourth century AD. Quarrels with imperial Rome had long obstructed trade with Egypt and the Mediterranean. To the south-eastward the rise in about AD 100 of another powerful trading state, Axum in Ethiopia, probably reduced the opportunities of Kushite trade along the shores of the Red Sea and across the Indian Ocean. In about AD 320 a king of Axum led an army northwestward into the land of the Kushites and completed their downfall. Under this and other blows, Kushite civilisation vanished so completely that even its name and memory were lost for many centuries.

ANCIENT NORTH AFRICA

Before about 2000 BC a large part of what is now the Sahara Desert consisted of well-watered grasslands where many groups of Stone Age Africans lived and thrived. For many centuries these early peoples of the green Sahara moved back and forth across this whole wide region, hunting big game and herding cattle. We know this from the stone and bone tools they left behind them. We also know it because they were skilled painters and engravers on the walls of caves and on rocks. Many of their drawings and paintings are of the highest quality of any Stone Age art.

The Berber peoples

When great changes of climate came and the rains gradually began to fail, these Saharan peoples, like the wild animals they hunted, had to move elsewhere with their cattle. Some went southward into the grasslands of the western and central Sudan. Some went eastward into the pastures along the Nile, and, as we have seen, fought the Egyptians for their right to settle there. Other groups shifted northward into the Mediterranean coastal lands, where water supplies remained good. A few learned how to live with little water; they stayed in their old Saharan home, settling in oases where the water shortage was less acute, or travelling from one well to another. Some of the descendants of these early Saharans are there to this day, the veiled Tuareg of the great desert.

Nearly all these peoples of the Sahara and North Africa belonged to the same large group. Though of different African origins, they all spoke one or other dialect of an ancient African language called Berber, and have accordingly become known to Europeans as the Berbers. Like the Kushites, the Berbers formed cultures of their own. Most of them had nomadic habits, moving between wells and water holes and seasonal pastures with their herds and flocks. Their way of life meant that they never came together in a single state. But a minority of the Berbers also became traders, and settled in towns or founded towns of their own, and, later on, these towns developed into states with kings. Some of these Berber trading kingdoms were in North Africa. Others were in the grasslands of the western Sudan.

Much earlier, and as part of the background to this development, those who were living in North Africa had learned metal-working from their neighbours across the Mediterranean in Spain. At the same time they had developed trading links with other peoples living round the Mediterranean. As the climate of the Sahara was less harsh than it is today, they could use horses and donkeys for travel and transport across its wide plains and hills. Using these animals, they began to develop a regular caravan trade with Berbers and other Africans living in the western Sudan, south of the Sahara. With this trade they were able to bring West African gold and other products, such as ivory, northward to coastal lands along the Mediterranean. After about 1000 BC they used two main north–south routes across the Sahara. One connected what is now Morocco to the western Sudan. The other linked what is now Tunisia and western Libya to the central

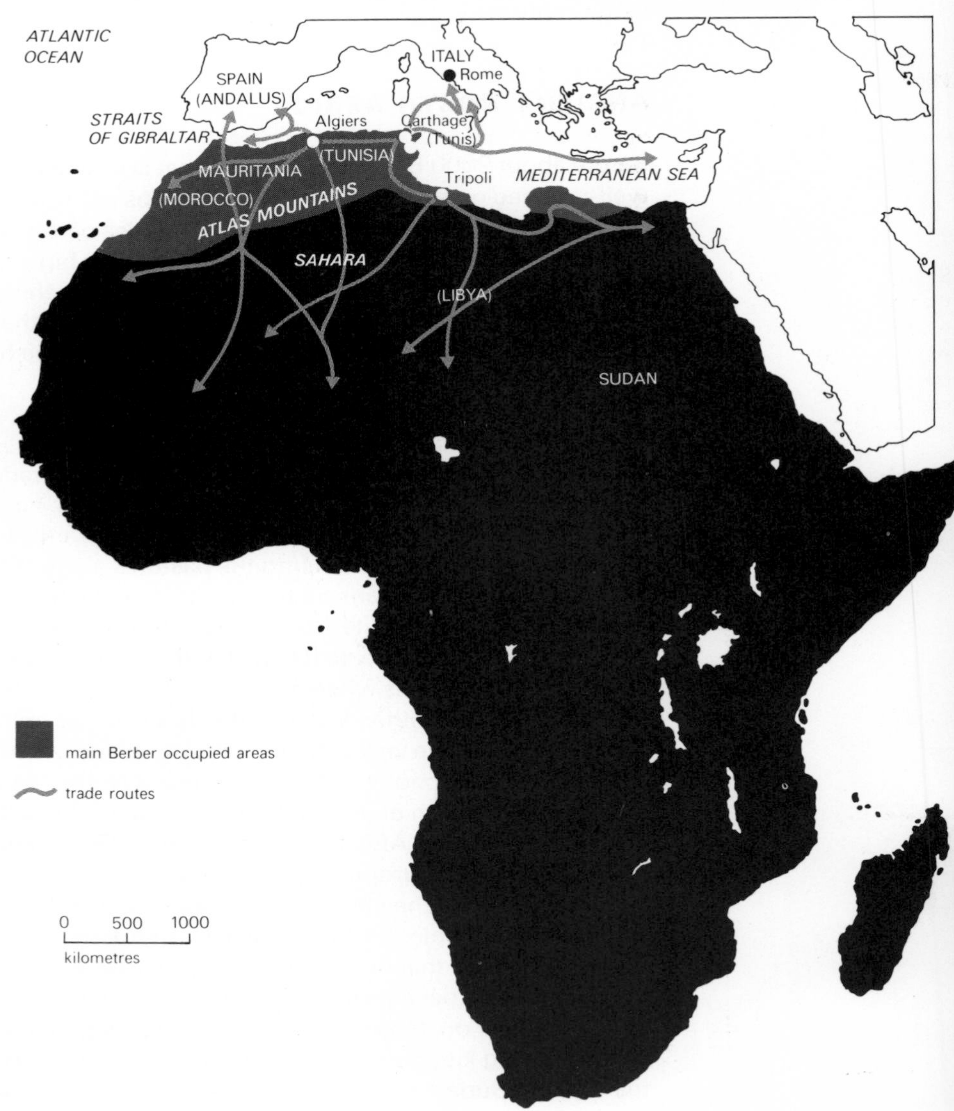

Ancient Berber trade routes across the Sahara. The sea routes across the Mediterranean are those of the Phoenicians

Sudan. These trails are marked for us today by the rough drawings of chariots and horses made on wayside rocks by Berber caravan-men of long ago.

This is how the great Saharan trade came into existence. It was to last for centuries and prove of deep importance to the history of much of Africa. There will be much to say about this later. Meanwhile you can see how the Berbers of the Sahara began linking the peoples of West Africa with those of North Africa, across the great desert, some three thousand years ago. The trading links they forged became of great value to many peoples, not only in Africa but also in Europe and Asia; and they remained of great value until comparatively modern times.

The early trans-Saharan trade was useful to the Berbers of the fertile northern coastlands. But it attracted foreigners as well. It helped to stimulate the growth of the powerful Phoenician city of Carthage. This was for a long time the wealthiest market along the western shores of the Mediterranean.

Carthage and Rome in Africa

The Phoenicians came from Syria. They were a Semitic-speaking people related to the Arabs and the Jews. Living midway along the trade routes which joined western Asia and Egypt, they soon went into trade themselves. They were brilliantly successful. Soon after 900 BC they established little colonies in Spain, at

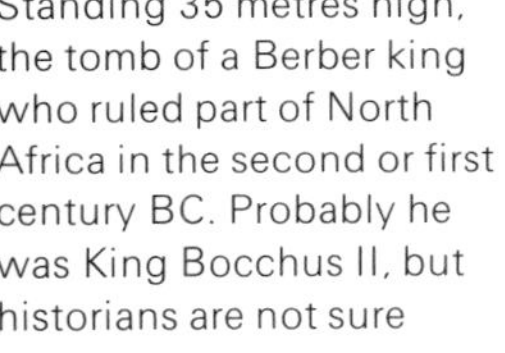

Standing 35 metres high, the tomb of a Berber king who ruled part of North Africa in the second or first century BC. Probably he was King Bocchus II, but historians are not sure

the other end of the Mediterranean. They mined Spanish silver and other metals. Not content with these, they ventured north across unknown seas as far as England, where they found Cornish tin.

Situated a few miles from the modern city of Tunis, Carthage was at first only a supply station for Phoenician ships travelling between Spain and Syria. But soon the wealth of North Africa (due to a favourable climate and fertile coastal plains) and the chance of trade with the Berbers, enabled the Phoenicians of Carthage to build their little port into a powerful city. By 500 BC or even earlier it had become an independent Phoenician state and commanded the trade of neighbouring lands. Carthaginian sailors took their ships out through the Straits of Gibraltar and southward along the coast of Morocco in search of gold and other goods. Carthaginian traders developed links with the Berbers who knew the secrets of the desert and conducted the trans-Saharan caravans, another source of African gold. Carthage became in these ways a strong trading empire.

Then the rulers of Carthage began to face rivalry from the rising power of the Roman republic. A long period of warfare followed. At one point the Carthaginian general Hannibal crossed into Europe with an army including battle elephants which the Carthaginians, like the Kushites, had learned how to use. These he led across the snow-covered mountains of the Alps and down into Italy against the Romans in their own country. In the end the Romans had the better of it. In 146 BC they took the city of Carthage and largely destroyed it, afterwards rebuilding as a city of their own. Seizing control of Carthaginian trade, the Romans ruled for several centuries in much of North Africa, but mainly in what are now Tunisia and eastern Algeria, developing there an African branch of Roman civilisation. Some Berber kingdoms survived further to the west, either as allies or subject-states of Rome.

Enter the 'Ship of the Desert'

But through all these great events the Berbers of the Sahara remained masters of their desert. And soon after the beginning of the Christian era they benefited from one of those technical developments which have often changed the course of history. Thanks probably to the Romans, now in control of Arabia and Egypt as well as much of North Africa, they got to know the value of the Arabian camel for transport under desert conditions.

Berber caravan-men soon discovered that the camel was a better means of desert transport than the horse or donkey, mainly because of its broad feet which are good for travel over sand. The camel can also go without fresh supplies of water for longer than other beasts of burden. With the 'ship of the desert' at their disposal, the Berbers of the Sahara could now enlarge the volume of their trade.

This brought changes in the grassland countries of the western Sudan. Arabic writers of the Middle Ages indicate that it was the growth of trans-Saharan trade that led to the formation of several new Berber states in the western grassland region to the south of the Sahara. These southern Berber kingdoms, based on trading towns, began to expand their dealings with other African neighbours. Among such neighbours were the Soninke (Son-in-kay) people. It was the Soninke who controlled the export of West African gold towards the north. With the expansion of trans-Saharan trade, the Soninke now felt the need to build a stronger state of their own. Out of their efforts came the empire of Ghana, for several centuries the strongest and most advanced power of the western and central Sudan. Thus the distant beginnings of Ghana, of the 'land of gold' as the Arabs later called it, were linked to the trans-Saharan trade and the arrival of the camel in Roman times.

Before following the rise of Ghana, other important developments must be considered. Among these was the rise in Africa of early Christian kingdoms.

EARLY CHRISTIAN KINGDOMS

Rome became a Christian empire in the fourth century AD under a Roman emperor who moved his capital from Rome in Italy to a new city at the eastern end of the Mediterranean. This became Byzantium, situated on the European side of the narrow channel of water which separates Europe from Asia Minor. A very creative inheritor of Greek civilisation, the Eastern Roman Empire had its centre at Byzantium for many centuries.

Spreading under Roman rule, Christianity took root and flourished in North Africa. Missions from Byzantium founded churches and cathedrals. Many African bishops were appointed. Some of these were men who acquired great learning and influence. The most famous among North Africa's Christian leaders was Saint Augustine, who was born in Numidia in 354. Augustine's writings were to have a deep effect on Christian thought.

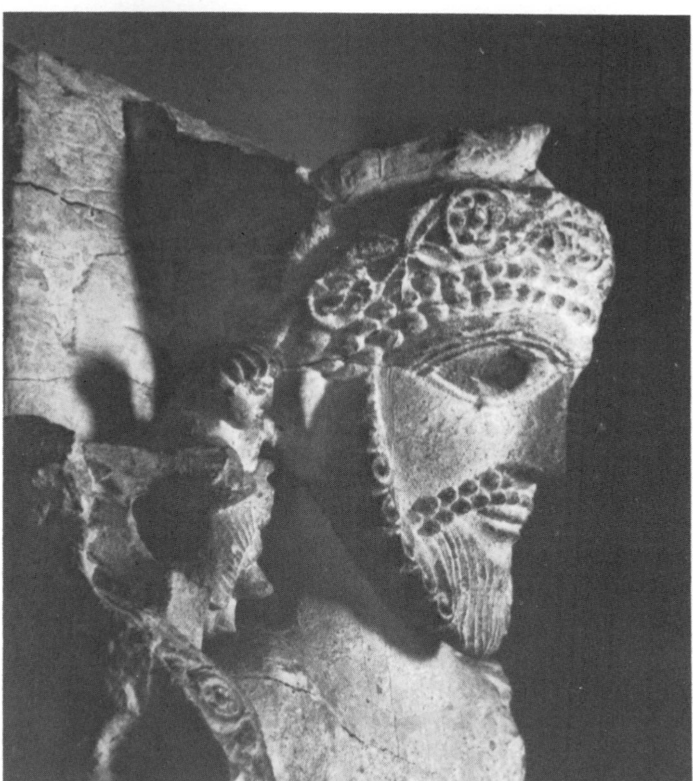

Before the Copts of Egypt became Christians, they worshipped many local gods, including the god of the Nile, shown here

Early Christian kingdoms

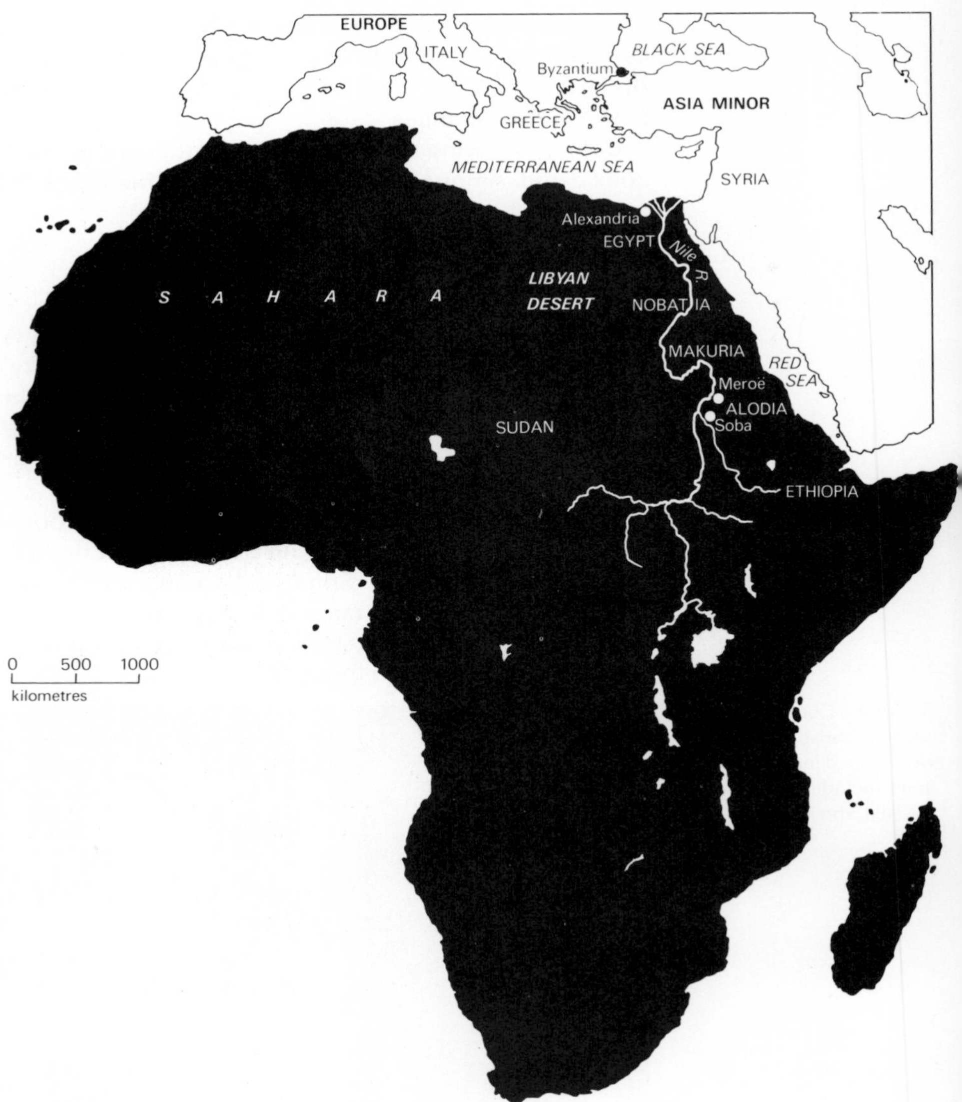

Egypt also became a Christian land. Long before Christianity was the official faith of the Roman Empire, the message of the Gospel began to spread through Egypt as a religion for the poor and humble. Roman rule was harsh. Taxes were heavy. Revolts of farmers were brutally suppressed. Looking for spiritual comfort, Egyptians found it in Christianity.

The Egyptians of earlier times had worshipped their god Amun as 'the light of the world'. But the light promised by Amun had become a distant one, guarded by the priests of Amun in dark temples barred to ordinary people. Now the new message of Jesus, saying 'I am the light of the world, he that follows me shall not walk in darkness, but shall have the light of life', was preached by poor men in the streets and slums of Egyptian towns, and poor men accepted the message.

A sort of Coptic 'political cartoon' from the fourth or fifth century AD, painted on stone. It shows a delegation of mice negotiating with a fierce cat. It is not certain who these animals are supposed to represent. The original is at Bawit in Egypt

The Copts

Gradually, in this way, a Christian community developed that was separate from the rest of the Christian world. Its beliefs and organisation formed a national Church which became a rallying point for patriotic feelings, and which afterwards became known as the Coptic Church. The name was taken from the Greek word for Egyptian, Aigiptoi, or, as it became in daily use, Qibt and then Copt.

This Christian or Coptic culture of Egypt created handsome churches, fine libraries, much religious painting and sculpture. The Christian gospels, and then other books, were translated from Greek into Coptic, the last surviving form of the language of Pharaonic Egypt, and written down in a Coptic alphabet modified from the Greek alphabet.

In the fourth century, political and spiritual differences led to a major split between the Coptic Church and that of Byzantium. Although the argument was about religion, one of the main reasons for their disagreement was that the Egyptians did not want their way of life to be altered by the government of Byzantium.

The Copts largely won out in this long politico-religious struggle. The Greeks of Byzantium continued to govern Egypt, but the Coptic Church maintained its independence. And when in the seventh century the Arab generals of the Prophet Muhammad conquered Egypt, the Copts were able not only to keep their religious independence, thanks to Muslim tolerance, but also to seize the churches and monasteries of their Greek opponents. Coptic Christianity has ever since remained alive in Egypt, though as a minority religion.

Early Christians in Ethiopia and Nubia

Christianity spread more deeply into Africa. Not long after 300 the Axumites of Ethiopia, at the southern end of the Red Sea, were converted by Christian monks from Syria. In its early years this new national religion of Ethiopia was an off-shoot of the Coptic Church in Alexandria, and its followers used Greek for its writings and religious services. But the leaders of the Ethiopian Church eventually decided to do away with Greek and, as the Copts had done in Egypt, began

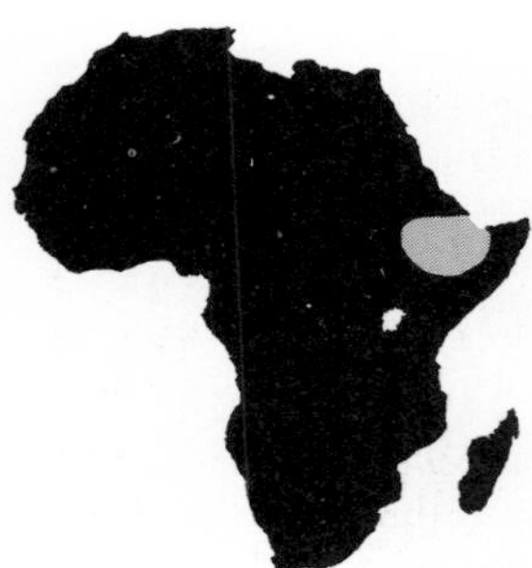

Early Ethiopia: Axum

writing their own language. They did this by altering the Sabaean script which their Axumite predecessors had borrowed long before from south Arabia. This national form of writing was done by learned monks, and the Ethiopian Church developed a rich literature which told of its long history as well as its religious beliefs. Strengthened by its intensely patriotic Church, Ethiopia stayed true to its faith and is today the oldest Christian state in the world.

Early Christianity in Africa had yet another chapter of brilliance. This unfolded along the southern Nile among the descendants of the Kushites and their neighbours of the eastern Sudan. Here in pleasant palm-shaded towns on the banks of the Nubian Nile, formerly ruled for so long by Kushite kings and queens, there arose a Christian civilisation of inner Africa. Its towns to some extent renewed the artistic and political triumphs of Meroë.

This Nubian Christianity came from Egypt, a country that began to become partly Christian soon after the life of Christ. Converted in the sixth century by missionary monks from Alexandria in Egypt, the Nubian descendants of the Kushites had at first three kingdoms. One was Nobatia in the north, another was Makuria in the middle, and the third kingdom was Alodia in the distant south. In

Carved out of the rock in a single 'piece', the church of Saint George at Lalibela in Ethiopia, dating from the twelfth or thirteenth century AD

about 700, or possibly a little earlier, Makuria and Nobatia were fused into a single kingdom, and this, with Alodia, lasted for many centuries.

Like Kushites who ruled there before them, the Christian Nubians excelled in skilful use of their sun-scorched land. They were good farmers, shrewd water engineers, craftsmen clever with their hands. They built comfortable towns, shading them with palms and other trees. They laid out pleasant gardens watered by canals. They wore loose cotton robes and sandals cool to the feet, just as do the Nubians of today. They developed a vigorous love of learning, taking over the Coptic form of the Greek writing and modifying this once again so as to be able to write their own language. They established libraries and schools. They built handsome churches, decorating these with fine wall paintings.

Unhappily, most of their writings are lost, and we know little of what they said about their country. We have to rely on the writings of Muslim Egyptians who traded with them or visited them. One of these wrote about Christian Nubia not long before AD 1000. He describes Soba, the capital of Alodia, as a city of 'fine buildings, great monasteries, churches decorated with gold, many gardens'. He adds that Alodia was rich in grain, and possessed many horses and camels, and that its learned men wrote Nubian in the Greek alphabet, by which he meant a modified Coptic alphabet.

These African Christians lived on good terms with Muslim Egypt until soon after 1250. Then came a time of troubles which ended in disaster. Unprotected by tall mountains, as Ethiopia was, they were invaded by Arab Muslims from Egypt. Soon after they were also invaded from the south by other Africans who had been converted to Islam by some of their Red Sea neighbours. Yet Makuria, which included the northern kingdom of Nobatia, was able to defend its independence until early in the fourteenth century, and Alodia even longer. Then the great chapter of Nubian Christianity was at last at an end.

Africa and the world of long ago

These pages have suggested some of the many ways in which Africans helped to shape the progress and development of the ancient world.

Egyptian civilisation was built by Africans in an African land. They set a towering example of government, administration, wealth-production and early forms of science. What the Egyptian Africans thought and did was of deep importance for three thousand years, and in many different ways. Egyptian scholarship had a profound influence. This went far and wide. 'The names of nearly all the gods', wrote the Greek historian Herodotus in the fifth century BC, 'came to Greece from Egypt.'

Other African achievements have their place in this record. The trading enterprises of the Kushites and the Axumites, the early caravans that crossed the Sahara between North and West Africa, the vigorous commerce of the Nubians and other African neighbours: all these were important African activities in the world of their time.

2 Varied lands and peoples

SIGNPOSTS TO A HIDDEN AFRICA

Kingdoms and empires in ancient Africa left many signposts to their greatness. These include tombs and temples, pyramids and palaces, as well as wall inscriptions, writings on reed-paper scrolls, and even a few history books such a: that of Herodotus. It is often hard to trace the detailed story of the ancient Egyptians, the Kushites, the Berbers, or others mentioned in Chapter 1, but there is no difficulty in seeing the chief stages of their progress.

What can be said about other Africans, about all those who lived in the plains and forests south of the Sahara Desert? Are there any signposts to the history of those long-hidden regions?

The ancient world has left us few such guides. Even the Greeks of Egypt, a restlessly adventuring people who were always eager to learn about distant land: knew next to nothing about Africans south of the Sahara. They learned a little more when their sailors and sea-merchants began visiting the coast of East Afric soon after the beginning of the Christian era. About AD 150 an Egyptian Greek captain wrote a 7,000-word sailors' guide to the ports and trade of the East African seaboard. About the lands of the interior, however, he had nothing to say No doubt the Berber caravan-men knew a great deal, at least about the western Sudan, but the information they brought to the thriving cities of North Africa has long since been lost. Even the enterprising Romans sent only a handful of explorers southward across the Sahara, and Roman records say little of what the found there.

In later centuries there were contacts between European countries and the coastal peoples of Africa. But signposts to the history of these coastal populations, and still more to the history of the inland countries of Africa, remained few and hard to read. Many reports that came back to Europe were wrong, and some were ridiculous. Often these reports were more remarkable for what they had misunderstood than for what they could really explain.

Because of this there arose a widespread belief in Europe that the Africans of inland Africa, especially those of Africa south of the Sahara, had no history of their own, built no civilisations, and made no progress. Historians now know tha such beliefs were mistaken. The Africans of inland Africa, or of any other part of Africa, were inferior to no-one else; their history has proved it. Yet they made few

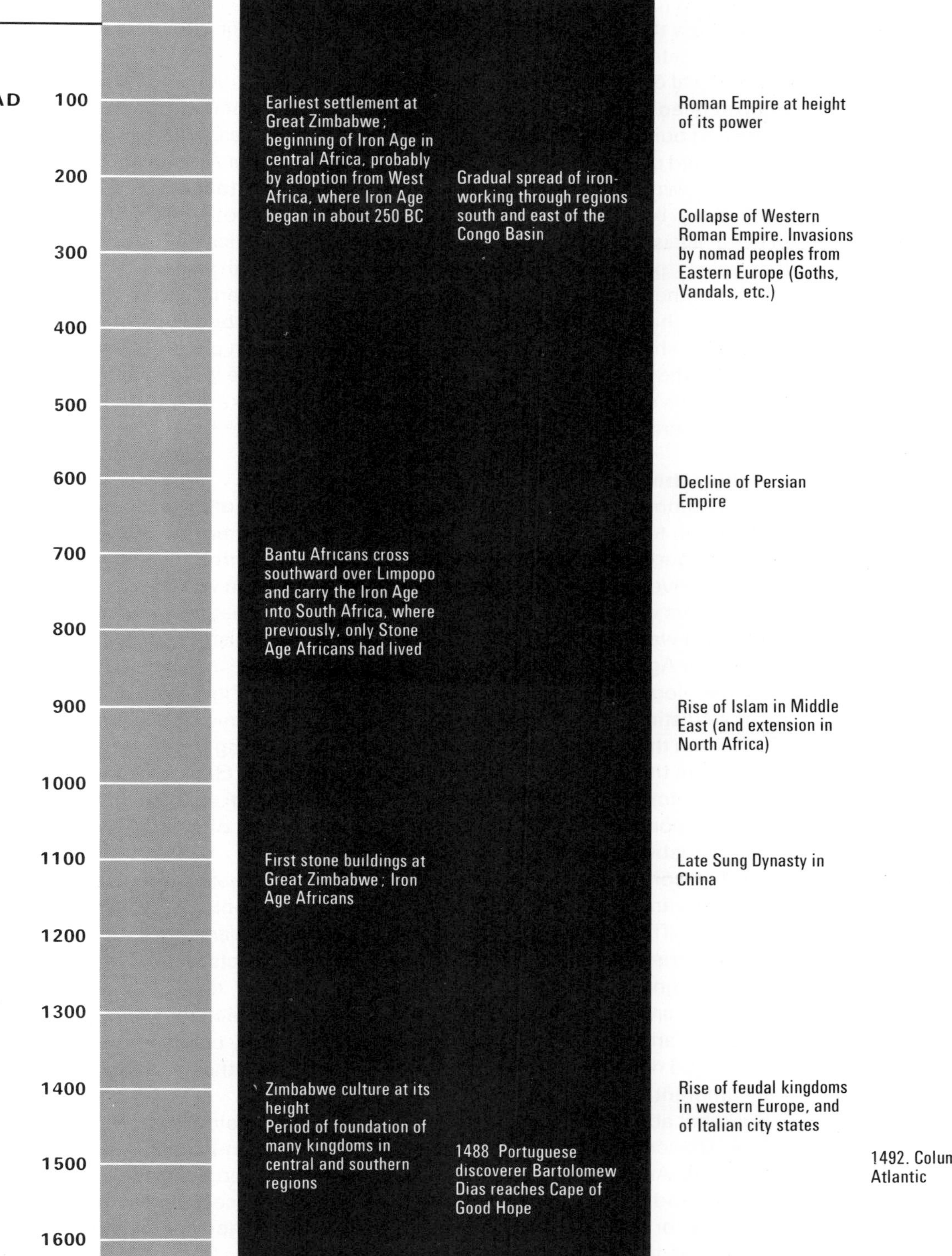
AD 100
Earliest settlement at Great Zimbabwe; beginning of Iron Age in central Africa, probably by adoption from West Africa, where Iron Age began in about 250 BC
Roman Empire at height of its power
200
Gradual spread of iron-working through regions south and east of the Congo Basin
Collapse of Western Roman Empire. Invasions by nomad peoples from Eastern Europe (Goths, Vandals, etc.)
300
400
500
600
Decline of Persian Empire
700
Bantu Africans cross southward over Limpopo and carry the Iron Age into South Africa, where previously, only Stone Age Africans had lived
800
900
Rise of Islam in Middle East (and extension in North Africa)
1000
1100
First stone buildings at Great Zimbabwe; Iron Age Africans
Late Sung Dynasty in China
1200
1300
1400
Zimbabwe culture at its height
Period of foundation of many kingdoms in central and southern regions
Rise of feudal kingdoms in western Europe, and of Italian city states
1500
1488 Portuguese discoverer Bartolomew Dias reaches Cape of Good Hope
1492. Columbus crosses Atlantic
1600

written records, and were seldom or never visited by travellers from the rest of the world. How then can we know their history? The answers are provided by historical detection and its methods.

Historical detection relies chiefly on three kinds of evidence. The first comes from archaeology, which is the study and explanation of things men in the past made and built, such as pottery, tools, ornaments, graves, houses, cities. The second kind comes from the histories of themselves that African peoples have handed down, by word of mouth, from one generation to the next. This is called oral history, because it is remembered and recited but not written. The third kind of evidence is that of books or reports written about Africa by Africans themselves, principally in Arabic, or by Arab or European visitors.

Each of these three kinds of knowledge gives a different type of information. And when they are all brought together it is possible to build up detailed and sometimes sharply clear pictures of the past. Many such pictures are now available, the patient work of long research. When these in turn are fitted together, the story of African development begins to take shape. An example may be useful here.

Reading the signposts of Zimbabwe

At the beginning of Chapter 1 you read how a white South African explorer of a century ago found the tall ruins of Zimbabwe; and how he and other treasure-seekers thought that some 'lost people' from outside Africa must have raised those massive walls. Then you read that this explanation was wrong, and that the true builders were the local Africans. Why is it certain that the great walls of Zimbabwe were built by Africans during the period of history known in Europe as the Middle Ages?

Archaeologists began studying Zimbabwe, or Great Zimbabwe as it is usually called to distinguish it from nearby stone ruins of the same kind, as long ago as 1905. From then till now they have toiled away at putting together the information they have found. Today the pieces in this archaeological jigsaw puzzle are almost all in place. Such pieces of information are of various sorts, each of them important for the work of historical detection at other places as well as at Great Zimbabwe.

The first sort comes from studying pottery and other objects, such as iron spearheads and bowls of carved stone, found by archaeologists while digging in these ruins. They compared objects of this kind with others they found elsewhere. This comparison showed them that the Zimbabwe objects were made by Africans, not by foreigners.

Next, the archaeologists studied the actual way in which the walls of Zimbabwe, and of nearby ruins, were put together. They could see that the builders had developed their skills from one style to another, and that these styles were different from those of any foreign country.

But what about the age of the ruins? Here the archaeologists have had two guides. One consists in objects of obviously foreign manufacture that were found in the ruins. Among these were fragments of Chinese porcelain, the broken bits of old plates and bowls imported from across the Indian Ocean and carried inland to Zimbabwe for the dwellings of its kings. Their knowledge of porcelain manufacture in China showed that these fragments were from plates and bowls

The stone ruins of Great Zimbabwe seen from the air. On hillsides nearby, but outside this picture, are the ruins of other large buildings. From right to left, the enclosure within the big surrounding wall measures about 130 metres

made between about AD 1200 and 1500. The archaeologists therefore had a useful start towards solving the problem of Great Zimbabwe's age.

But it was only a start. These Chinese objects might have reached Great Zimbabwe long after the main building period, or, alternatively, long after they themselves were made in China. But archaeology can apply another kind of age test. This stems from a brilliant invention by an American scientist, W. F. Libby, some thirty years ago, known as the Carbon-14 Test. Carbon-14 is an isotope of carbon that is radioactive, and loses its radioactivity at a known rate across the years. This means that an old lump of wood or any other carbon-containing material, even iron, can now be tested to see how old it is. The test gives no exact answers, but it does give answers that are fairly reliable to within a couple of hundred years.

Applying the Carbon-14 test, archaeologists working at Great Zimbabwe have learned that Africans first settled there in about AD 300. They have found that the earliest buildings in stone, which fortunately also included pieces of timber, were raised in about AD 1100, and that the great walls which still survive were built between about AD 1350 and AD 1400. In this way the evidence of the foreign pottery, suggesting that Zimbabwe flourished after about 1200, is confirmed. Applied to other ruins and objects, Carbon-14 tests have provided many other approximate dates.

Putting the evidence together

Having got so far, the historians had to ask another kind of question. What did the Africans of the country of Great Zimbabwe remember about the history of these ruins and the work of their ancestors in building them? What was the oral history of this country? The first point to note is that this question was very seldom asked till a few years ago. It is easy to see why. In the 1890s the country of Zimbabwe was invaded by British colonists from South Africa who turned it into the colony of Southern Rhodesia. They were people who had no interest in the Africans whose land they took and used. Yet a few scientists did get to work on the question; and they have come up with interesting answers.

They have found that the Africans of this country remember a lot about their own history. It is clear from this remembered history, told and retold down the centuries, that an important kingdom arose here soon after 1400 under King Mutota; and that Mutota and his son Matope extended the power of this kingdom, during the fifteenth century, till it reached all the way across modern Rhodesia and Mozambique as far as the Indian Ocean. Oral history also tells us that by 1490 this kingdom ran into trouble, and split into two kingdoms. The first of these two kingdoms was then ruled by a line of kings whose title continued the royal title of Mutota, that of Mwana Mutapa or, as Europeans called it, Monomotapa. This kingdom was in the northern part of the country that would long afterwards become the colony of Southern Rhodesia. A second kingdom, based on a capital in the western part, was ruled by another line of kings whose title was Changamire. All these kings and their peoples were Africans of the Shona branch of the Bantu language family. Their descendants live in the same country today, and they call it Zimbabwe after the famous capital of those early times.

The empire of Mwana Mutapa

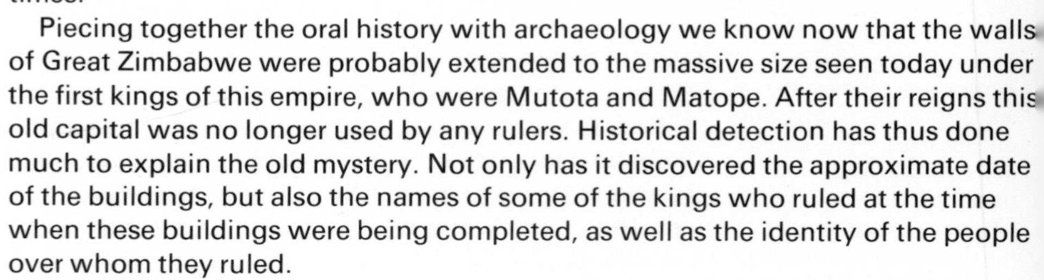

Piecing together the oral history with archaeology we know now that the walls of Great Zimbabwe were probably extended to the massive size seen today under the first kings of this empire, who were Mutota and Matope. After their reigns this old capital was no longer used by any rulers. Historical detection has thus done much to explain the old mystery. Not only has it discovered the approximate date of the buildings, but also the names of some of the kings who ruled at the time when these buildings were being completed, as well as the identity of the people over whom they ruled.

Then there is the third kind of evidence. What do old books say about Zimbabwe and its kings? The answer is that they confirm the findings of archaeology and oral history, but add useful details rounding out the picture.

The 'Meadows of Gold'

The first book of any value about the kingdoms of this country was written as early as AD 945 in the bustling city of Cairo, a major centre of trade and learning. Its author was an Arab scholar called al-Masudi, a geographer of those times. He called his book *The Meadows of Gold and Mines of Precious Stones (Muruj al-*

Dhabab wa Ma'adin al-Jawhar) partly, as he explained, because he thought that an attractive title would 'excite a desire to know its contents, and make the reader eager to understand history', but also because he was writing about the distant lands from which gold and precious stones did in fact reach Cairo and other wealthy markets.

Al-Masudi was not content to collect information from travellers. Like Herodotus long before him, he went to see for himself. He tells how he took ship with sailors and merchants of the port of Siraf, on the Persian Gulf, and sailed across the perilous seas far south along the East African coast, and how he safely returned after seeing and hearing new things. He says he went as far as the island of Kanbalu, evidently one of the offshore islands of modern Tanzania or

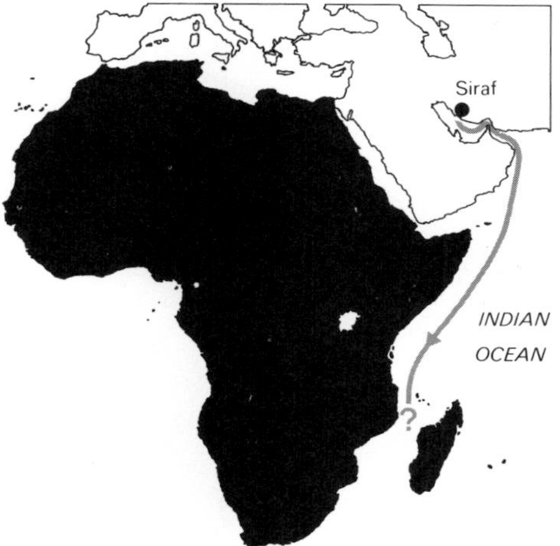

al-Masudi's voyage, made in AD 916

Mozambique. Somewhere in that region, perhaps near the mouths of the Zambesi River which flows into the ocean from Mozambique, al-Masudi heard news of a powerful African king who ruled over other African kings, and whose country was rich in iron, ivory, and gold. Historians believe that this 'kingdom of Zanj' described by al-Masudi (who used the Arabic word 'Zanj' for Africans), was possibly the forerunner of one or other of the later kingdoms of the Mwana Mutapa. The people certainly exported a great amount of ivory and gold. Most of the ivory, says al-Masudi, went to India and China, while the gold was bought by traders of many lands.

Centuries after al-Masudi and just before 1500, Portuguese sailors from Europe arrived on these eastern coasts. They too heard news of a powerful kingdom somewhere in the interior, and found that the Swahili cities of the seaboard were buying gold and ivory from it. The Portuguese collected news about this gold-rich inland kingdom from Swahili traders who went back and forth between the coast and the interior. These traders told the Portuguese as little as they could, for they rightly feared that the Portuguese would try to capture the gold and ivory trade for themselves. But they told a little, and the Portuguese were also able to meet Africans from the inland kingdom. A Portuguese merchant who gathered information on the East Coast soon after 1500 recorded the following description:

> Beyond this coastal country lies the great kingdom of Monomotapa [Mwana Mutapa] which belongs to black men who go naked from the waist up. These ar warlike men, and some of them are great traders. They wear swords carried in wooden scabbards, which are made with gold and other metals, and they wear them on the left side, just as we do. Their king lives in a town called Monomotap in a very large building, and it is from there that the traders carry gold to the coast

This 'very large building' interested the Portuguese; they continued to gather what information they could find. Another of them described it soon after:

> It is a large fortress, which is built of large and heavy stones, a very curious and well constructed building which is said to be built without any cement. And in other districts of that country there are fortresses like this, and in each of these fortresses the king has a governor. He is a great king, and those who serve him d so on bended knee, and with much reverence.

A modern photo of one of the emirs (rulers) of northern Nigeria today. He is the man who is third from the left. Nowadays these rulers remain important people but do not have political power

Now it is clear from our other sources of information that this African capital was probably Great Zimbabwe, and that in any case the other 'fortresses' were those whose ruins may still be seen such as Naletele or Dhlo Dhlo. Here, then, is another confirmation of the accuracy of the findings of archaeology and oral history. Only in the use of these royal buildings were the Portuguese mistaken. They were not fortresses but unfortified royal residences. Their rulers felt no need for strong defences. Until later invasions by the Portuguese and others they had no enemies who could seriously endanger them.

Thus the various sources of information combine to show that the old African state of Zimbabwe began some six or seven centuries ago. Other states are now known, whether from oral history or other evidence, to have begun still earlier. The Mossi people of the Volta River region of West Africa have a line of kings who have ruled for about a thousand years. The Kanuri of north-eastern Nigeria can claim much the same for their ruling family, whose first king came to the throne around AD 900 and whose last king of that same line ruled until as late as 1846. And it is not only the peoples with kings who remember their history. Others who have never or seldom had kings do the same, though with less detail. For example, the history of the Luo group, who live in Uganda and Kenya, can be traced by oral history back to the fifteenth century and even earlier.

Putting all these different kinds of evidence together, historians have combined to build a record of the African past that is rich in detail, change and movement. All this confirms that the black peoples, like the white peoples, can look back on a long road travelled through many stages of development and civilisation since primitive times.

THE BATTLE WITH NATURE

Peoples everywhere have developed in the same basic ways. Members of every community have had to work together to solve their problems; to find out how to grow more food and make a wider range of tools, to evolve more efficient ways of government and self-defence, and to use these inventions so as to support larger populations and better conditions of life.

It is also true, of course, that communities and peoples have developed differently in different lands and continents. They have faced different problems of soil and climate, natural resources, and other such factors, and have had to find different solutions. To understand the nature of African solutions – why Africans developed as they did, and not in some other way – we must think about the sorts of problems they faced.

In certain important ways Africa was, and still is, an extremely difficult continent for man to master. Harsh obstacles have faced people who have settled in most of its regions. Endurance, ingenuity, and wisdom have been required to overcome such obstacles.

Obstacles to settlement

Although many people outside Africa have always thought that the intense heat was one of those obstacles, this is not in fact true. Over most of the continent the average temperatures are fairly comfortable all through the year. Even in the

This is an outline of Africa with an outline of Europe over it. It shows you how big Africa is when compared with Europe

central regions along the Equator, between the latitudes of about ten degrees North and ten degrees South, temperatures seldom rise much above 27° Centigrade, and often they are lower, partly because cloud or dust lessens the intensity of the sun's heat.

Great variations must always occur in a continent as large as Africa. Summer heat in the central Sahara and the eastern Sudan is certainly intense, and has been so for at least four thousand years. Around AD 550, for example, one of the earliest Christian missionaries to the Nubians said that it was so hot there, during summer days, that 'he was obliged to take refuge in caves, full of water, where he sat undressed but for a linen robe such as the people of the country wear'. It is just the same today, except that nowadays people take refuge, whenever they can, not in caves but air-conditioned buildings. Yet these same regions in wintertime, around January, can be so cold that you need two blankets at night, while the days are often chill and bracing.

What, then, were the chief obstacles to human settlement? They had to do with climatic and other natural problems in which heat played only a small part.

First of all, look at the rainfall map on page 43. Though simplified, it shows the general situation that has existed in Africa for many centuries. Along the Equator, in the centre of Middle Africa, lies a region of very high rainfall, ranging from between 1800 and 2500 millimetres every year. Both the days and nights can be hard to bear, not because they are very hot but because they are very humid. This is the country, as you might expect, of dense and steaming forest. The vegetation of these vast equatorial forests is so luxuriant that a person may walk for days and scarcely see the light of the sky, while huge trees and dense undergrowth crowd together so that pathways narrow into tunnels. Until our own century the only good 'roads' through these rain forests were the great Congo River and its tributaries.

At a few points on the western coasts, in the 'bend' of Nigeria and Cameroon and out on the far western tip of the Guinea Coast, the rainfall is higher still: and here, too, the season of the rains, falling between July and December, brings stifling weather and great quantities of water.

On either side of the equatorial region, to the south as well as to the north, there is a belt of lesser average rainfall, ranging between an annual 1750 and 1000

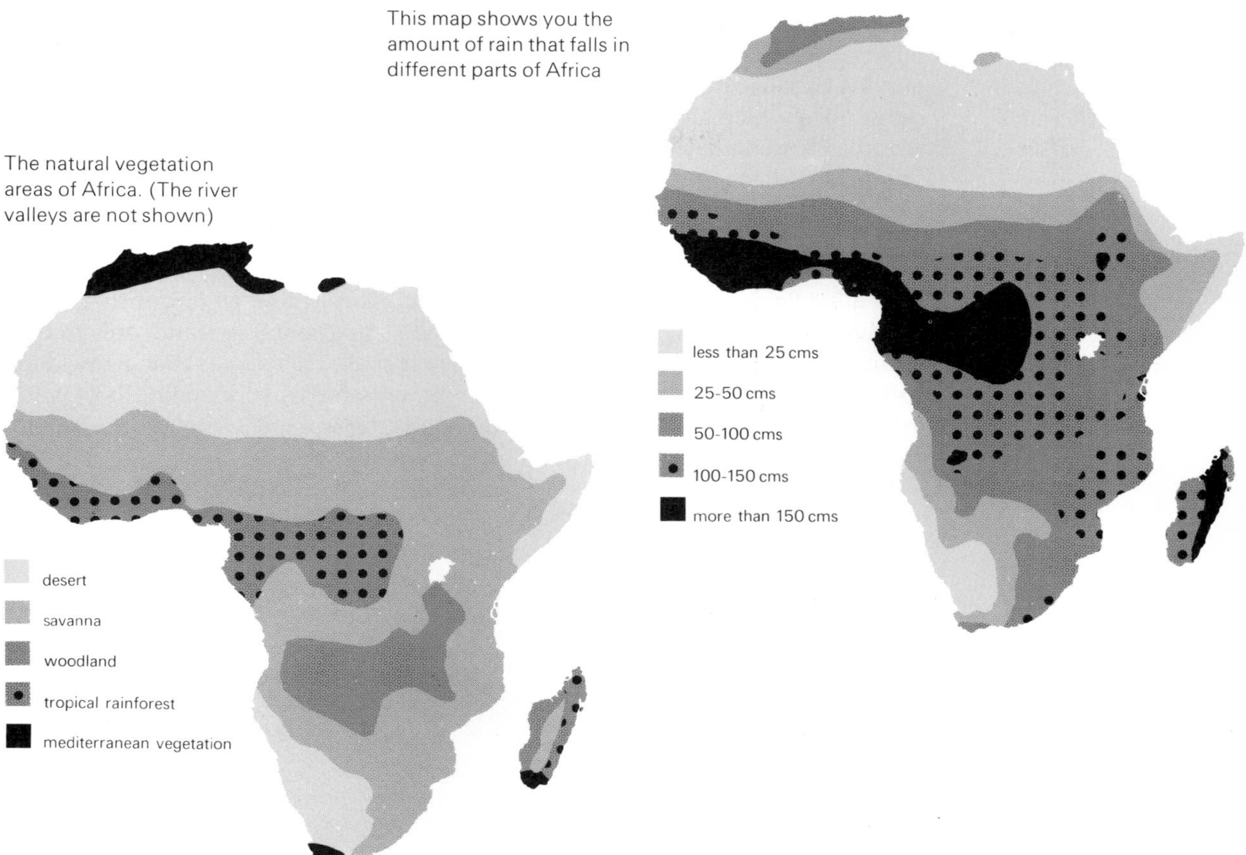

This map shows you the amount of rain that falls in different parts of Africa

The natural vegetation areas of Africa. (The river valleys are not shown)

millimetres. Then, again farther to the north and farther to the south, is a second belt of varying width where rainfall averages between about 760 and 200 millimetres a year. At least 500 millimetres of rainfall a year is needed to grow most crops. In some years this belt suffers from drought. Beyond this in the north there is the Sahara Desert, and in the far south-west is the Kalahari Desert, where whole years may pass without a drop of rain. Several other regions also suffer from severe droughts.

Again, of course, there are many variations. In the north-east the land rises into tall mountains often covered with snow; even near the Equator there are isolated peaks, such as Kilimanjaro and Ruwenzori, where snow lies on the upper slopes for most of the year.

Belts of varying rainfall have helped to produce belts of varying vegetation. The 'rain forests' of the equatorial regions, of the Basin of the river Congo, thin away into broad plains of tall grass and scrub to the north and south, and these again into savanna lands of short grass and thorn. In the savanna lands there is little or no timber for building or for shade, while most of the trees that do grow in these grasslands and steppes are of little value to mankind.

The kind of soil found in different areas is another influence on settlement. In most of Africa, with exceptions in the highlands of East Africa, the far south of

South Africa, the coastal lands along the Mediterranean, and at a few other points, the soil is both shallow and poor in quality. This matters least in the forest regions because there the quantity of dying vegetation forms a deep compost on the surface which has great fertilising value. But the grasslands and thin woodlands generally have soil too poor to support more than a few annual crops one year after the other, before losing their fertility, while grass for the pasturing cattle is also soon exhausted.

This poor soil is partly produced by the way the rains fall. The rains seldom fall gently; often they fall in great tempests of water. Dramatic thunderstorms, forked with great flares of lightning, pour down their rains in sudden floods that swell the rivers, sweep away or thin the surface soil, and drench the land, only to be followed by long periods with little or no rain at all. This means that many lands suffer badly from loss of soil, or soil erosion, whether by sudden floods of water that carry it away, or, in dry seasons, by winds that snatch it from the surface in clouds of dust.

The physical features of Africa

The Anopheles mosquito that carries malaria from one human to another

The water snail that carries bilharzia or schistosomaiasis

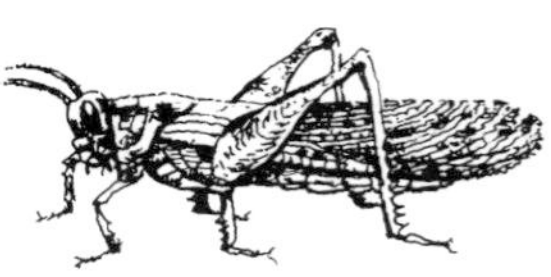

The locust has destroyed crops in many parts of Africa since ancient times

The tsetse fly carries the parasites that cause African sleeping sickness in humans, cattle and horses

A tough continent

In many ways, then, this was indeed a difficult continent, and needed a stubborn and courageous people to master it and make it yield the means of human life. While a few peoples were lucky in finding easy homelands, along some of the great rivers or the shores of lakes, or in the fertile eastern highlands of what are now Kenya, Uganda, northern Tanzania, Ruanda and Burundi, or in the temperate and comfortable lands of the extreme north and south, most Africans could survive and prosper only by meeting these severe challenges of climate and soil.

Sometimes they were helped by the lavish growth of nature in Africa, by its tall forests or great herds of animals that were good for meat, such as antelope and buffalo; but these same advantages also had disadvantages. The forests were hard to penetrate; often they were hard to live in. The animals included dangerous beasts such as lions, leopards, and rhinoceros in the grassland plains, crocodiles in the rivers, and poisonous snakes.

Most Africans also had to survive diseases peculiar to their tropical regions. These included malaria, carried by mosquitoes; certain other sicknesses, such as bilharzia carried by water snails, or debilitation caused by hookworms; and, among the worst, the disease carried by tsetse fly. Scientists believe that the tsetse fly, carrier of sleeping sickness for human beings and nagana for cattle, has existed in Africa since the earliest human life. It is present, as the map below shows, over wide areas of the continent; and wherever it is present there could be and there can be no breeding of cattle or horses, while stock brought in from other regions may not live for long.

In the north-east and east especially, Africans have had to bear with other troubles, such as invasions of locusts, big grasshoppers which breed in multitudes and consume all grass or grain wherever they settle in their flight from

The areas of Africa affected by the tsetse fly. (Some areas are more seriously affected than others)

place to place. In a few hours a swarm of locusts can destroy the farming work of many months, and overnight whole communities can be threatened with starvation.

Nevertheless Africans were able to build their own cultures in every habitable region. It is this major achievement that forms the central theme of African history.

AFRICANS TAME THEIR LAND

In the beginning Africa was populated by small groups of wandering hunters. They lived mostly in the open plains and woodlands, and survived by killing game and gathering wild plants.

Then man in Africa learned how to domesticate cattle, and, soon afterwards, how to grow food. This first occurred in the valley of the Nile and the green Sahara. After about 3000 BC good breeds of cattle, acclimatised to African conditions, were gradually taken southwards by a variety of stock-raising peoples. Cattle became numerous in the Sudanese grasslands, south of the Sahara, and in the eastern highlands. Little by little these cattle continued to spread southward as more and more peoples learned how to handle and use them until, by about a thousand years ago, they were common as far as the southern tip of the continent. At the same time, there were still many regions where people could not raise cattle because of dense forest or the presence of tsetse fly.

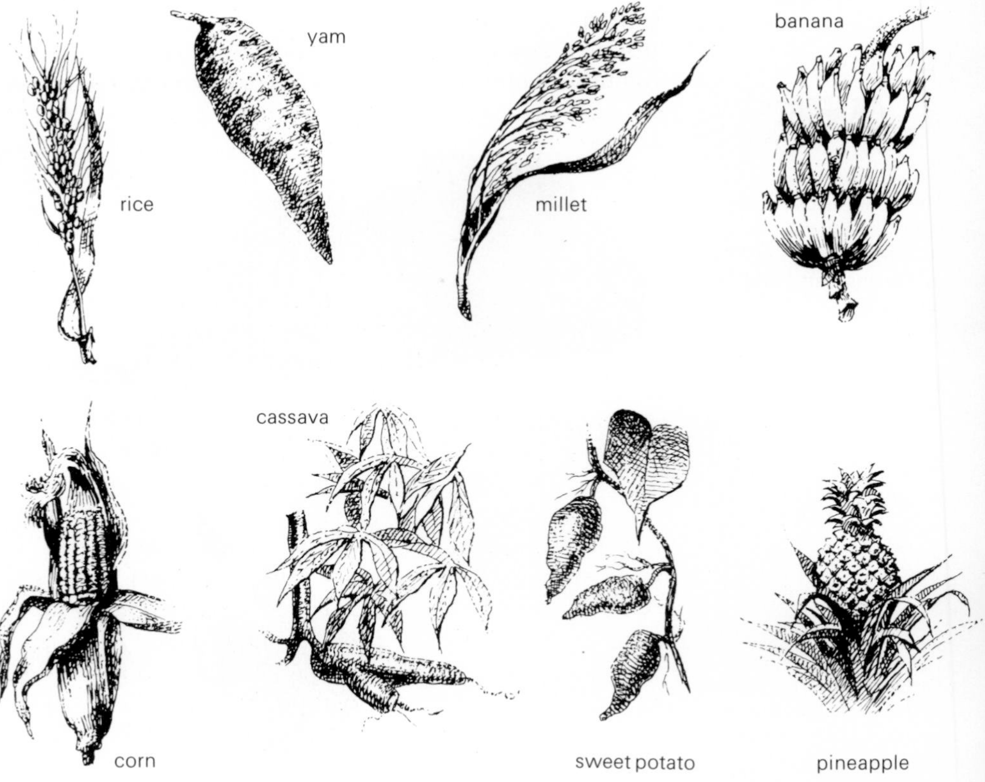

When the first Europeans arrived on the coasts of West Africa they found Africans using the plants and fruits shown in the top row. Later, Europeans brought to Africa useful fruits and plants they had discovered in America; some of these are shown in the bottom row

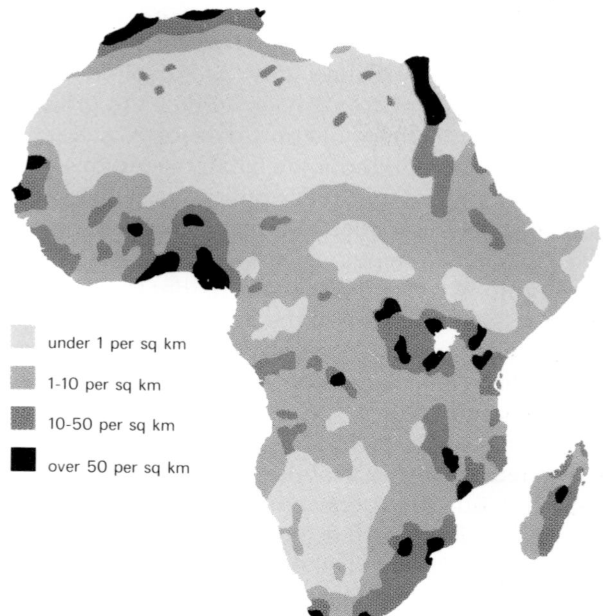

A population density map of Africa showing the average number of people per square kilometre. This refers to modern times, but the relative densities were probably not much different in the past

The farming of crops moved gradually southward not long afterwards. Mostly these crops were rice or millet. They began to be raised in the western Sudan perhaps as early as 2000 BC, and at about the same time, though still in small quantities, in parts of East Africa. By about two thousand years ago such crops were being grown throughout most of the grassland countries south of the central Congo forests. Yet here again there was a difficulty. Africa did not have many good food plants of her own. Millet was probably the best food plant that most Africans had, as well as several useful roots, such as yams, and fruits such as bananas.

As time went by, other fruits and plants were brought in from other continents. One of the best varieties of food-banana probably arrived around AD 300 or 400 from south-east Asia in the ships of Indian Ocean sailors. Much later, after about 1600, some valuable American crops were introduced by the Portuguese and other Europeans. These included corn, cassava (an edible root-tuber), sweet potatoes, pineapples and one or two others. African farmers welcomed these valuable additions to their food supply, and quickly learned how to grow them.

The growth of population, and the gradual mastering of nature, depended always on the growth of food supplies. This growth occurred in several main stages.

Settlement, food surplus, division of labour

Once cultivation and cattle raising were understood, even by primitive methods, Africans could begin to settle in a chosen place and stay there for several years. They could seldom stay for very many years, because they could not grow enough grass or other crops on the poor soil, after a year or two of pasturing or cropping. But little by little Africans learned the secrets of better farming, and, as they learned, they could stay a little longer and each settlement could support more people.

Once again you need to remember the great variety of Africa's vegetation. The peoples who lived in the dense forests could often stay in the same place for many years at a time, adding fruits and wild food-plants to their crops of yam and other roots. But they, in turn, found it very difficult to grow grain or keep cattle, so the size of their settlements could only develop slowly.

As settlements throughout the habitable regions grew gradually larger, the same general process took place which we saw in the valley of the Nile. People began to be able to produce a surplus of food. In the fertile valley of the Nile this gave rise to rich and populous cities. Elsewhere, in conditions nothing like so good, the surplus of food was much harder to produce, and was therefore much smaller. Yet in Africa south of the Sahara, from rather more than two thousand years ago, this surplus began to be large enough to support groups of craftsmen who specialised in making tools and other useful objects, to exchange for the food their farmers grew.

Thus, as in the Nile valley and a few other regions in early times, there occurred what is called a division of labour. Most people produced food in these small communities, but others concentrated on producing equipment for the food-producers. This led in turn to early divisions in society and created new problems of law and order. Gradually the settled communities of Africa south of the Sahara became large enough to feel the need for more complex forms of government. Political history began in these wide central and southern regions, just as it had already begun in the Nile Valley and in Africa north of the Sahara.

Local leaders became chiefs, and chiefs became kings. . . . Here is a splendid wood-carving of King Shamba of the Bushongo kingdom in the Congo Basin long before our time. He probably ruled the Bushongo people in the seventeenth century

As their methods of producing food improved these small communities grew in numbers, until they decided to appoint chiefs to rule over them and settle their disagreements. Groups of neighbouring communities came together under stronger chiefs or kings. Some groups in society began to have more power than others. New specialists appeared, such as men trained in warfare or in government. So each community began to consist of groups with different skills, different duties, different kinds of work.

Such divisions in society south of the Sahara seldom went as far as in the Nile Valley. Most of these communities remained very democratic. For a long while each member continued to have a say in the way the laws were made and kept. Only in much later times did this early democracy begin to fade.

Another important influence on society was the types of equipment available. The size of the food surplus that Africans could generally produce, and therefore the size and complexity of their communities and systems of government, depended to a large extent on the kind of tools they had at their disposal. So long as they had to work with tools of stone or bone or wood, they found it difficult or impossible to cut their way through dense forests, or to till the soil. After the introduction of farming, their next big breakthrough came with their development of metal tools.

There is some evidence that copper was the first metal to be worked south of the Sahara. Copper is found in surface ores at several places in Africa and is easy to work once the secret of doing this is learned. But copper is a soft metal and not much good for tools. Mixed with tin it can be made into bronze, which is much harder. This was the alloy that the ancient Egyptians mainly relied on. But bronze south of the Sahara played little or no part in human development. Here the Africans went straight from copper to iron, or from stone to iron. And iron proved to be the metal which enabled them to tame their continent.

Iron, the 'democratic metal'

Iron has been called the 'democratic metal' because, unlike copper or tin or their alloys, it could be made in relatively large quantities once the essential operations were understood. Good surface ores of iron are abundant in most African regions, and there are few regions without any at all.

The use of iron and how to make it was probably discovered by a western Asian people called the Hittites, around 1500 BC. This knowledge remained a closely guarded professional secret for centuries. It spread slowly elsewhere, partly for this reason, and partly because other peoples were content with the bone, stone, or bronze equipment they already had. Even the ancient Egyptians, as we have seen, scarcely used iron until after 600 BC.

But, once established in Africa, the use of iron spread with remarkable speed. It was developed by a variety of African peoples, probably from methods evolved in North Africa and Meroë. On this point the evidence is not yet clear, nor does it greatly matter; people in every continent have borrowed useful ideas from others since history began. We do know however that the iron-making crafts developed by African peoples took forms of their own. Even if they borrowed the original know-how from the north, they developed it along new lines. They showed energy and speed in passing this valuable knowledge from one region to the next.

Carbon-14 tests have proved useful in tracing the dates at which this great step

Small sculptures in terracotta, or baked clay, from the *Nok Culture*. They were made more than 2000 years ago, and show us what fine artists the people of the *Nok Culture* were

forward, from the use of stone and bone and wood to iron, was taken in different places. The first people known to have made iron, south of the Sahara and Nile Valley, were a people of central Nigeria, although further research will probably show that they had neighbours who made the change to iron at about the same time. Carbon-14 tests indicate that these Nigerians (distant forefathers of people who live in central Nigeria today) were making simple iron equipment as early as about 300 BC.

This early iron-making culture is called the *Nok Culture* after the modern village where its first remains were discovered shortly before the Second World War. It had one foot in the Stone Age and the other in a new Iron Age. Its people went on using stone tools, as others did, but they began to make and use iron tools as well. This is known for certain from the primitive little blast furnaces, which they used for smelting ore, whose remains have been found by archaeologists. As it happens, the Nok people were also fine sculptors, and left behind them many excellent figures in baked clay. From the skills which formed these clay figures there afterwards developed the magnificent sculpture in clay and brass and bronze for which many Nigerian peoples were to become famous, notably those of the ancient cities of Ife and Benin.

Why was iron so important?

Whether for cutting through the forest or clearing woodland, for hoeing fields, or for improved hunting, iron heads for tools, spears and arrows were a big advance on those of stone, bone or wood. They still used these materials but gradually the growing supply of iron-headed equipment made it possible for man to increase his mastery of nature. This was a major technical change in improving man's command of his environment, comparable to that which occurred in the twentieth century when petrol-driven vehicles took over from horses.

The process of change that now started meant that one forward step led on to another, and each in turn expanded the possibilities of further growth. Iron-headed tools helped to produce more food. More food meant that more people could be fed, or better fed. Settlements could become larger. They could also last longer in any one place, and stores of food could become larger between one harvest and another. As settlements grew larger and lasted longer, other changes took place. Farming methods improved. The bigger food surplus that could now be grown gave support to more specialists in iron-making and other crafts. With more specialists, there could be more tools, an ever stronger command of nature, a better chance for mankind to grow in numbers.

These discoveries in farming and stock-raising and metal-working were the outstanding advances of the period before about AD 1000. They gave the Africans the essential keys to their success in populating their vast and difficult continent.

The techniques of iron-making then understood in Africa south of the Sahara moved quickly across the central and southern parts of the continent. Only three or four centuries after the Nok people began making iron, others were doing the same as far away as the hills of East Africa and the grassland plains south of the Congo Basin.

Much more research is needed before the full story of this spread of iron-making can be told. But already we know from Carbon-14 tests, and from other evidence, that the fires of early types of blast furnace were flickering through the African night as far as the middle of modern South Africa by as early as AD 1000.

The 'land of flames'

Several areas of metal-working became well known in large regions because traders often sold their products some distance away. One of these was in what is now the Katanga province of the Republic of Zaïre (Congo) and the neighbouring land of northern Zambia. At least twelve hundred years ago Africans living in Katanga had begun to exploit the rich veins of copper ore which Europeans were also to find and work in the colonial period. These early African metal-workers became successful copper producers, trading their copper ingots far and wide. This helped their communities to grow in size and strength, and brought wealth to the trader chiefs whom they had appointed to rule over them.

Another famous iron-making centre was Malawi, for many centuries the homeland of the Nyanja-speaking group of Bantu Africans and today a republic. One of the meanings of the word Malawi is 'land of flames' – the flames of Malawi's countless little blast furnaces in times of long ago.

African methods for making iron objects will be discussed in Chapter 6. An important point to remember here is that these techniques gave rise to a new period of social growth during which most peoples in Africa steadily multiplied in numbers, and developed the cultures and civilisations which form the greater part of African history.

PIONEERS AND FRONTIERSMEN

Armed with the skills of farming and metal-working, bold groups of young men and women split away from the little communities of those early times, and began spreading across a continent that was still almost empty of mankind. Step by step, thrusting onwards, they pushed out the frontiers of settlement across the horizons of the world they knew. Some cut deep into the rain forests. Others moved across the long low skylines of the grassland plains. Many found new homelands, never populated before, or populated only by rare families of nomad Stone Age hunters.

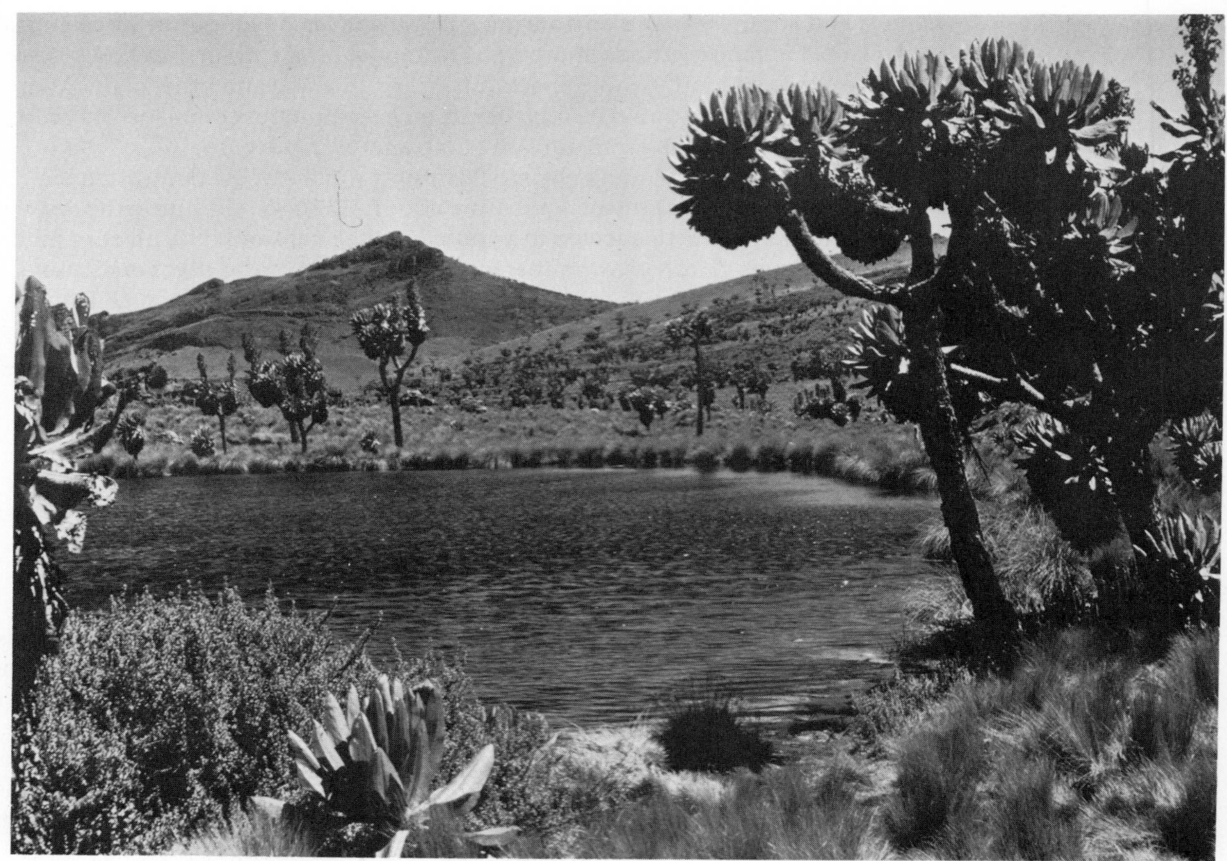

'And they went to places where no man had been before. . . .' At 4000 metres on Mount Elgon in Uganda: these strange 'trees' are a huge plant called giant groundsel (*senecio*)

This was the period of the 'founding heroes', of all those remote pioneering leaders whom Africans still remember and respect as their 'first ancestors', the men and women who led their forefathers into new lands and new ways of life. Even today, Africans recite legends and tales that praise their 'founding ancestors'. Often these stories contain a core of truth. Of the Chwezi leaders who undoubtedly formed kingdoms in southern Uganda seven centuries ago, the Nyoro who live there now say that they were so strong and brilliant that:

> one could not even look them in the face, their eyes were so bright it was like looking into the sun. And they went to places where no man had been before, and nothing could prevent them. They made things never made before. They were mighty hunters. They were good traders.

A few peoples become many peoples

With the historical knowledge of today the general meaning of such tales can be explained. Pioneering and new settlement were closely linked, as in other continents, with the need for food. People moved because they were drawn by the love of adventure, but much more because they wanted fresh pastures or fields to cultivate. With increasing supplies of food provided by farming and iron-headed tools, settlements began to grow larger than could be fed even by the increased quantities of food they could produce. Whenever this happened, and it happened more and more frequently, some people had to go away in search of a new home somewhere else.

In some regions this 'splitting up' of early peoples began several thousand years ago. Indeed, it had been happening since remote Stone Age periods. But it began happening more frequently after iron tools and weapons gave better control of nature. Little by little, as the centuries passed, the few original languages of Africa increased in this way to hundreds of languages, so that today there are more than a thousand different African languages. Each is the possession of people whose ancestors in distant times moved away to form a separate community and, in doing so, built a new and separate way of life, and developed a new and separate language.

This was how the great solitudes of ancient Africa gradually became populated with numerous and thriving communities. It was a process that began far back in time, during the Stone Age, and for long was very slow. Much about it remains

his map shows how storians think the Bantu-speaking peoples may ave spread during the ast 3000 years

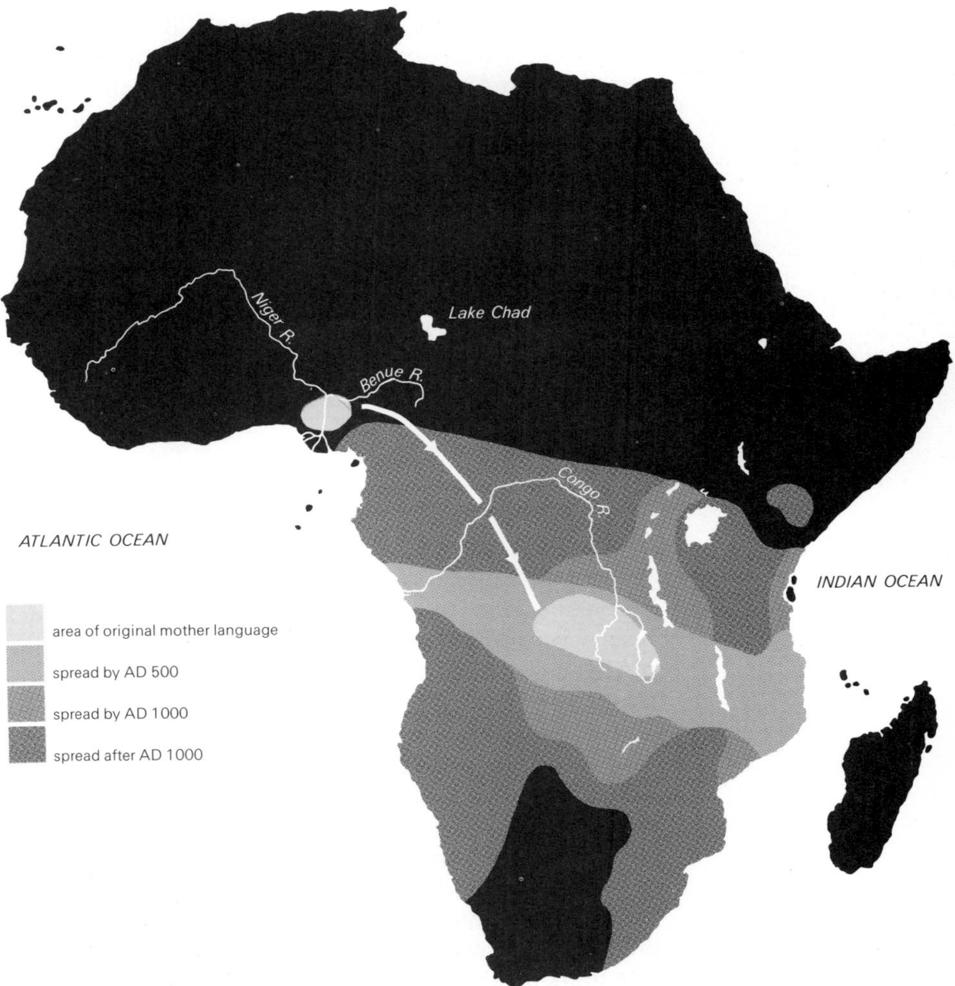

unknown. But historians can say a little about this early development. Of great importance, in this matter of peopling the solitudes of Africa, was the development of all those peoples who speak one or other of the languages of th Bantu group. (The word *bantu* simply means 'people', being the plural of the ro -*ntu*, 'humanness', just as the word *muntu* is the singular. So *bantu* means people, and *muntu* means a person.)

The original mother language of all the many Bantu languages of today is believed by language experts to have taken shape in the region of the Niger and Benue rivers, in the eastern part of West Africa, some thousands of years ago. B the principal region of early development of the people of the Bantu group lay i the grasslands of the eastern Congo Basin, or what are now known as the provinces of Katanga and Kasai in the modern Republic of Zaïre. From there the Bantu spread far and wide to the east and south and west. By AD 1000, if not earlier, there were well established settlements of Bantu people as far away as th south-eastern parts of modern South Africa.

This process of populating Africa was far advanced by the time that European began to travel through Africa. Peoples like the Bantu had tamed their wild continent, and were settled in its every region. The Europeans found hundreds c independent African states, some small and others large; and many of these stat already had a long history of their own development. After 1885, during their colonial invasions, the Europeans shuffled all these independent states into abo fifty colonies.

Here lies one of the reasons why modern Africa has political troubles. The colonies have in their turn become independent states. But their progress depends partly on forging national unity from the many smaller units of earlier times. This poses problems. But such problems can be understood only by understanding the history of Africa before the colonial period began. Understanding the Africa of today means understanding the Africa of yesterday

THINGS AREN'T ALWAYS WHAT THEY SEEM

Before we go on with the development of African history, and meet some of the outstanding men and women who helped to make that development, we shoul tackle a difficulty. It is one that white observers have often stumbled over. The Europeans who have gone to Africa have come mostly from countries with a history very different from the Africans. They have come from countries that hav not been cut off, as was most of Africa, from the revolutionary development of science and machine invention which began in Europe several centuries ago.

The wrong conclusion

When they went to Africa they found peoples who had no machine-made industry, but who lived by the earlier skills of hand-labour. These peoples had in fact solved many tough problems, but Europeans did not know this. The ways o African life seemed simple to them; the thatched huts and hoes and spears and hand-shaped pots. So they jumped to the conclusion that the Africans were primitive peoples who had invented nothing.

In thinking like this, Europeans and other whites forgot that the mother of invention is necessity. Individuals may invent things out of sheer curiosity, or out of personal interest in solving a problem. But communities *accept* such inventions only when they need or want them. If the Africans had no wheeled transport, it was partly because their way of life had no need for it. If they had no potter's wheel, it was largely because they could make all the pottery they needed by shaping clay with their hands. If they had no plough, at least south of Ethiopia, it was chiefly because of the types of farming they had developed. If most of them had no knowledge or means of writing (though here, as will be seen, there were important exceptions) it was mainly because their village life called for none. Whenever they did find a need for writing, they soon discovered the means.

There were other reasons why Africans stayed content with the inventions they had made, with the methods of farming, metal-working, and community-living that they knew, and why they looked for no others until they began to feel the pressures of European competition or domination. These reasons lay in their religious beliefs, which, like most religious beliefs, were very slow to change. As will be explained in Chapter 6, African religion taught that a man should walk in the ways of his forefathers, should avoid the temptations of personal wealth, should share his goods with his neighbours and look for happiness in equality with these neighbours. This attitude helped people to live together in peace; but it discouraged individual enterprise.

A many-flowered growth

African kinds of religious belief also favoured a wide diversity in local ways of life. Nothing in Africa is more interesting than the many different ways these peoples found in solving the same sort of community problems. In doing this they were successful again and again. Far from remaining primitive, these societies have shown a many-flowered growth of human genius that goes down into the same deep soil of early courage, invention, and development.

Most of the Europeans who conquered Africa seventy years ago believed that African ways of life were savage and deplorable. They thought of African life as if it had no civilising value of its own, no capacity for progress or improvement. They declared that Europeans must shape the rules for African law and order. In thinking like this they were blind to the facts. For the Africans had worked out their own solutions to their own problems. In finding these solutions, Africans had evolved their own civilisations. What these were we shall now see.

3 Traders and empires: the western and central Sudan

AN AFRICAN WORLD OF TRADE

Civilisation in Europe greatly developed during the Middle Ages between AD ' and 1400. New states were formed, new cities founded, new skills developed. for much of this period of early growth, important though it was, the European were outshone by African neighbours.

This was particularly true of commerce and commercial production. The gre centres of banking and exchange lay in Africa, not in Europe. None of the new towns in Europe could compare in wealth or magnificence, in the power of the merchants or the quantity of goods they handled, with the leading cities of Afr The greatest of these was Cairo, the capital of Egypt, for long the heart and foc of trade across the continents.

Gold for coins and commerce

How can we be sure of this? One convincing answer comes from a lucky accident. Tens of thousands of business letters and contracts have survived fro the Cairo of around AD 1000. Scholars have found them in the storehouses of synagogue and cemetery. They were stored there by Jewish traders who made rule to keep every document on which the name of God was mentioned, and m business documents of those days mentioned God in one way or another. The Jewish merchants were members of a much wider trading network operated b Arabs, Berbers, and other peoples of Africa and western Asia. This network reached from the Atlantic shores of Africa across the world to India and China, northward into Europe and far southward over the Sahara Desert into West Afr

These business documents of about nine hundred years ago tell a fascinatin story. We read of merchants of North Africa who made their fortunes trading w the countries around the Indian Ocean; of goods bought in West Africa and so in Cairo for Eastern silks and spices; of regular routes by land and sea that linke host of thriving cities in a far-ranging community of commerce.

In all this evidence of world-wide trade, there is repeated emphasis on the central importance of certain African products, and, most of all, of gold. It is ea to see why gold was so important. Long-distance trade required a convenient a standard means of pricing and payment. This called in turn for the use of mone and the best form of money, although cheques and similar means of payment

AD 100	Berber traders of the Sahara begin to use camels instead of horses, and desert transport becomes less difficult		Romans in Britain	
200				
300	Probable origins of ancient empire of Ghana (not in region of modern Ghana, but in western area of Western Sudan), stimulated by trans-desert trade in gold and other goods with Carthage and other Phoenician cities in North Africa			
400			Romans leave Britain	
500				
600				
700	Muslim Arabs occupy Tunisia (Uqba ibn Nafi)		Beginning of Viking raids in Britain	
	Caliphate of Cordoba in southern Spain (al-Andalus)		Anglo-Saxon kingdoms. King Offa of Mercia (English Midlands) builds a great dyke, from the Dee to the Severn, to mark his border with the Welsh	
800		Growth of Trans-Saharan trade between West and North Africa; origin of trading cities of West Africa such as Gao. West African gold very important in economic life of whole Mediterranean region		
900				Flourishing Muslim civilization in Spain
1000	Ancient Ghana at height of its power		Central Europe invaded by nomads from Eastern Europe and Western Asia	
1100				
1200	Decline and fall of Ghana as rival states become powerful, among them Mali			
1300			Rise of Venice, Florence and other city-states in Italy. Big feudal conflicts in England	
	Mali empire at height of its power	Rise of Kanem-Bornu		
1400		New gold-export trade from Ashanti (modern Ghana); rise of cities of Timbuktu and Jenne		India a powerful empire
1500	Songhay empire at height of its power		1492. Columbus crosses Atlantic	Spain colonizes Hispaniola (Haiti), Cuba, and other Caribbean lands
1600	1591. Moroccan invasion of Songhay empire, which then decays		Big extension of the slave trade to the Americas, including Brazil (found by the Portuguese in 1500)	
1700				

were sometimes used, was gold coins.

In those times there was a severe shortage of gold. Even the wealthy traders of the splendid city of Cairo did not have enough; nor did the Indians and Chinese. Right up to the second half of the thirteenth century, near the end of the Middle Ages, none of the governments of Europe could afford to use gold for their coins their countries were far too poor and backward.

An African 'world of trade'

Only the Africans proved able to meet this shortage. They did this from two large regions (look at the map on p. 60). The first was the Middle African land of the Mwana Mutapa and its neighbours, tied into world trade by Swahili merchants who travelled inland from their East Coast cities. The second, still mor important source of gold, was West Africa south of the Sudan, linked to the same great system of world trade by Sudanese merchants and by Berbers of the Sahara and North Africa. Through Swahili or Sudanese and Berber middlemen, both regions did much to support and enlarge the commerce of Asia and Europe. Africans produced and exported many hundreds of tons of gold. For several hundred years they ensured the supply of gold coins in many lands. They kept going a whole world of trade.

They had begun doing this long before, in the distant days of Carthage and Rome. But the world of trade powered by African gold became wider and busier than ever before after the followers of the Prophet Muhammad had united many peoples of Africa, Asia and Spain in the same Muslim faith. More trade routes were opened; more merchants used these routes, and more often. Business

Luxury goods even from distant England found their way to West Africa in the great days of the trans-Saharan trade. This bronze jug was made in England in the reign of King Richard II (1377–99), and is decorated with his royal badge. But it was found in the palace of the king of Ashanti when the British, 500 years later, invaded that country at the end of the nineteenth century

letters, contracts, cheques and above all purses of gold coins passed in growing volume from one end of this trading world to another. No business network as valuable as this had occurred in the world before.

As time went by the peoples of Europe, rising out of their poverty in the early Middle Ages, began to look to Africa for the gold they required. After about AD 1300 the first gold coins made in England since Roman times were minted from metal brought across the Sahara from West Africa. To obtain this gold the English, and others like them, sent out their own manufactured goods. They had few to offer, but did the best they could, so as to compete with North African, Asian, or south European merchants. Centuries later, in 1896, the invading British fought a battle against the Ashanti Empire, then in command of most of modern Ghana. They found there a fine vessel of silver made in England before AD 1400, and stamped with the badge of the English King Richard II, who reigned from 1377 to 1399. No doubt it was one of the objects that the English had sold, through Arab and other 'middlemen' traders, in order to buy gold from West Africa.

The cooks of Awdagost

Comfortable merchant cities grew out of this trade. Some have survived to this day; others have altogether disappeared. For a long time none was more important than Sijilmasa to the north-west of the Sahara, or Awdagost to the south-west (see the map on p. 60). These were the main northern and southern 'terminals' of the old trans-Saharan trade. They were hospitable towns where travel-weary merchants and their guides could rest and recover from weeks of harsh and dangerous travel across the sands of the desert, and where they could meet their business colleagues and make their deals.

Founded in AD 757 by local Berbers, Sijilmasa stood at the north-western entry of the desert. Largely because of its key position, Sijilmasa became the chief northern centre of the gold trade. Its merchant rulers were able to mint gold coins of their own. These coins, or *dinars* made with the excellent metal of West Africa, became famous for their reliable quality and weight. For a long time, Sijilmasa *dinars* were the dollars of the world of trade. Every merchant tried to get hold of them, being always sure of their acceptance by bankers or traders in Cairo and elsewhere.

Awdagost was Sijilmasa's chief trading partner on the southern fringe of the desert, though separated from Sijilmasa by many weeks of travel. In the ninth century it was an independent Berber state; later it came under the control of the strong West African empire of Ghana. A startling glimpse of the value of the trade which passed between Awdagost and Sijilmasa is offered in the book of a tenth-century Arab traveller. He was shown a cheque made out by a certain trader of Awdagost, in favour of a partner in Sijilmasa, for a sum worth at least a hundred thousand pounds in the money and prices of today.

By about AD 1000 Awdagost had grown into a large and handsome town. It had stone houses surrounded by well watered gardens, according to another Arabic account of 1067, and 'a market filled every day with a crowd so great that you cannot hear yourself speak above the noise of their talk', where 'gold dust is the means of buying and selling' between local people and travelling merchants. The same account notes that Awdagost was famous among these merchants for its clever African cooks, for the 'nut cakes' and 'honeyed pastry' and 'all sorts of

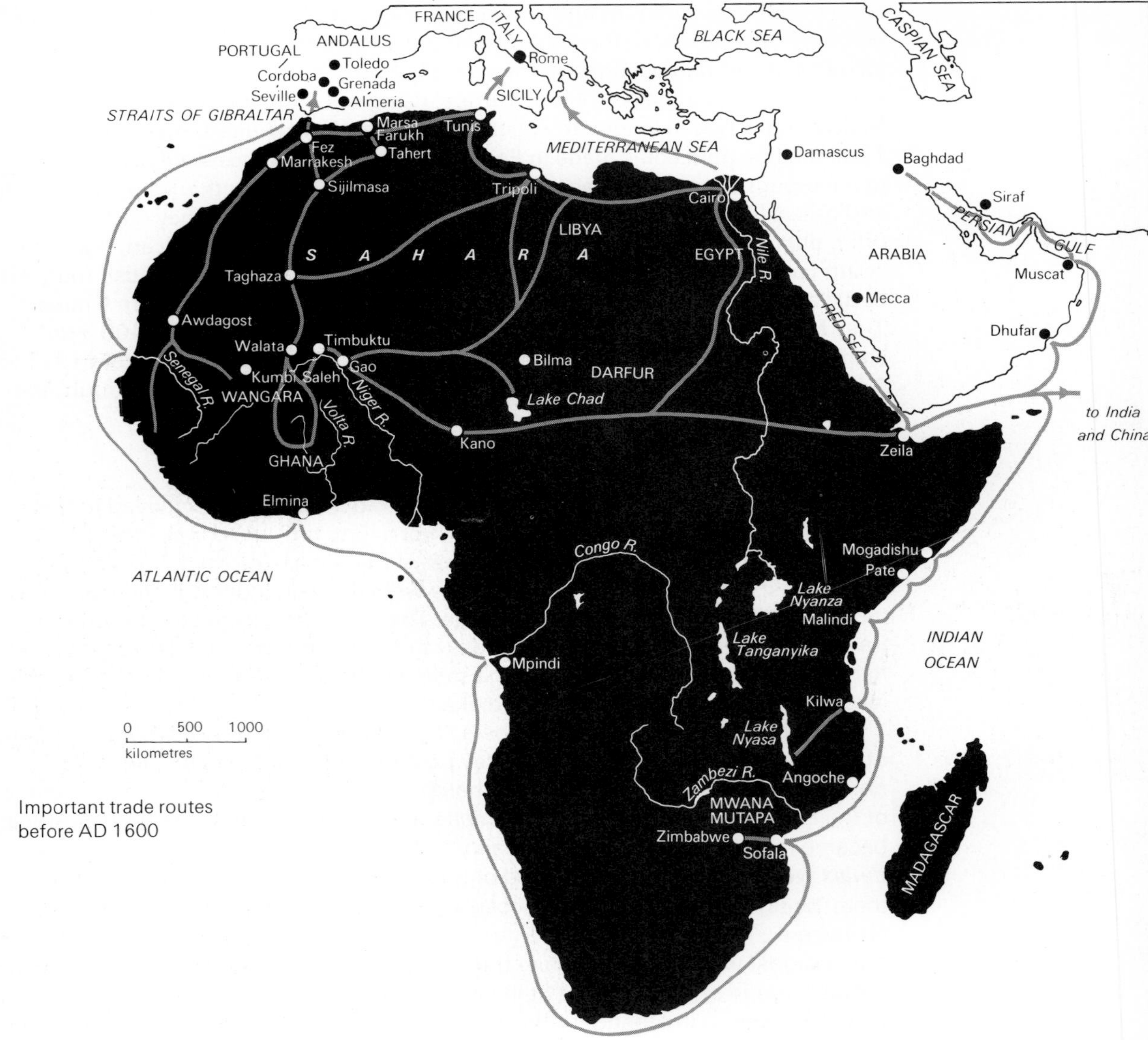

Important trade routes before AD 1600

sugar delights' made by those ladies. It is easy to imagine how keenly the trans-Saharan merchants longed to reach the shady cool and good drinking water of Awdagost, with its comforts of good cooking, after weeks of thirst and hunger while crossing the great desert.

Crossing the desert: 'don't get out of sight'

When one thinks about the hardships of trans-Saharan travel, it is easy to understand the reputation of Awdagost and Sijilmasa. The Sahara had to be crossed by riding camel or on foot. Mostly it was crossed on foot because merchants wanted as many goods as possible to be carried on their camels. Also merchants wanted to spare their valuable camels from unnecessary effort. In each

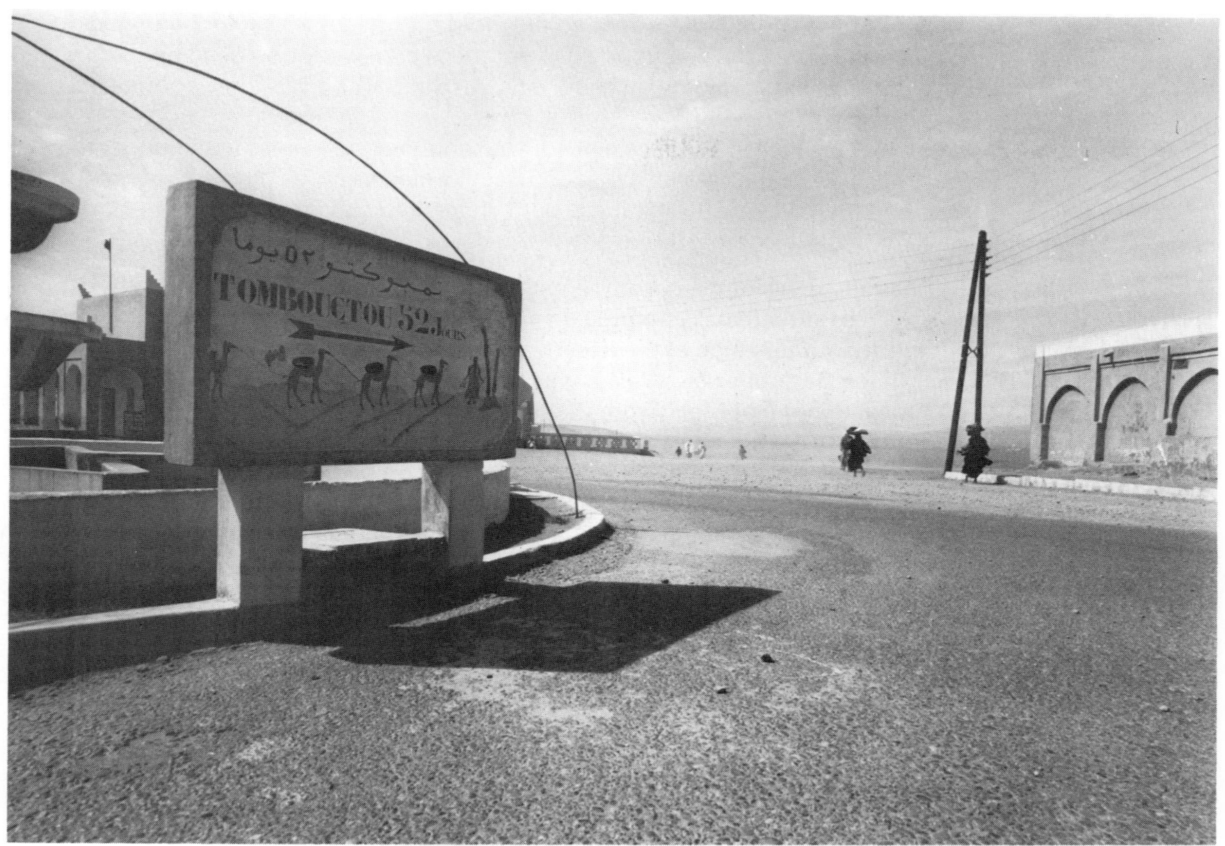

How far to Timbuktu? This Moroccan signpost says it is '52 days' across the wilderness of the Sahara Desert

direction, between north and south, the journey across the Sahara took as much as two or three months to complete.

Another writer in Arabic, a Moroccan Berber called ibn Battuta, tells how in 1352 he travelled to Sijilmasa with the aim of visiting West Africa. There, he says, 'I bought camels and a four months' supply of forage for them', and set out for the south with several merchants. They journeyed across a desert for twenty-five days until they came to the salt-producing settlement of Taghaza, 'where there are no trees, but only sand'.

> We spent ten days at Taghaza in discomfort, because the water is bad and the place is plagued with flies. Here the caravans stock up with water for the crossing of the desert which lies to the south of Taghaza, a crossing that takes ten nights of travel without any water to be found on the way.

Caravans travelled by night because it was cooler. On this particular journey, as it chanced, the travellers were lucky; they found water in pools left by a rare storm of rain. At this stage, ibn Battuta explains, 'we used to go ahead of the caravan, and when we found a place suitable for pasturage we would graze our camels. We went on doing this until one of our party was lost in the desert.' After that, he adds wryly, 'I neither went ahead nor lagged behind.' He soon had another proof of the wisdom of this.

We passed another caravan, and they told us that some of their party had got separated from the main body. One of these men we found dead beneath a shrub of the sort that can grow in sand. And yet there was a well only about a mile away from where he died.

Next we came to a place, called Tarasahla, where there is water under the surface. Here the caravans halt and usually stay for three days so as to rest and mend their waterskins, fill these with water, and sew on them covers of sackcloth as protection against the wind.

Then the perils of the desert began again. Ibn Battuta says that it was two months after leaving Sijilmasa before he and his companions reached the first oasis town on the southern side of the desert, a market called Walata.

In ibn Battuta's day, Walata was the northernmost town of the powerful West African empire of Mali. From Walata the trails ran through mainly grassland country to market cities along the river Niger, and on to the capital of the empire. Once in Walata the travellers were safe and could rest before resuming their journey. This old desert haven still exists, though it has long since lost its importance as a trading station. To this day its people decorate their houses with fine painted designs, and remain proud of their long history.

Other regular routes crossed the Sahara. Caravans used them for centuries. Along them passed the gold and ivory of West Africa in exchange for the silks of the East, for the famous swords of Damascus in Syria, for the metalware of Europe, and for other useful or beautiful things that West Africans were glad to buy.

AFRICA'S KINGDOM IN EUROPE

Many lands were a part of this world of trade. None of them was more admired by its neighbours, or more comfortable to live in, than a rich African state which took shape in Spain. This was Andalus. Beginning in the eighth century, Muslims from North Africa built a civilisation in the southern and central parts of Spain that was justly famed for its strength and brilliance, and lasted until conquest by Spanish Christians in the fourteenth and fifteenth centuries.

Andalus was on the northern side of the Mediterranean, but it belongs to the history of Africa. Its leading population was of Berber or North African Arab origin. Its fortunes were repeatedly linked with the rise and fall of North African rulers. Its cities held a leading place in the long-distance trade of Africa.

Abd al-Rahman of Cordoba

The story of Andalus is one of civilised achievement, but also of violent drama and adventure. Its first king, a young soldier called Abd al-Rahman, was the son of a prince of Arabia and a Berber princess. After many adventures, he made his way to his mother's distant Berber homeland in the western part of North Africa. There many ambitious and discontented men rallied to his flag, and the young prince looked around for a kingdom to rule. He was encouraged to cross the straits of Gibraltar into southern Spain, where many Berber settlers were already living. In 756 he founded the Caliphate or state of Cordoba, and opened the way for a brilliant Muslim development.

He and his successors reigned until 1031 by which time Andalus included the greater part of Spain, while northern Spain consisted of several small Christian kingdoms. After a period of confusion, Andalus came under the rule of another line of rulers from north-west Africa (the Almoravids) and these in turn, soon after 1200, by a third line of Berber kings (the Almohads). Yet such was the vitality and wealth of Andalus that repeated wars and upheavals, with all their squandering and waste, could not prevent the growth of splendid cities. The arts of peace flourished in spite of all the wars.

The great mosque at Cordoba, in southern Spain, which the kings of Andalus began to build in the eighth century. Spanish Christians long ago converted it into a church. This great building is one of the glories of Andalusian architecture

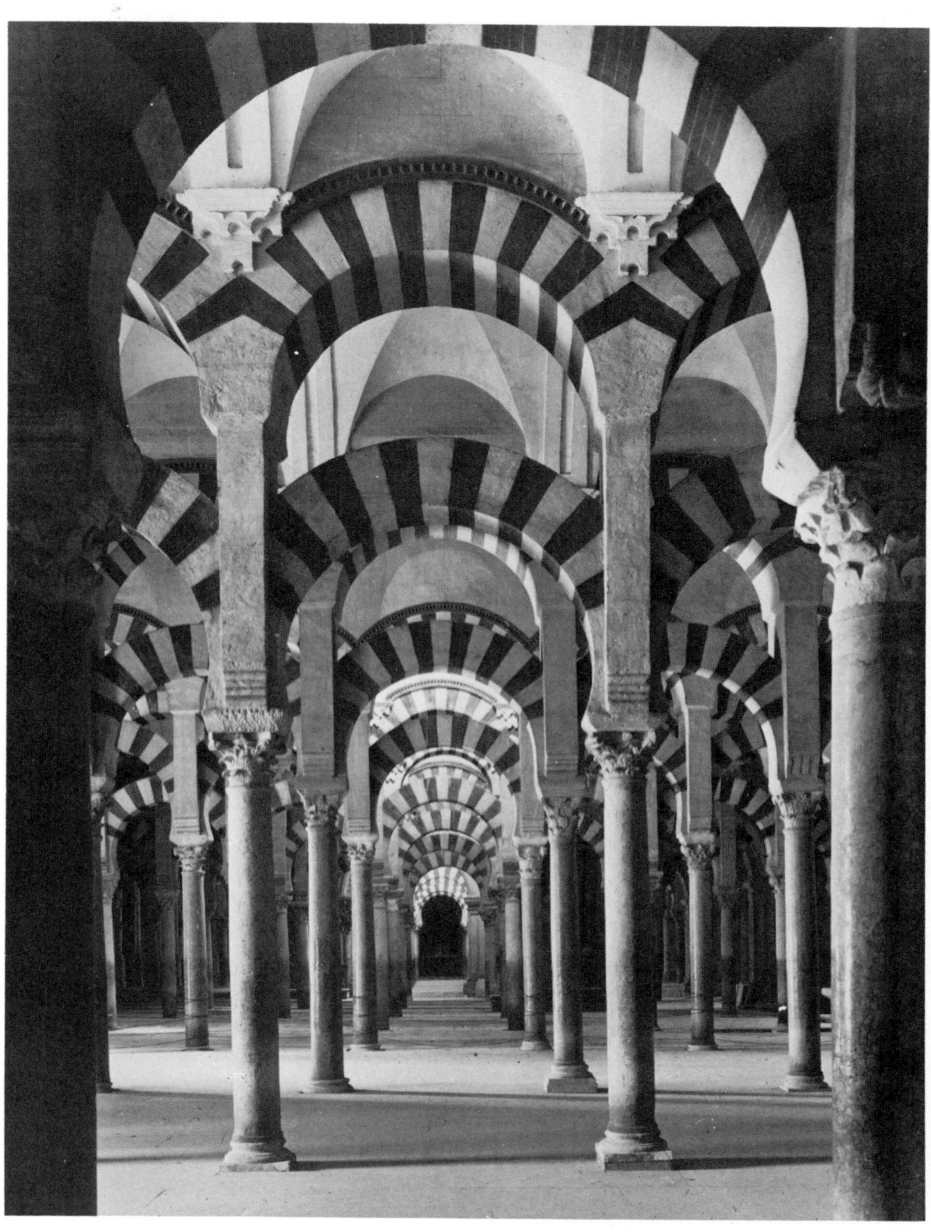

Craftsmen and scholars

Those who travel through southern Spain today may still see some of the glories of this African civilisation in Europe. The great mosque of Cordoba, long since converted to Christian use; the Alhambra at Granada, a palace built upon a rock; the fountains of Seville: these are examples of an architecture that was supreme in the world of its time. Much in the daily life of southern Spain still tells the haunting tale of long ago, not least the songs and dances of Andalusia whose tone and rhythm reflect the proud if distant memories of Andalus, and, behind those again, the artistic gifts of Africa.

Andalusian civilisation was possible because rulers could accumulate great wealth, and exploit the labour of ordinary people. Good farming, skilled use of water for irrigating fields and fruit groves, and the breeding of high-quality cattle were matched by the skills of craftsmen clever in many kinds of manufacture. Cordoba alone was said in the tenth century to have thirteen thousand weavers working in silk and wool as well as in cotton. Almeria became famous for its ships, Toledo for its swordblades, Seville for its wines. Much was developed, much invented. A ninth-century record even speaks of a Cordoban inventor who tried to design a flying machine. In these cities there lived philosophers and writers who studied natural science, theology, geography, history, and law. These men stood at the head of the scholarship of their times.

Some Andalusian scholars wrote books about West African history. Al-Bakri was one of these scholars. His important *Book of the Roads and Kingdoms* was completed in 1067. This was just a year after the Norman conquest of England, but al-Bakri has nothing to say on that subject. To the geographers and historians of Andalus England then was an obscure land of which they knew little; and they had their eyes fixed on the kingdoms that really counted for their own civilisation at that time. Thus al-Bakri's book contains the best description we have of the distant West African empire of Ghana.

A wide trading partnership

This Andalusian interest in the affairs of Africa is easy to explain. All the great Andalusian rulers sought to enclose both North Africa and Spain within their power. This was because both these regions were centres for the production and exchange of valuable goods. So it came about that the kingdoms of West Africa and North Africa were often partners with Andalus in the same wide enterprise of business growth.

This partnership was forged early in Muslim times. Two little states in North Africa formed the main links with West Africa. One was the kingdom of Tahert in what is now central Algeria. Tahert was founded in 776 by Berber Muslims who combined a strong belief in human equality with a notable skill in trade. So democratic were their kings that they were even said to sweep out their own houses, modest palaces which they refused to make luxurious. So enterprising were their traders that they rapidly established good links with other Africans to the south of the Sahara, in West Africa, and, through their Mediterranean port of Marsa Farukh near modern Mostaganem, with the cities of Andalus.

A second important 'linking' kingdom of North Africa was Sijilmasa, already mentioned, whose kings and peoples had much the same ideas about religion and trade as those of Tahert, and were in close alliance with Tahert. Both Sijilmasa and Tahert traded with the rest of North Africa, and with Egypt and western Asia.

You can see how this international trade was fruitfully widened if you look at the map on page 60. At the far northern end, Andalus traded with France and Italy, Germany and England. At the eastern end, Egypt traded with western Asia, India, and still farther afield. At the southern end, increasingly after 800, Berber merchants traded with West African peoples who lived in the grassland regions of the western and central Sudan. In one form or another, this network of far-ranging trade endured for centuries, and influenced all whom it enclosed.

SOUTH OF THE SAHARA: GRASSLAND EMPIRES

Against the background of this wide trade network, we need to think now about what had been happening in the broad plains of the western and central Sudan, south of the Sahara, since the introduction of cattle-raising, cultivation, and the working of metals. As in other countries, these skills helped the growth of population, while trade encouraged the foundation of towns. New states arose, and new political systems.

Challenge of changing times

Here there is a useful parallel with the eastern Sudan. Chapter 1 described how the peoples of the eastern Sudan, south of Egypt, met the challenge of changing times with the formation of the Kushite kingdom of Meroë, and afterwards of the Christian kingdoms of Nubia. Much the same kind of development, but Muslim not Christian, occurred in the central and western Sudan.

Little or nothing is known about this area's origins and earliest growth. What seems certain is that the same basic factors were in play; the enlargement of settlements as skills improved, the changing problems of government, and the opportunities of long-distance trade. These are the chief factors which explain the rise of powerful empires such as we shall look at now: Ghana, Mali, Songhay, Kaŋem-Bornu, and some smaller states. Indeed, these factors are important in explaining the early rise of states in every part of Africa, and no doubt in every part of the world.

The earliest of these West African empires, Ghana, perhaps began to be formed when the Romans still ruled North Africa, and when West African gold, if still in small quantities, helped to fuel the economy of the Roman empire. For the Berber traders of those days certainly traded with West Africans, and these West Africans were presumably organised in early states. This is what the traditions of Ghana suggest. They were written down, long afterwards in 1650, by an African historian of the city of Timbuktu in the central Sudan. They suggest that Ghana was founded before AD 400. What is certain is that Ghana was founded by African people who had to solve new problems of government.

A period of great development

The great period of Muslim long-distance trade through North Africa, Andalus and Egypt, which opened in the eighth century, also marked the beginning of a period of important development in West African countries south of the Sahara. This development continued at one level or another for more than a thousand years. It brought the growth of rich and varied cultures, partly Muslim and partly not, and saw the rise of powerful states.

These states were strong in trade. They were mostly centred on rich market cities where their kings and merchants lived. These West African cities were the magnets that drew traders south across the Sahara, and from far away in the forest lands of West Africa. In these cities were to be found the ambassadors of other kings, the agents of distant bankers and merchants, the businessmen who ran the long-distance trade, and, as time went by, scholars, theologians, and legal experts. Like the empires of which they were the heart and centre, they were cities of international fame. Tales of their magnificence reached far across the civilised world; even the threadbare kings of northern Europe could share in their prosperity. Though often magnified by distance and ignorance, such tales were founded in truth.

It would be wrong, of course, to think that these empires and cities came into existence merely by the influence of foreign trade and ideas. They were the creation of West Africans in response to the needs of West Africans. And although their rulers began to accept Islam in the eleventh century, these states were rooted in the customs, beliefs, and development of West Africa itself.

GHANA: 'THE LORDS OF GOLD'

Ancient Ghana

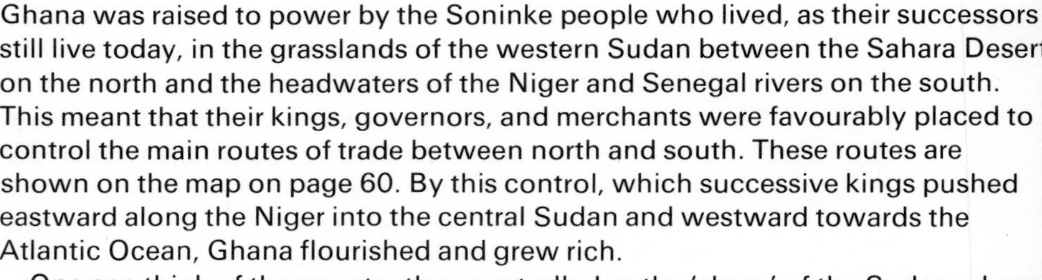

Ghana was raised to power by the Soninke people who lived, as their successors still live today, in the grasslands of the western Sudan between the Sahara Desert on the north and the headwaters of the Niger and Senegal rivers on the south. This meant that their kings, governors, and merchants were favourably placed to control the main routes of trade between north and south. These routes are shown on the map on page 60. By this control, which successive kings pushed eastward along the Niger into the central Sudan and westward towards the Atlantic Ocean, Ghana flourished and grew rich.

One can think of the country they controlled as the 'shore' of the Sudan whose grasslands run along the southern edge of the Saharan 'ocean' of sand and rock. Many of the big market towns of West Africa were situated along this 'shore'. They were like ports facing the Sahara, to the north of which were other ports such as Sijilmasa. Regular caravans of laden camels, of 'ships of the desert', passed several times a year between these ports to north and south.

At the height of its power, around 1000, Ghana controlled most of the southern ports. But its kings also controlled the routes which led southward from Ghana to the country, lying round the headwaters of the Niger River, from where the gold came. In other words, they had control of the export of gold. And they used this control to their advantage. Well before 800 the rulers of North Africa knew of Ghana as 'the land of gold'. The importance of this export trade was shown even in one of the titles of the kings of Ghana: 'Lord of the Gold'.

Taxes and revenues

Gold was not the only source of ancient Ghana's wealth. Thanks to its position and wide-ranging power, Ghana also controlled the trade in salt, another essential product.

For many centuries the kingdoms of Europe were able to make coins in gold only by getting the gold from Africans. Here are some examples of European gold coins made from African gold

Almoravid gold dinar, 1109

Spanish Christian gold maravedi, 1188–1230

Florentine (Italian) gold florin, 1252 and after

English gold coin of Charles II, 1663. The little elephant under the king's head shows that this coin was made from African gold

West Africans needed large and regular supplies of salt because salt is necessary to health, especially in warm countries. Except for those who lived along the distant ocean, West Africans could not produce enough salt for themselves. They needed to import it. As it happened, the best sources of salt lay far north or north-east in the Sahara, at places such as Taghaza and Bilma. Even today the saltpans of Bilma are visited every year by caravans numbering many thousands of camels, seeking the salt that is plentiful there.

As they were well placed to control the import of salt as well as the export of gold, the Soninke people developed a valuable two-way trade which included other items, such as Saharan copper and manufactured goods carried from North Africa. This may explain much of their political success, but it also shows how they could grow militarily strong. For the export–import trade brought in money for the kings of Ghana which was sufficient not only for the support of government and governors of distant provinces, but also for armies and military equipment. They could buy and maintain horses for their mounted troops. They could support metalsmiths to make iron heads for spears and lances. These were superior to the stone or bone weapons which were still used by many of their neighbours.

Al-Bakri's book of 1067 tells something of how these royal revenues were raised: 'The king puts a tax of one *dinar* of gold on every donkey-load of salt which enters the country, and two dinars on every donkey-load of salt that goes out of it.' Al-Bakri does not explain why the export tax was double the size of the import tax. Perhaps the reason lay in the government's wish to keep as much salt as possible inside the country, so as to prevent a shortage. Copper imports, partly for the making of luxury goods in alloys such as bronze, were taxed more highly. Five *dinars* were paid for each load of copper. Manufactured goods from across the Sahara, likewise chiefly for the kings and rich men, were taxed even more highly.

It is unlikely that coins were used in Ghana, whether for purposes of trade or taxation. Al-Bakri probably gives these values in *dinars*, because that was how North African merchants calculated what they had to pay. The *dinar* was the standard gold coin of the Muslim world of those days, though another word for it, *mitcal*, was often used in West Africa.

Gold exports were also taxed. Most of the gold came from the country of Wangara, some eighteen days' journey by foot to the south of Ghana's capital. Wangara was the country which lies today in the northern part of the Republic of Guinea, where gold was smelted from ore lying near the surface, and also panned in rivers. You can see this on the map on page 60. Most of the gold-traders were Mandinka people, whose homeland was Wangara. Even today, the traders of this people are often called Wangara by other West Africans.

The Mandinka carried their gold to the markets of Ghana, and the merchants of Ghana also went south to buy it on the spot. Here again the king found a useful source of money from which to meet royal expenses, whether for government or military upkeep or for laying on the lavish public feasts for which the kings of Ghana became famous. Al-Bakri says that 'all the pieces of gold found in the mines of the empire belong to the king'.

The gold trade, in other words, was a state-controlled business run for government profit by the kings of Ghana, acting through their governors and other officials. They probably did not control the mines themselves, for historians think that Wangara was already a half-independent province at the time when al-Bakri wrote about it. But the ruler of Ghana undoubtedly controlled the export of Wangara's gold from mines and alluvial pans. 'If he did not do this', al-Bakri explains, 'gold would become so plentiful as to lose its value.' By controlling gold exports, that is, the king could decide how much he could put on the market without undermining its selling price. Other kings and governments in other land would afterwards find this policy of monopoly, of single control, a useful one.

At the same time, al-Bakri adds, 'the king does not bother about gold dust, which he leaves to the public'. The gold-dust trade, then, remained in private hands. Gold-dust was widely used as a means of buying and selling in the markets of the empire.

The secrets of Kumbi Saleh

All this activity in trade and government centred on the capital where the king lived and held his court. Where was this capital?

Like other kingdoms of the same type, Ghana probably had several different capitals in the course of its long history, because kings in those days moved around with their armies and officials according to the political and military needs of the moment.

But it is obvious from al-Bakri's book that, by the eleventh century, Ghana had had its capital fixed in one place for a long time. And thanks to the recent work of archaeologists, we can be fairly certain where this place was. It lies at a point on the map on p. 60 called Kumbi Saleh, some 320 kilometres to the north of Bamako, capital of the modern Republic of Mali.

There is little to be seen there now save a few mounds of soil. Digging into these mounds, however, archaeologists have discovered the traces of a capital so large that it may have contained, they say, as many as twenty thousand inhabitants, making it one of the largest towns in the world of that time. The archaeologists found not only a town of stone dwellings but also traces nearby of a separate town without buildings in stone.

Did the capital of Ghana really have two separate towns? Al-Bakri's book confirms the evidence of the archaeologists. He says that it was composed of 'two towns lying in a plain. The one that is inhabited by the Muslims' – by traders, that is, who had come from the north – 'is very big and has a dozen mosques with prayer leaders, scholars, and salaried teachers. There are plenty of lawyers and learned men.' Another town, inhabited by the king, lay 'six miles away, while the land around is covered with dwellings made of stone and timber'. Thus the long-distance traders were given a suburb of their own where they could build their mosques and dwellings in the styles of their own North African lands, while the king and his subjects lived in other urban centres or suburbs, presided over by the palace and its officials.

The comfort and solidity of the city built at Kumbi Saleh a thousand years ago is shown by stone dwellings uncovered in the Muslim suburb. These had thick walls against midday heat or midnight cold, because temperatures in these grasslands can sharply change between day and night. Some of these dwellings had two storeys with several rooms on each. Here the merchants from northern 'ports' such as Sijilmasa had their permanent residences and warehouses, while smaller houses nearby provided for visitors from the cities of distant lands such as Tunisia, Libya, and Egypt.

Such was the capital of the 'Lords of the Gold' at the height of their commercial and political power. Long afterwards, when all but the memory of Ghana had disappeared, fabulous stories were still told about its everyday life. In about 1650 a Timbuktu historian completed a book in which he told some of the tales that were still remembered about Ghana. He told, for example, how one of its kings had kept a thousand horses for his personal use, and how each of these horses had its own carpet and silken halter, and three grooms to care for it. He also told how feasts were offered by the kings to thousands of their subjects.

King Tunka Manin

Were these only legends spun by love of story-telling? To some extent, no doubt, they were. But they were more than that; they were drawn from the memories of a splendid past. There are passages in al-Bakri's book to illustrate this. Al-Bakri wrote them down in 1067 from accounts given to him by Andalusians who had visited the capital of Ghana, or possibly by men of Sijilmasa who had travelled between Andalus and Ghana. They describe the magnificent court of King Tunka Manin.

Travellers told al-Bakri that this king, who had come to the throne of Ghana in 1063, was 'the master of a great empire and has great power. He can put into the field an army of 200,000 warriors, of whom more than 40,000 are archers.' Even if this was an over-statement, the king's military power was undoubtedly a large power, and compared well with that of other big empires in Asia, Africa, or Europe. Far away in the fogs of northern Europe, three years after Tunka Manin became king, Duke William of Normandy invaded Saxon England. But the total of the warrior-knights who went with William was only about 4,000.

Not surprisingly, these powerful lords of Ghana were awesome figures, and their courts the scene of grand and glittering ceremony. According to al-Bakri:

> When this king gives audience to his people so as to listen to their troubles and set them to rights, he sits in a pavilion around which ten pages stand, holding shields and gold-mounted swords.
>
> On his right hand are the princes of his empire, splendidly clad and with gold ornaments in their hair. The governor of the city is seated on the ground in front of the king, and all around him are his ministers in the same position.
>
> The gate to his chamber is guarded by dogs of an excellent breed which never leave the king's place. They wear collars of gold and silver decorated with the same metals.
>
> The beginning of a royal audience is announced by the beating of a kind of drum they call *deba*, which is made of a piece of hollowed wood, and the people gather when they hear this sound.

Then the king, wearing a head-dress of gold-embroidered stuff, and fine garments of white cotton, listened to the lawsuits that were brought before him, and gave judgements.

For long afterwards the scene would be repeated in much the same way at later courts of other powerful states in the western and central Sudan. The royal ways of Ghana set an example many kings were to follow. Where had these ways come

King Tunka Manin of ancient Ghana had 'dogs of an excellent breed. . . .' What did they look like? Perhaps like this royal dog on a Kushite tomb-engraving dated to about 110 BC

from? Who had first thought of them? Perhaps they were invented by early ruler of Ghana several centuries before King Tunka Manin's reign. Yet we may note, a another sign that all parts of African history are somehow connected together, even if we cannot always understand how, that some of these customs strangely echo those of the ancient kingdom of Meroë in the eastern Sudan, whose end, in the fourth century AD, had come so near to Ghana's probable beginning.

Thus the kings of Meroë had also possessed their favourite royal dogs, equipped with fine collars; some of these dogs are still to be seen in pictures engraved on royal tombs at Meroë. This does not mean that the first kings of Ghana necessarily took over their customs from the last kings of Meroë. What it does mean is that the ancient history of Africa comes out of a broad reservoir of customs and beliefs that were shared and developed by many different peoples even if they often lived far apart.

Invaders and rivals

The royal ways of behaviour, state organisations, trading networks and military arrangements of Ghana evolved over a long period. Unfortunately, we know littl more about these matters than what is told in al-Bakri's book. Although the Timbuktu historians of the seventeenth century asserted that forty-four kings had reigned in Ghana from first to last, today we know only two or three of the royal names, and almost nothing of their history.

There is a little more information about the last years of the empire. They were overshadowed by invasions. These, too, were a result of the general development of West Africa. Growing strong in their turn, these neighbours coveted the power of Ghana. Eventually they overthrew the ancient empire.

The first big invasions were connected with the rise of western Berber peoples who became known as the Almoravids. They were followers of a pious Muslim teacher who was probably Wajaj ibn Zallu al-Lamti, or, as we would say, Wajaj son of Zallu of the Lamtuna people, who were a section of the western Berbers.

Among those who studied under Wajaj was Abdulla ibn Yasin, whose name was to be well remembered. He became one of those dynamic Muslim chiefs who called on Muslims to make war not only on non-Muslims, but also on other Muslims who were considered lax in their faith. Ibn Yasin set going a great movement of the western Berbers. They eventually unified Morocco, founding a new capital there, Marrakesh, in about 1070. Their armies crossed into Andalus and gave that country, then divided among rival princes, a new unity and line of kings. These Almoravid kings of Andalus ruled for about a hundred and fifty years.

Other Almoravid armies marched south-eastward against Ghana. As with most wars of religion, loot and destruction were also on the scene. In about 1054 the Almoravids seized and plundered Awdagost, then part of the empire of Ghana, and in 1076, after long wars, they did the same with the capital of Ghana itself. Then their southern effort was largely over. They retreated from Ghana, or were driven out, and the capital was rebuilt.

Yet they had deeply disturbed the balance of power in the western Sudan. Though the Soninke people of Ghana recovered, they were soon in trouble again. A neighbouring West African people followed where the Almoravids had led. Soon after 1200 these new invaders took and destroyed the capital at Kumbi Saleh, which never recovered.

But the victors' success was again brief. Within a few years they were themselves defeated by another rising power. A new empire was on the threshhold of the times.

ANCIENT MALI: THE LAND OF THE LION PRINCE

Ancient Mali

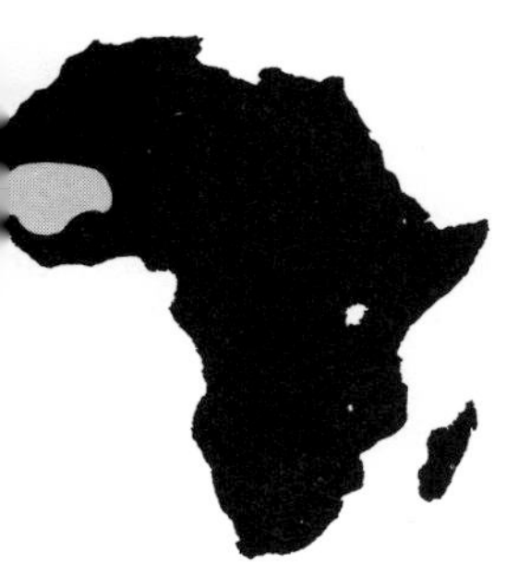

The rise of Mali, and its rule over wide West African lands, was largely the work of the Mandinka people of Wangara, the ancient land of gold production, and of neighbouring areas. After about 1250 Mali steadily expanded to become one of the largest states of any part of their world, whether in Africa or not. Mali became famous for the wealth of its rulers, for the peace which prevailed in its territories, and for the influence of its learned men.

This reputation reached outside Africa. Several countries of Europe were now beginning to emerge from the poverty and ignorance of the Middle Ages. Magnificent city-states such as Florence developed in Italy. As early as 1252 the bankers of Florence gave a fresh impulse to long-distance trade within Europe by

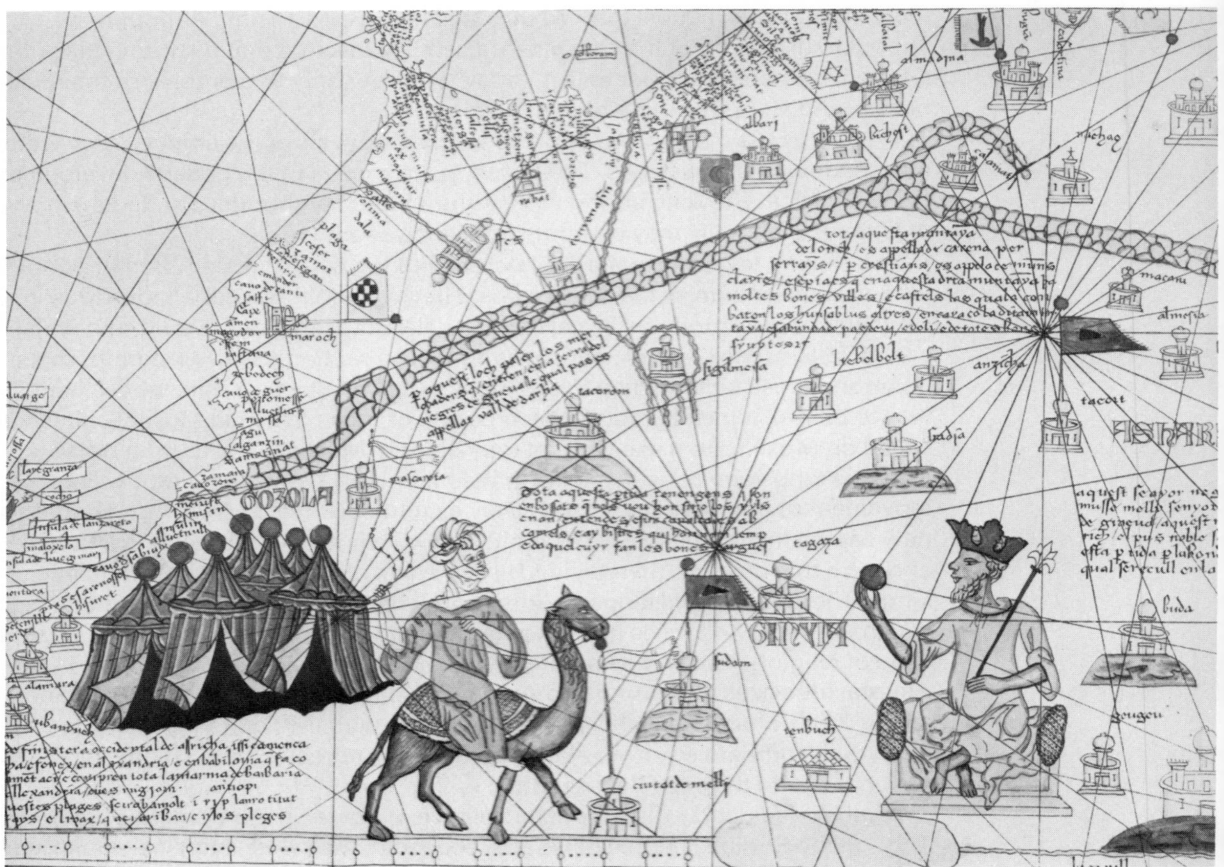

A detail from Abraham Cresques's map of Africa. Top left, you can just see the Straits of Gibraltar, and, below them on either side, the north and north-west coasts of Africa. Almost in the centre is the ancient trading-city of Sijilmasa

the production of a new gold coin, the *florin*, which they made in metal brought from Africa. Such advances led Europeans to take an active interest in the sourc of gold, and thus in Mali.

Yet it was hard for Europeans to collect information about Africa. Between them and Mali stood the barrier of Muslim kingdoms. Luckily Jewish communities in North Africa were on good terms with the Muslims. Gradually, through Jewish channels, European kings and merchants were able to satisfy a little of their curiosity. They could do this thanks mainly to a great school of map makers who drew their information from North African traders, and were established on the western Mediterranean island of Majorca.

In 1375 one of these Majorcan map-makers, Abraham Cresques, completed a new atlas for the emperor of Germany, which showed, with fascinating details, something of the grandeur of Mali's reputation. He included the many cities of North Africa and the 'wall' of the Atlas Mountains dividing these from the Sahar and the Sudan. He sketched the oasis cities of the desert, the tall tents of their rulers, and a veiled Berber figure riding a camel towards the capital of Mali. Ther enthroned in majesty, is 'Musa Mali, the Lord of the Blacks', holding a sceptre a an orb of gold.

Mali dominated the life of the western Sudan, and much of the central Sudan, for nearly two centuries. Its influence ranged from the Atlantic far towards the east, and towards the north and south on either side.

Emperor Kankan Musa

The dates of the reigns of the earliest kings of Mali, members of the Keita (pronounced Kay-ta) section of the Mandinka people, are unknown. First as local chiefs and then as kings of a small state, they ruled for several centuries before AD 1200, and were generally subject to the emperor of Ghana.

Around 1240, in the midst of Ghana's final troubles, there came to power in Mali an outstanding leader whose title was Mari-Djata (pronounced Jar-ta), who set about the systematic expansion of his little kingdom. According to ibn Khaldun, who wrote about these Mali kings in 1400, Mari meant Prince and Djata meant Lion. Mari-Djata, the Lion Prince, set about reorganising the lands of the western Sudan, the regions of the old empire of Ghana, into a new system of government. He had much success.

Other kings carried on his work. They overcame their rivals and pushed the power of their government east from Wangara until it reached far down the Niger, and west towards the Atlantic. Of these kings the most successful was Kankan Musa, who came to power in about 1312 and ruled until 1337.

Mansa Kankan Musa's reign (*Mansa* means 'lord' or ruler in the Mandinka language) marked the high point of Mali. Those who followed him had varying success. Gradually their power weakened as other people grew in wealth and strength and embarked on political expansion. By 1650 Mali was once again little more than the land of Wangara and its immediately neighbouring areas. Yet the memory of Mali, and especially of its greatest ruler, Kankan Musa, stayed vivid in men's memories. Even in recent years the historians of the Mandinka still taught the oral history of Mali in a school they maintained near the little town of Kangaba, where, many centuries ago, the empire had begun to take shape. Here students have gathered every year to learn about the Lion Prince and his deeds, about Kankan Musa and Mali's other kings, and the life of those times.

At the court of Mali

It was to the court of the prestigious ruler of Mali that the Moroccan traveller ibn Battuta was going when he crossed the Sahara in 1352. This is fortunate for us, because ibn Battuta was a keen observer. He had already visited Egypt and the Swahili cities in East Africa, India, and China, staying with Muslim scholars of those lands, working for their rulers, finding out how they lived and governed. Yet even so his journey in Mali could still impress him.

Travelling for months through the Mali empire, from its northern outpost at Walata to its capital of Niani on the Upper Niger, down the Niger by canoe for hundreds of miles, and then north again on his journey home, he says that he found 'complete and general safety'. Travellers in Mali had no reason to fear thieves or bandits, since among 'the admirable qualities of the blacks there is the small number of acts of injustice that you find here, for of all peoples the blacks are those who most hate injustice, and their emperor pardons nobody who is guilty of it'.

Ibn Battuta was received at the capital of the emperor of that time, *Mansa* Suleyman, and was present at lavish ceremonies. He reports a public occasion:

On certain days the emperor holds public audiences in the palace yard, where there is a platform with three steps shaded by a tree. They call this platform the *pempi*. It is carpeted with silk and has cushions, and over it they raise a big silken umbrella which forms a sort of tent. This is topped by the model of a bird in gold about the size of a hawk.

The emperor comes out of a door in the corner of the palace, carrying a bow in his hand and a quiver [of arrows] on his back. He wears a golden skullcap that is bound by a strip of gold with narrow ends shaped like knives. Usually he wears a red tunic of velvety stuff made in Europe.

His musicians go in front of him, carrying two-stringed guitars made of gold and silver; and behind him come three hundred armed servants. He walks in a leisurely fashion, on purpose, and stops every now and then. When he reaches the *pempi* he stops again and surveys the assembled people, and then he mounts the *pempi* in a sedate manner as though he were a preacher going up into the pulpit.

As he takes his seat the drums, trumpets, and bugles are sounded. Three servants go out at a run to summon his deputy and military commanders, who come in and also take their seats.

Then the king listened to the speeches of his governors and considered difficult lawsuits brought to him for judgment. In this he behaved in much the same way as King Tunka Manin of Ghana. But there was one large difference, for the kings of Mali were more than the leaders of the religion of the Mandinka. Unlike Tunka Manin, they were also Muslims. With many of their subjects, they had made the pilgrimage to Mecca and were devout in their faith. They had become important figures in the Muslim world.

Drawing of a wall decoration on a house in the old trading town of Walata. This was once an important 'stop' on the journey across the Sahara between Morocco and Mali

Islam comes to West Africa

When and why did Africans accept Islam? There are several answers. To begin with, back in the eighth and ninth centuries, the ideas and teachings of Islam reached West Africa by means of traders from the Muslim states of North Africa such as Tahert and Sijilmasa. These teachings spread in the towns and cities.

By the eleventh century a number of West African kings had accepted Islam, though at first only as another religion alongside the local religions they had already. Many African traders did the same. They were persuaded by various reasons. Until later times, most of these reasons were practical and political rather than religious.

One reason was that accepting Islam could improve relations with the Berber traders from the north, nearly all of whom belonged to one or other of the sects or 'brotherhoods' of Islam. African kings and traders had their own belief in God, but they were usually ready to agree that belief could take different forms. Accepting Islam, they could thus find common ground with other Africans who had also become Muslims. This helped to overcome disunity, at least among traders and townspeople.

Another reason was that the teachings of Islam were concerned with much more than spiritual matters. They also taught new laws and ways of everyday life, so as to improve government and increase trade. This side of Islam was and is known as *fiqh* (pronounced *feek*), the study of civil law. Much of what was taught by *fiqh*, especially in matters of business, credit, and methods of handling property, could now be useful to the growing numbers of townspeople of West Africa.

In the grassland cities of West Africa by the reign of Kankan Musa, early in the fourteenth century, many schools of Muslim learning had grown up, where *fiqh* and other aspects of Muslim law and belief were taught, discussed, and reshaped for application to local conditions. These schools were visited by wandering scholars from North Africa and Egypt. The cities of West Africa became part of a wide community of learning.

This in turn points to a third reason why West Africans began to accept Islam. Islam was a world religion, linking all its members in a great community which Muslims call the *umma*, the 'family of Islam'. By accepting Islam, West Africans could become members of a world civilisation which stretched far across Africa and Asia. Their kings could share in the prestige of famous Muslim rulers in Egypt and other lands.

As early as the eleventh century, for example, the kings of the little state of Gao, in the central Sudan, began importing finely inscribed tombstones of Spanish marble from Andalus. These handsome tombstones, brought on camel-back across the Sahara, were more than a sign of wealth. They shed on the kings of Gao a little of the distant glamour of the Andalusian rulers in whose realm these stones were inspired and carved.

Welcoming membership in a world-wide community, West Africans began to make the pilgrimage to Mecca, holy city of Islam, which all good Muslims are supposed to visit at least once in their lives. Nowadays these pilgrims usually go by truck, and increasingly by plane. But in the days of Mali they had to walk or ride a camel to get to Mecca and back again, and the journey lasted many months each way. You can see how far away it was if you look at the map on p. 60.

Famous pilgrimage

The magnificent *Mansa* Kankan Musa made a famous pilgrimage to Mecca in 1324. He set out on his journey, determined to show the world something of his wealth and majesty. His pilgrimage caused a sensation that was talked about for years afterwards.

A Timbuktu historian, Mohammed Kati, who wrote early in the seventeenth century, tells us that Mansa Musa took with him some eight thousand courtiers and servants. When this vast company from Mali reached Cairo, the emperor thoroughly made his point about his wealth and power. We know this because a Cairo historian, al-Omari, wrote about Mansa Musa's pilgrimage only twelve years later, and described the remarkable impression that it caused.

Kings were judged by the splendour of their gifts. So Musa is said to have taken with him some eighty loads of Mali gold, each weighing about 135 kilograms, while five hundred of his servants each carried a staff of gold weighing about 2 kilograms. Most of this the emperor gave away in Cairo, while his courtiers also used their gold for shopping in the fashionable markets of the Egyptian capital. They gave away or spent so much good Mali gold that the Cairo coinage, suffering from a shortage of precious metal, seriously declined in value.

Kings were also judged by their political power. The king of Egypt expected his visitors to show him respect by kissing the ground before his feet or at least by kissing his hand. But the emperor of Mali, al-Omari records, had no intention of doing any such thing. His realm, after all, was far wider than Egypt, and, at least in gold, far wealthier. This put the Cairo court officials in a difficulty. How could they bring the two great men together if the visiting monarch refused to obey the rules? It was the monarch of Mali who solved the problem. Understanding that some compromise had to be found, he told the officials that he would certainly kiss the ground in the king of Egypt's presence; not in respect for the king, he said, but for God 'who created me and brought me into the world'.

No fool himself, the king of Egypt accepted this compromise and the rulers were able to have a friendly meeting, after which the Egyptian king 'sent gifts of clothing for the Mali emperor, for his courtiers, and for all those who were with him, as well as saddled and bridled horses for the emperor and his chief officers'. Both sides were evidently satisfied.

After this pilgrimage it is likely that Muslim influence considerably increased in the western and central Sudan, just as, with the overthrow of the Christian Nubian kingdoms at about the same time, the influence of Islam was likewise increasing in the eastern Sudan.

Society grows more complex

What were these Muslim methods of government?

Mali had risen to power under much the same system of government as Ghana before it. Chiefs of leading family groups were appointed to rule over other family groups. As they became kings they gained more power. Growing wealthier by taxing their subjects they used this power to safeguard their power at home, and make conquests abroad. But at this point they began to be faced with difficult problems of administration. It was now that the teachings of Islam came to their aid.

Like his successors, Mansa Musa ruled from Niani, his capital. His power came from his administration and army, and from being the senior living member of the Keita family group. As such, people looked upon him as a great religious figure. They respected him because they believed that he enjoyed God's special blessing. In one way or another, whether in Africa or not, most kings in history used to have this kind of religious importance.

For practical affairs, the emperor ruled through ministers who lived at Niani and through governors in the different provinces of his empire. This, too, was much like ancient Ghana. By the fourteenth century, however, the old simplicities of 'family rule' were not enough. Development in West Africa had led to deeper division in society. Now that the empire was large and wealthy, Mansa Musa had to find ways of satisfying the ambitions of rival families, as well as the needs of traders and townspeople who had aims and ambitions of their own. To cope with these new situations, as well as with the fact that many townspeople had now accepted Islam, Musa adopted new methods of government.

He set up Muslim courts alongside the existing courts which dispensed justice by traditional Mandinka law. He appointed a Muslim chief judge, the *An Faram Kuma*, whose task was to look after the working of these new courts. He introduced Muslim customs into court ceremony, and into the ways in which he dealt with his ministers and governors.

Designed to meet the growing complexity of society, these new laws and customs were to have a deeper effect in the later empire of Songhay. Meanwhile in Mali the old, traditional forms of government remained important. These were developed, but not changed very much.

The minister in charge of all transport, and of fishing on the Niger, was the *Hari Farma*. His colleague in charge of forests and their produce was the *Sao Farma*. The minister concerned especially with farming was the *Babili Farma*, while the emperor's minister of finance was the *Khalissi Farma*.

Division of labour had meant that specialist groups had grown up who handed on their skills from father to son. In Mali, each of these groups was obliged to pay a yearly tax. Every metal smith's family, for example, had to give a hundred arrowheads and a hundred lanceheads of tempered iron. The fishermen of the Niger and its tributaries had to give a number of bundles of dried fish, according to what they could afford. The masons had to give a number of days of unpaid labour. Other groups paid their taxes in other ways.

Society became more divided as it became more complex. Most numerous of all groups were the farmers of the countryside. They had little or no political power and had to work for their lords, and to fight in wars. Beneath them again were persons who had lost their right to be treated as free men, either by capture in war or by some serious offence. They were regarded as permanent servants. North African writers often called them *abid*, the Arabic word for permanent servants. European writers have translated this as meaning 'slaves'.

But we have to be careful about this word 'slave'. It usually meant something very different from what our modern world has understood by it. We shall come back to this important point. Meanwhile, we should note that the 'slaves', or permanent servants in Africa, usually lived in a kind of slavery that was very tolerant and easy-going, so that 'slaves' often lived and worked in much the same way as other people.

In those days men seldom worked for wages. It was customary to buy 'slaves' who were servants for life, or at least until they were sold again. Once bought, these permanent servants had to do what they were told. But they possessed many rights. They could marry their master's daughters, own their own property, go into trade on their own account, and win influence and power. Often they became military commanders. Sometimes they became kings.

Such 'slaves' were costly to buy and maintain. Usually, they were luxuries that only rich men could afford. Writing of the cake-makers of Awdagost, of those famous ladu cooks of the eleventh century, al-Bakri notes that each had cost the man who owned her for her cooking skills, a hundred pieces of gold or more, or as much as the price of a couple of small cars today.

Another specialist group who grew to importance under the empire of Mali were traders known as *dyula* (pronounced joo-la). Working in small companies, often with their own escorts of mounted guards and couriers, they established a specialised trading network within West Africa, forging valuable links with many peoples living in the forests or along the seaboard. Sometimes their trading stations grew into cities ruled by Muslim law and custom.

So you can see that Africa today looks back upon a distant past. Even now there are companies of *dyula* in parts of West Africa, each under its leader, or 'chairman' called *dyula mansa*. Or a *dyula* leader may be called *Shehu Wangara*, 'Commander of the Wangara': of the people of that ancient land where the empire of Mali took shape nearly a thousand years ago.

SONGHAY: THE EMPIRE OF THE ASKIAS

Songhay

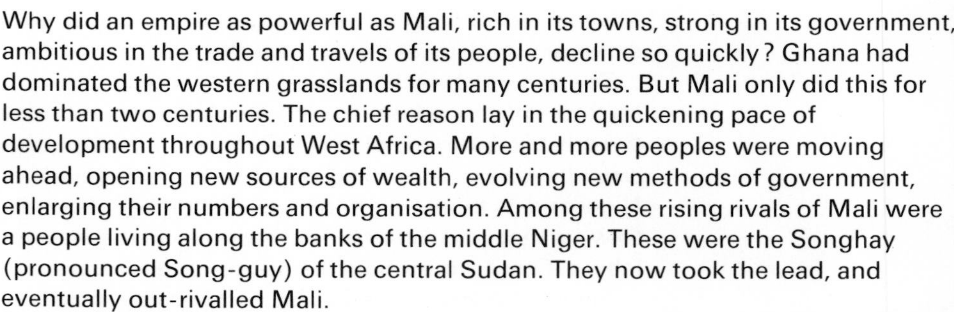

Why did an empire as powerful as Mali, rich in its towns, strong in its government, ambitious in the trade and travels of its people, decline so quickly? Ghana had dominated the western grasslands for many centuries. But Mali only did this for less than two centuries. The chief reason lay in the quickening pace of development throughout West Africa. More and more peoples were moving ahead, opening new sources of wealth, evolving new methods of government, enlarging their numbers and organisation. Among these rising rivals of Mali were a people living along the banks of the middle Niger. These were the Songhay (pronounced Song-guy) of the central Sudan. They now took the lead, and eventually out-rivalled Mali.

The Songhay were another West African people, like the Soninke of Ghana and the Mandinka of Mali, who had gone into the long-distance trade in early times, and thrived on it. How early they did this we do not know, but one of the ancient chariot trails of the Berbers, during Carthaginian times, came down through the central Sahara to a point on the middle Niger near Songhay country. Regular caravans began using this route after the rise of Muslim states in North Africa. It seems likely that Gao, near the southern end, was founded as the chief Songhay trading centre even before AD 700.

Then the North African trading kings of Tahert and Sijilmasa, already in touch with Ghana, grew interested in Gao as well. They sent ambassadors and merchants, and a new partnership developed. Gao flourished on this. By about 850 its people had grown strong enough to need a king of their own. Still surviving as a riverside market, Gao today is one of the oldest towns in the world.

Gold from the forest country

The early kings of Gao were possibly subjects of the emperors of Ghana. But with the collapse of Ghana, Songhay and its kings became independent for a while. Then for fifty years they were subjects of the emperors of Mali. But in about 1375 the first of a new line of Songhay kings, whose title was *Sunni*, threw off the overlordship of Mali, and embarked on new development.

The reasons for this development are important in West African history. Like their neighbours, the Songhay were steadily getting a stronger control of nature. They became good farmers, fishermen and metal-workers. So they grew in numbers, and they worked out more efficient ways of government. This was happening in many African countries. But now the Songhay acquired a big advantage over their neighbours. Around 1350, or soon after, new supplies of West African gold began to reach West African markets. The old supplies had come mainly from the country south of the western Sudan, from Wangara and nearby. Now gold began arriving from the country south of the central Sudan, produced by the Akan people of forest country in the country that is modern Ghana today. The Akan began washing gold from their rivers and mining it from their rocks.

New markets sprang into life to handle this new trade in gold and other products of the forest country. One of them was Begho (pronounced Bee-go), a *dyula* market-town founded on the northern fringe of the Akan forests. Another, still more important, was Jenne (pronounced Jen-nie), a new town on the middle Niger which soon became a major meeting-place for traders travelling between Begho and the markets of Mali. A third was Timbuktu, founded somewhat earlier, which now began to expand with the growth of this new trade. It was through Timbuktu that Akan-produced gold began to be sent to North Africa along the caravan routes of the central Sahara.

The rulers of Mali tried to control this trade of the central Sudan and Sahara. For a while they succeeded. But the Songhay, who were well placed to extend their power from Gao, then took a hand in the game. Their kings played it with skill and daring, none more boldly than Sunni Ali.

Sunni Ali and Askia Mohammed

The name of Sunni Ali may often be heard even now, five centuries after his reign, when people of the West African grasslands talk about their past. He was one of the great warrior-kings of history, a natural leader skilled on the field of battle and also in the council chamber. Uniting courage with cunning, Sunni Ali transformed the little trading kingdom of Gao into a large empire, thrust its influence across the grasslands of the central Sudan, enclosed rich cities such as Jenne and Timbuktu within its domains, and met with no major defeat in all the twenty-eight years of his reign.

Sunni Ali was the true founder of the empire of the Songhay, exploiting both the decline of Mali and the rise of the new trade with the forest peoples of the south. He ruled from about 1464 to 1492. Power then passed to a weak successor, who almost at once lost it to a provincial governor called Muhammad Turay.

Turay took the title of *askia*, a senior rank in the Songhay army, and was the first of a line of nine askias who ruled the Songhay empire until its collapse under

Tomb at Gao of the great Songhay emperor, Muhammad Askia, who died in 1528, when King Henry VIII was ruling England. This large structure is typical of Sudanese building then and since, it is made of hardened clay plastered to a framework of timbers. You can see the ends of these timbers sticking out of the clay walls

invasion from North Africa. He is remembered today as Askia the Great because of his many conquests, the shrewdness with which he governed, and the changes that he introduced. He extended Sunni Ali's conquests far to the west and north. By the time of his death, in 1528, the Songhay empire had become as large as Mali had ever been.

Under Askia Muhammad the trading cities grew in size and wealth. Jenne, in the words of a Timbuktu historian who completed his work in 1655, became a 'great, flourishing and prosperous city, one of the great market centres of the Muslim world'. Trading caravans travelled to Jenne from south and north. Its scholars and writers became famous.

New problems of development

States such as Songhay grew larger and wealthier. They enclosed cities within their power as well as peoples of the countryside. And so their problems of government also changed. Divisions within society became deeper, with some men winning far more freedom of action than others, or more authority and prestige, or more wealth than most people. And the kings, trying to stay safely on top of this rising pyramid of power, had to reinforce their position against rival bids for leadership.

These problems, of course, also faced kingdoms in all parts of the world. They had to adapt to the same basic changes, the same new strains and conflicts, the same new dangers of upheaval. Shakespeare's historical plays, which he wrote around 1600 about the Tudor kings of England, are full of scenes that a Songhay audience would have understood. Though with large differences of detail, these scenes might well have been written about struggles for power in the Songhay empire. The empire faced difficulties of two sorts. One was the rivalry for political leadership among ambitious men, and the other the rise of cities which wanted to be independent.

Ghana and Mali had been ruled by leading families whose supremacy was generally accepted, for traditional reasons, by the Soninke and Mandinka peoples. For a long while the Songhay adopted the same system. Like Mansa Musa of Mali, or Tunka Manin of Ghana still earlier, Sunni Ali divided the empire that he built after 1464 into a number of provinces. In each of these he appointed a governor and other officials, as well as staffing his own court with secretaries and ministers. The most important of these governors and ministers were appointed from families which stood at the head of the various sections of the Songhay people. Such appointments, in other words, were made by right of birth. The sons of leading men could expect to be given posts of political power or privilege.

This might have continued to work if it had not been for the growing prosperity, and therefore political power, of Timbuktu and other cities. But these cities were now filled with men increasingly divided from the peoples of the countryside, and therefore from the traditional lords and laws of Songhay, by two differences. In the first place, they were traders or lawyers concerned with problems of business, credit, the buying and selling of property, and other aspects of a new economic system in which the people of the countryside had little interest or share. In the second place, they had solved these problems by accepting the laws and ideas of Islam. In accepting such laws and ideas, they had become Muslims; often they had become devout Muslims.

There arose in Songhay a clear conflict of interests, as well as of beliefs, between the Muslims of the towns and the peoples of the countryside who remained loyal to Songhay religion. Sunni Ali was the first king to meet the full impact of this conflict. Generally he was shrewd and strong enough to contain it. He balanced the interests of the towns against those of the countryside. Mostly he sided with the second. Resenting this, Timbuktu revolted against his rule, whereupon Sunni Ali took an army into the city and harshly punished its leading families. That is why the historians of Timbuktu afterwards wrote of Ali as a cruel tyrant; it is also why the Songhay of the countryside remembered him, and still remember him, as the greatest of their kings.

When this dominating figure died in 1492, the conflict erupted again. Seeing that royal power had passed to another 'man of the countryside', the traders of the cities called for revolt. They found a leader in Muhammad Turay; and Askia Muhammad Turay, as we have seen, grasped his opportunity.

But Turay, however successful, could not ignore the rivalry of town and countryside. It was his biggest problem, and no amount of wishing would make it go away. Basing his power mainly on the trading cities, with their strong Muslim faith, Turay still had to find a way of meeting the rivalry of chiefs of leading families outside the cities. Partly he absorbed them into his system, sending them out as governors or using them as ministers. Though staunchly Muslim himself, making a pilgrimage to Mecca in fairly grand style, he was careful to retain ceremonies at court that belonged to Songhay history and religion. Yet this was not enough. He needed another way of buttressing his power.

He did this in much the same way as did the kings of Europe at about the same period. He began to appoint to his service men of humble birth. Often these were 'slaves' whom he had captured in war and who had therefore lost their freedom. Such men stood outside the network of loyalty to leading families in Songhay. This meant that the king could expect from them a purely personal loyalty to himself. There appeared in this way a new group in society: of 'king's men', as they may be called. After 1500 they formed the basis of the regular civil services of later times.

This in turn increased the influence of the cities. They alone could supply the educated 'king's men' – the clerks and secretaries, the lawyers and judges, the diplomats and negotiators – that were needed by the growing complexity of government and interstate relations.

The writers of Timbuktu

Of all the cities of Songhay, Timbuktu was the most important under the rule of Askia the Great and his successors. Gao remained the political capital of the empire, but Timbuktu became its commercial and intellectual centre. Its schools of learning, whether of theology, law, history, or other studies, became known throughout the Muslim world. Scholars from distant lands arrived to teach or learn. By late in the fifteenth century these schools formed a group of 'colleges', like the universities of Oxford and Paris in their early days.

Many renowned West African writers and teachers, whose names are still remembered and whose books are still studied, lived and taught in Timbuktu. One was Muhammad Kati, who was born in 1464, travelled with Askia the Great on pilgrimage to Mecca, and wrote a valuable history book, called the *Chronicle of the Seeker for Knowledge*. A second was Abd al-Rahman al-Sadi, the author of another book of value for the history of the central and western grasslands, the *Chronicle of the Sudan*. A third was Ahmad Baba, author of Muslim law books that are used in West Africa even today.

Christian Europe began to learn of all this only with the publication in Italy of a remarkable description of parts of West Africa by a man called Leo Africanus, originally a citizen of Granada in Andalus. Leo finished his book in 1525. It was published for a wide audience in 1550; it caused a great sensation, of much the same kind as that which greeted the first news of America. Leo's book opened for Europeans the vision of an African world of which they knew almost nothing, and it did this in vivid detail.

His readers were astonished by what he had to report, but perhaps by nothing as much as by his account of Timbuktu:

> There you find many judges, professors, and devout men, all handsomely maintained by the king, who holds scholars in much honour. There, too, they sell many handwritten North African books, and more profit is made there from the sale of books than from any other branch of trade.

Timbuktu was governed by its chief Muslim judge or *qadi*. He was usually a member of a local leading family which produced scholars such as Ahmad Baba. These city rulers cherished their power. Having opposed Sunni Ali, and paid for their disobedience, they worked well with Askia the Great and his successors. Yet they were never completely loyal to the Songhay cause. When an invading Moroccan army came in 1591 they saw another chance to regain their independence. They took it, only to find that Moroccan rule could be harsher than anything they had known before.

Disaster from the north

Songhay had come into conflict with Morocco, in about 1550, over control of the central Saharan sources of salt. Then the Moroccans developed another ambition. They decided to invade Songhay in an attempt to get hold of the sources of gold. In 1591 a Moroccan army crossed the Sahara and defeated the Songhay army at Tondibi near Timbuktu. It proved, in the end, a fatal enterprise to nearly all concerned.

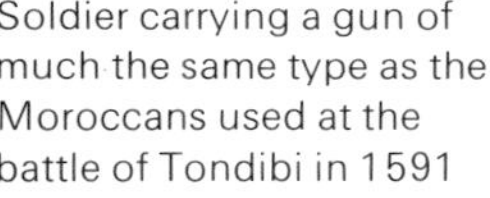

Soldier carrying a gun of much the same type as the Moroccans used at the battle of Tondibi in 1591

The Songhay were defeated for a number of reasons. The battle of Tondibi signalled the appearance south of the Sahara of a new weapon. Until now the spear and lance and arrow had been the weapons of warfare. Now the gun appeared. At Tondibi and for a long time afterwards, true enough, the gun was a remarkably poor one. The Moroccans used a type called arquebus, which was wildly inaccurate beyond a range of about one hundred yards, and very hard to reload. But the noise of their firing frightened the Songhay horses, and may well have scared the Songhay horsemen as well.

The Songhay army had other troubles. It was weakened from having had to pu down a rebellion of the empire's western governors. And it seems likely that it suffered from defeatist advice given by some of the emperor's advisers. These were men who hoped that a Songhay defeat would free the way for cities such a Timbuktu to become independent.

Once defeated at Tondibi, the Songhay never recovered their power. They wer on fighting for years, launching sudden raids on the invaders or relying on guerrilla tactics of harassment. But they had lost control of the cities of the empire, and it was the cities that held the keys to power and wealth. Meanwhile number of peoples of the countryside, long restless under the sometimes oppressive power of the cities, threw off their loyalty to the Songhay lords and revolted against them.

The cities fared little better than the Songhay lords. Having hoped for independence, they found themselves in the power of the Moroccan governors, and these, under urgent orders to send home gold and other valuables, saw to it that their troops took whatever could be found.

But the Moroccans also failed in the end. They seized much loot in Timbuktu and Gao, but were unable to gain command of the trade routes to the south where the gold was mined. Their expeditions were thrown back, their troops cut off by roving units of Songhay cavalry. The Moroccans paid a high price for their invasion before they were through with it, for it is said to have cost them the lives of 23,000 men. Eventually the king of Morocco tired of sending reinforcements, decided to cut his losses and pull out. Moroccan governors continued to rule in Timbuktu for many years, but with little power outside the city walls and often challenged even inside them. Yet the Songhay empire had been destroyed.

OTHER GRASSLAND STATES

While the Askias ruled Songhay, between 1493 and 1591, another powerful empire developed in the eastern grasslands of the central Sudan. Kings of the Saifuwa section of the Kanuri people had come to power there before AD 1000. Like those of Mali and Songhay, and by much the same methods, they gradually increased their power. By the 1600s this empire of Kanem-Bornu controlled wide regions to the west and east of Lake Chad.

Kingdoms based on trade

For them, too, the trans-Saharan trade was important, but this time along the north–south routes of the eastern Sahara that linked Kanem-Bornu with the trading cities of southern Tunisia, Libya and Egypt. In time, facing problems

gs built up small
ofessional armies. . . .
ese bronze figures of
rtuguese soldiers with
ns were made by an
ist of Benin around 1600

similar to those of Songhay, they also built up civil services of 'king's men' and formed small armies of professional soldiers. Their best-known ruler, the emperor Idris Alooma, who ruled between about 1571 and 1603, or at about the same time as England's Queen Elizabeth I, strengthened his forces with a special corps of musketeers trained by specialists from Egypt.

Between Kanem-Bornu and Songhay lay the city-states of the Hausa people in what today is the central and western part of Northern Nigeria. You can see this on the map on p. 85. Seven of these cities were chiefly inhabited by Hausa; and seven others were formed by close neighbours of the Hausa. Most of them arose soon after AD 1000 as small settlements, each surrounded by a defensive stockade. These settlements grew with time into strong cities with power over the surrounding countryside.

he Hausa states

In the book he finished in 1525 Leo Africanus reported them as wealthy kingdoms. Their kings borrowed the methods of self-rule worked out in Songhay to the west and Kanem-Bornu to the east. Like the rulers of those empires, the Hausa kings flourished on trade and on the taxation of trade between north and south. Growing stronger, they also built up civil services and small professional armies, equipped their cavalry soldiers with chain-mail armour and good steel weapons, and built palaces for themselves. With all this, of course, ordinary people suffered by having to pay heavier taxes, work harder for powerful lords, and endure the dangers and ravages of war. Yet there was also a lot of economic development.

Leo described another of these states as inhabited by 'people who are in general very civilised. They have many weavers and shoemakers, and they export their goods to Timbuktu and Gao.' Their great city of Kano 'was encircled by a wall made of beams of wood and pounded clay, and its houses are built of the same materials. Its inhabitants are civilised artisans and rich merchants.' Kano is still a rich city today.

Kings and constitutions

The kings of these states were firmly established on their thrones but, like other African monarchs, they were not dictators. They could govern only within the rules of their constitutions. These constitutions were unwritten, like that of Brit to this day, but the rules were well known. As constitutional monarchies, kingdoms whose rulers have to obey the rules of accepted law and tradition, th governments were carefully balanced between two sorts of officials. One sort consisted of noblemen who were given high posts; the other, offsetting the power of these nobles, consisted of 'king's men' who were personal henchmen the king. Playing off one sort of officials against the other, the kings manoeuvre between the two; in practice they had to win the agreement of both before taki any major decision, such as going to war. Having begun their existence before 1300, some of the Hausa cities still exist today as thriving, though no longer independent, centres of trade and local government.

It was not only in the grassland regions of the Sudan that African civilisation grew and developed during these centuries. Much the same process occurred among other peoples living in the forest lands of the tropics, in the grassland plains to the south of the tropical forests, or along the coasts of the Atlantic and Indian Oceans. Before returning to West Africa, we shall read about this proces of growth and change in another large region, that of the eastern seaboard and the inland countries of East and Central Africa, the home of the Swahili and the many neighbours of Middle Africa.

4 East and Middle Africa: ocean ports and inland kingdoms

CITIES OF THE EASTERN SEABOARD

We have seen that development in the medieval world was strengthened by West African production of gold and other goods, and by African trade across the Sahara with kingdoms in North Africa, Egypt, western Europe, and western Asia. This circuit of long-distance trade in the west was paralleled by another wide circuit in the east. Look at the map on p. 89. A community of merchants of many nations joined the coastal peoples of East Africa with those of India and Arabia, and reached, as time went by, from Egypt at one end of this eastern world to China at the other. This trade in the east had far-reaching consequences for Africans and other peoples, as did the trade in the west. Just as the vast sand-ocean of the Sahara became encircled by thriving merchant cities and strong kingdoms, so also did the waters of the Indian Ocean. The people of India played a big part in this wide circuit of eastern trade.

Even before 500 BC small ships were making their way along the coasts of Arabia and India, looking for new trade and business contacts. Gradually they improved their equipment and navigation. As they did so, they were able to venture out of sight of land and trust themselves to the ocean winds. They discovered the *monsoons*, the reliable 'trade winds' of the Indian Ocean which blow for months from north-western India towards East Africa, and then just as regularly back again from East Africa towards India. Many sailors began to use these winds.

Whether in this way, or by coasting voyagers from the Red Sea, the seaboard peoples of East Africa were drawn into a system of ocean commerce, beginning about two thousand years ago. These seaboard Africans belonged to Bantu-speaking groups who had made their homes here earlier, and had developed farming, fishing and the use of metals. They did not think of themselves, then or later, as forming a single people or nation, but all of them spoke various forms of the same Bantu language, and Arab visitors began calling them the Swahili, a word which derives from the Arabic for 'coastal plain'. This general name has stayed with them and with their language.

The Swahili became skilled and enterprising traders. They made friendly contact with inland producers of gold and ivory. They brought these goods down long trails from the interior to their city-ports on the Indian Ocean, and sold them

Date	East and Middle Africa		Elsewhere	
AD 100				
200				
300				
400				
500				
600				
700	Southern Bantu peoples establish themselves in northern parts of South Africa		Empire of the Franks in France Anglo-Saxon kingdoms in England	
800				
900	Early Arab settlements along East African coast; origins of Swahili civilization			
1000	Swahili towns begin to be built in stone, and to grow rich as trading centres		Vikings discover North America Period of Christian crusades against the Muslims in Palestine	
1100				
1200	Earliest stone-building at Great Zimbabwe			
1300	Rise of Shona kingdoms in Zimbabwe		Anglo-French wars in France	
1400	Formation of new kingdoms in Angola and southern Congo Basin		Holy Roman Empire in Germany	
1500	Rise of Luba kingdoms in Katanga (Congo Basin)	1505. Portuguese raid and burn on East Coast	Rise of Spanish empire, fuelled by wealth looted from the New World	
1600	Portuguese wars of invasion in Angola kingdoms Rise of Lunda kingdoms in Kasai region (Congo Basin)	1652. Dutch form small settlement at the Cape of Good Hope; origins of modern South Africa	Dutch, and then English dominate Indian Ocean, pushing aside the Portuguese	Period of major African slave trade to the Americas, mainly from West Africa
1700				
1800				

to Arab and Indian merchants for cottons and other imports. At the same time they developed coastal trade in their own ships.

Growing prosperous in these ways, the Swahili after about AD 900 developed a successful civilisation, taking many ideas from the Arabs but transforming them for their own use. In the course of time they built cities of stone at many points along the nearly 5,000 kilometres of the sea coast of what are now the countries of Somalia, Kenya, Tanzania, Mozambique, and their offshore islands such as Zanzibar. Like West Africans, the Swahili and their inland neighbours of East and Middle Africa progressed by their own success in overcoming natural obstacles. They increased their numbers and developed political systems, solving new problems. But long-distance trade above all proved vital for the Swahili in their development.

Sinbad the sailor: tales of the ocean trade

The Indian Ocean trade was important from very early times. But it really began to flourish after about AD 650 with the rise to power of the Arabs under Islam. The Muslim Arabs rapidly enlarged this trade, settling their agents or governors in the ports of India, East Africa, south-east Asia, Indonesia, and South China, and linking all these ports in an extensive business system. And then, having become literate through the teachings of Islam, the Arabs also began to write about their achievements and adventures. In later times the Swahili would write and tell their own stories of the sea. But in the centuries just after 700 it was the Arabs, chiefly those of Iraq and the Persian Gulf, who told the best tales of this ocean trade.

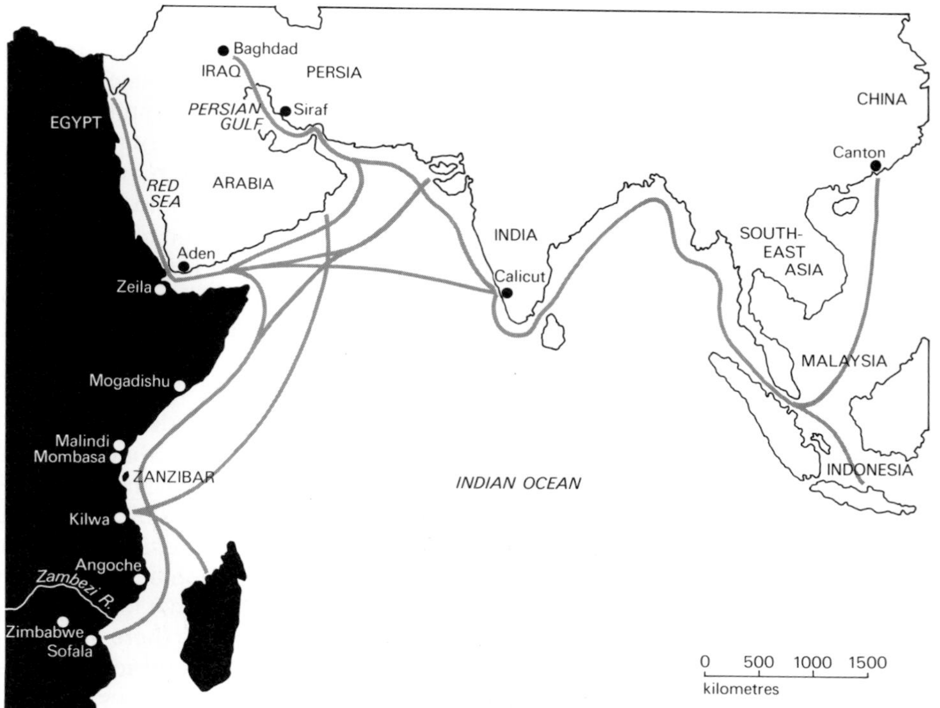

Eastern trade routes, pioneered by Arab sailors long before the arrival of the Europeans. Only a few of their ports of call are shown here

Blessed with a favouring wind, we sped upon the foamy highways of the sea, trading from port to port and from island to island, selling and bartering our goods, haggling with merchants and officials wherever we cast anchor.

In such words as these, the fabulous Sinbad the Sailor used to speak to his listeners in the great inland city of Baghdad and tell of his seven long journeys from the Persian Gulf to Africa and India. He told of the marvels he had seen on these journeys. Some of these marvels really existed, such as 'the gigantic rhinoceros which grazes in the fields like a cow or buffalo', or the 'trees so huge that beneath one of them a hundred men could shelter from the sun'. Others we imaginary, such as the giant roc, a bird so big that its wings when spread 'enclosed the sky'.

Sinbad was a fictional character in folklore tales that were written down afterwards in a book of 'wonderful stories', *The Thousand and One Nights*, alon with the tales of Aladdin and his magic lamp. Yet Sinbad's stories had some trut in them. They told how the Arabs had discovered an African and eastern world c which they had known nothing, just as the Europeans were to do eight hundred years later in these same regions.

The Arabs voyaged to East Africa for a variety of goods. They were especially interested in ivory and tortoise shell, gold and other metals. Their most reliable writers had much to say on the subject. For example, the much travelled al-Masudi, in his book of 945 which he called *The Meadows of Gold and Mines of Gems*, discussed the importance of the African ivory trade. Better for carving tha Indian ivory, the African product was in great demand in the markets of the East 'The kings and military or civilian officials of China', wrote al-Masudi, 'would never think of visiting their emperor except in a palanquin (a chair carried by servants) that was decorated with ivory', while 'the Indians use ivory for many purposes such as sword hilts and games like chess'.

Reports about East Africa were made in still more distant countries. In about 1250 a Chinese customs inspector in one of the South China ports wrote that ships from the kingdoms of north-western India sailed every year on trading journeys to East Africa, and their crews sold large quantities of cotton cloth and porcelain to the East Africans. The cotton cloth has long since vanished. But eve today, along the shores of Kenya and Tanzania, a visitor can give himself a histo lesson by walking along the beach and gathering bits of broken Chinese cups ar pots and saucers, mute witnesses to the Indian Ocean trade of long ago.

The rise of Swahili culture

Using their share in the profits of this trade, the Swahili were able to build handsome cities from the grey coralstone that forms their coastline. Built near th beach, or on small islands close to the coast and sometimes surrounded by a defensive wall, these cities were the work of Swahili architects and masons working in styles of their own. Tall houses, terraced one against the other, lined narrow streets that led to a seaport 'square' where seamen gossiped and ships o many nations anchored. Most of the larger houses enclosed a pillared courtyard usually shaped as a rectangle, off which there opened a series of small rooms ke dark and cool against the brilliant light and sometimes stifling heat of this coastland. Skilled craftsmen decorated houses with painted pottery and plates

Objects relating to old Swahili civilisation found by archaeologists in or near the ruined city of Kilwa

1. Copper coin of King Hasan, dating from about AD 1200

2. Silver coin of King Hasan found at Kisimani on Mafia Island

3. Bronze lid, possibly of Indian origin, dating from about the fourteenth century AD

4. Bronze inkwell dating from about the tenth century AD

5. Two clay crucibles for melting copper, found at Kilwa and Kisimani

from Persia and China, arranging these in decorative niches carved in the coral walls. Much attention was given to the supply of fresh water for washing and sanitary purposes.

After about 900 the Swahili leaders began to adopt Islam from their Arab visitors and settlers, just as Africans in the Sudan, at the same time, were adopting Islam from the Berbers; and they did this for similar reasons. The Swahili wanted to join themselves to the world-wide community of Islam. With the growth of their cities, they needed new techniques of trade and government. This change was reflected in many aspects of their life, including their coral architecture. Becoming Muslims, they began to build handsome stone mosques. The best of these date from about 1200–1300, and were designed with finely carved windows and arches.

Although they adopted the faith of Islam, they no more became Arabs than did Muslim peoples of the western and central Sudan. They absorbed many Arab settlers by inter-marriage, and considered themselves a part of the Muslim world. Their leading families were careful to trace their origins from Arabia or Persia, even when these origins were largely imaginary. But Swahili civilisation remained African, weaving Muslim beliefs and laws into the fabric of its own culture. This can be seen in many details of their architecture as well as in the design of their pillared gravestones, which are in forms not found elsewhere. It can also be seen, still more convincingly, in their literature.

The Swahili were influenced by the poetic literature of the Arabs, but they had their own verse rhythms, their own styles of story telling. They loved to hear and tell their own heroic poems; sea-faring tales, epics of adventure, romances of love and daring. The poet and the story teller became men whom everyone admired, gathering an audience around a fire at night or else on someone's veranda. In its earliest period this literature was never written down. The means of writing came with Islam, probably around 1100, just as in the western and central Sudan. Nothing survives of this Swahili literature in Arabic until much later times. Later again, perhaps after 1600, the Swahili began writing their own language in an Arabic script, though the earliest known example of a poem written in this script dates from 1728.

Like Timbuktu and the cities of Mali and Songhay, the chief Swahili towns also grew into centres of Muslim learning and debate. The tireless ibn Battuta, when he was young and decided to travel the whole Muslim world, was careful to pay them a call. He tells in his memoirs how he took ship in 1331 at Aden, on the south coast of Arabia, and 'after four days reached Zeila [now in northern Somalia] which is inhabited by black people.' He was not pleased with Zeila, which he called 'the most stinking town in the world' because of the smell of fish and the slaughter of camels for meat. His own ship arrived there in the evening; the passengers preferred to pass the night on board.

Next, ibn Battuta sailed south along the East African coast to Mogadishu (today the capital of Somalia) and found it 'an enormous town'. But his real aim was to reach the city whose reputation outshone all others on the long East African seaboard. This was Kilwa, at that time the chief East African centre of the gold and ivory trade.

Kilwa deeply impressed this globe-trotter. Nearly thirty years later, having at last settled down in his homeland of Morocco, he still remembered it with admiration. By then he had visited or lived in nearly all the great cities of the Muslim world from Morocco to Peking, China. But Kilwa, he thought, was among the best built of them all.

He says that Kilwa city, established on a small island close to the coast of southern Tanzania, was 'very fine and substantial'. It is not a surprising judgment. For Kilwa by that time, 1331, had certainly become 'Queen of the South' among the cities of the world. It is easy today to see why by looking at its coral ruins among the trees and thorn thickets of Kilwa island. As archaeologists have lately made clear, the king of Kilwa at the time of ibn Battuta's visit, King Hasan II, lived in the splendid many-roomed palace of Husuni, just outside the main town on Kilwa island. There, among other signs of luxury, was a large eight-sided bathing pool on the summit of a cliff. Kilwa's chief mosque, much of which survives in partial ruin, was already a magnificent building of many domes and pillars. Later kings of Kilwa made it larger still.

Kilwa and its partners

This development of Swahili culture was not an accident. It came about in several stages. Each was largely in response to the growth of the ocean trade. By the 1330s, when ibn Battuta travelled here, several main centres of power and trade had taken shape. These were Mogadishu in the north, Pate (pronounced Pa-tay), Mombasa, and Kilwa in the south. By about 1400 there were more than thirty cities along the coast. Each kept its own independence, for these cities seldom or never combined in more than short-lived alliances, being often in sharp competition with one another. But Kilwa took a clear lead in the south, dominating all the ports of southern Tanzania and those of Mozambique. In this way Kilwa had control of the gold exports of the inland country, most of which came from the interior to the ports of Mozambique.

Control of this gold trade brought Kilwa wealth and success. As early as 1200 the king of Kilwa controlled enough trade to justify him in minting a currency of his own. These and later Kilwa coins were made from copper and silver, and were of several values. Similar coins were afterwards minted by the kings of Mogadishu and Zanzibar.

All these kings drew money from taxes on trade. They taxed their own merchants. They taxed the merchants from other Swahili cities. They taxed the foreign traders who came from Arabia and Persia, India and Ceylon.

Swahili merchants traded far and wide. When the Portuguese reached south-east Asia, soon after 1500, they found East African merchants in the ports of Malaysia and Indonesia. Usually the Swahili travelled the ocean in the large trading ships of India or Ceylon. But they used their own ships for trade along the African coast, and their 'sewn boats' became well known in those waters. Some of them were as large as seventy tons. They were called 'sewn boats' because they were held together by palm lashings instead of by iron clamps or nails, and so were safe from rust. In the handsome and busy harbours of the Kenya and Tanzania coast there were seamen and pilots who understood the winds and routes in every part of the Indian Ocean, and who used navigating instruments as good as any then known to Europeans, or sometimes better. Swahili ports were often full of foreign shipping, sometimes from very distant places. In 1417 and 1431 there were even visits by large Chinese fleets.

The Swahili cities were international in their outlook and welcomed visitors who came in peace. Chiefs and messengers on embassies of business or

In 1414 ambassadors from East Africa presented a giraffe to the emperor of China in Peking. Here it is with its keeper, in a Chinese painting made at the time

diplomacy arrived from African kingdoms far in the interior. Wandering scholars from Egypt or Arabia, India, or from other African cities, came for visits of discussion with Swahili colleagues. All these visitors could meet with many ordinary citizens engaged in many crafts; fishermen, farmers, fruitgrowers, shipbuilders, masons, metal workers, and others.

This was a civilisation that developed without serious interruption or invasion from outside until 1498. Then Portuguese sailed in from the Atlantic Ocean. They did not come in peace, but as pirates and destroyers. Yet some of these Portuguese had time to admire what others of their nation were about to destroy. We know from Portuguese reports of about 1500 and soon after how successfully the Swahili had continued their growth since ibn Battuta had admired Kilwa two centuries earlier.

Some of the best of these early Portuguese reports were written by Duarte Barbosa, a business agent of the king of Portugal who went out in one of the first Portuguese fleets, stayed many years, and returned to Portugal in about 1517. First he describes Sofala, which was for centuries the chief centre of trade with the gold producers of the inland country. He says that Sofala

> is inhabited by the Moors [he means Swahili Muslims] who are black, and some of them are brownish; some of them speak Arabic, but the most part use the language of their country. They wear cotton and silk garments from the waist down, and others wear cloaks about their shoulders and various sorts of hats.

Farther up the coast he admired the port of Angoche, afterwards re-named Antonio de Enes by the Portuguese, 'where there are many merchants who deal in gold and ivory, silk and cotton cloth, Indian beads', and who spoke Swahili as well as Arabic. Next there was Kilwa, 'a town with many handsome houses of stone and mortar, very well arranged in streets, and whose doors are of carved wood'. Around the town were 'streams and orchards and fruit gardens'. The people of Kilwa 'are finely clad in many rich garments of gold and silk and cotton, and they wore many bracelets and other ornaments of gold and silver, and the women have jewelled earrings'. Barbosa also makes it clear that Mombasa, today the chief port of Kenya, was already a fine city, and is a place of wide international trade.

If the Portuguese and other Europeans who came after them had been content to share in this eastern prosperity they could have gained much and given much. But they were not interested in sharing. First they meant to discover, then to conquer. The consequences were disastrous.

'Devil take you! What brings *you* here?'

In 1498, having crossed the grey loneliness of the South Atlantic, the Portuguese Admiral Vasco da Gama with three small ships went eastward round the southern tip of Africa in search of India. It was a big moment in history, the first European visit to the Indian Ocean and its surrounding coasts. But da Gama and his men discovered more than they were looking for. Sailing north along the East African seaboard, they came upon the civilisation of the Swahili: busy ports, splendid towns, rich traders, experienced pilots and seamen. They were astonished, but they were also delighted. After their months of ocean voyaging the sight of all this, says da Gama's logbook, 'made us so happy that we cried for joy'.

In 1498 the Portuguese admiral Vasco da Gama sailed eastward round the Cape of Good Hope into the Indian Ocean with three small ships. These drawings of them were made about fifty years later

They found developed people where they had expected to find savages. At one harbour (that was probably Quilimane on the Mozambique coast) the logbook says their ships were inspected by 'two gentlemen of the country who were very haughty and valued nothing that we gave them'. Unimpressed by da Gama's ships, these visitors told the Portuguese that they had already seen 'big ships like ours'. The Swahili, in fact, were very far from 'crying for joy' at the arrival of these European visitors. They at once saw trouble coming. They were right.

Da Gama failed to find Kilwa on this first voyage, as his ships were carried northward past its island on a strongly running tide. He went on to Mombasa. Here he was treated with sharp suspicion and he continued on to Malindi. Only in Malindi did he find a welcome. This was because the king of Malindi thought that the Portuguese might prove useful allies against his chief rival, the king of Mombasa.

At Malindi the Portuguese were able to hire an Arab pilot, ibn Majid. This pilot took them safely across the Indian Ocean to north-western India, though he cursed himself afterwards for doing it. Anchoring in the great Indian port of Calicut, da Gama followed the usual Portuguese custom on voyages of discovery. He sent ashore one of the Portuguese convicts whom he carried for this purpose. The idea was that the convict could secure a pardon by running the risk of being the first man to go ashore in an unknown and possibly dangerous port. The logbook of the flagship tells us what happened. On landing, the convict met a man from Tunis (on the coast of North Africa). This Tunisian understood Portuguese. More than that, he also understood something of the true meaning of this sudden arrival of Europeans where they had never been before. He greeted the first Portuguese to step ashore with some memorable words: 'Devil take you!' he said, 'What brings *you* here?'

The answer came soon. Da Gama returned to Portugal in 1499. After that, year after year, the kings of Portugal sent out fleets to loot and conquer these rich eastern cities. The coming of the Portuguese brought ruin to the whole trading community of the Indian Ocean.

Disaster and survival

These Portuguese were not an unusually greedy or violent people. But they were ruled by kings, nobles, and powerful merchants who believed that they should bother to get by peaceful trade only what they could not take by force of arms. Finding peace in the East – open harbours, cities with little or no defence, small armies or none at all – they thought it simple and sensible to use their guns and swords to take whatever they wanted. In the course of taking, they introduced more savage forms of warfare.

Dazzled by the wealth they found, contemptuous of non-European peoples, ignorant even of the ruin they caused, they battered down cities and sailed away with their loot. Many gave way to get-rich-quick temptations. A great European missionary in India, St Francis Xavier, in 1545 called it 'a power which I may call irresistible. Easy profits and easy plunder sharpen the appetites of those who get them. Bad examples and bad habits then sweep these men headlong into the abyss.' But in doing this, the Portuguese also swept away much peace and welfare.

The Swahili suffered with the rest. In 1505 the Portuguese viceroy in the East, Admiral Francisco d'Almeida, set out on a campaign of undisguised piracy. Hans Mayr, a German or Dutchman who was on board one of d'Almeida's ships, has left an account of it. Kilwa was taken and looted, then Mombasa. After the capture of Mombasa, d'Almeida

> ordered that the town should be plundered, and each man should carry to his ship whatever he wanted, and then they would divide up the spoils, so that each should have one twentieth part of what he had taken.
>
> This rule they applied to gold, silver and pearls [as well as other things]. Then everyone began looting the town and searching the houses, forcing open the doors with axes and iron bars.
>
> The Grand Captain [d'Almeida] took a good share for himself. A large quantity of rich silk and gold-embroidered cloths were seized, and carpets too; one of these, almost without equal for its beauty, was sent to the king of Portugal with many other valuables.

Other Europeans, English, Dutch and French, joined this hunt for eastern wealth. New conquests were carved from the countries of the Indian Ocean. Many Swahili cities continued to suffer. Some were abandoned. Others survived, sadly remembering their past glories. In a well-known Swahili poem of 1815 a poet sang of the ruin that had come upon his native city of Pate:

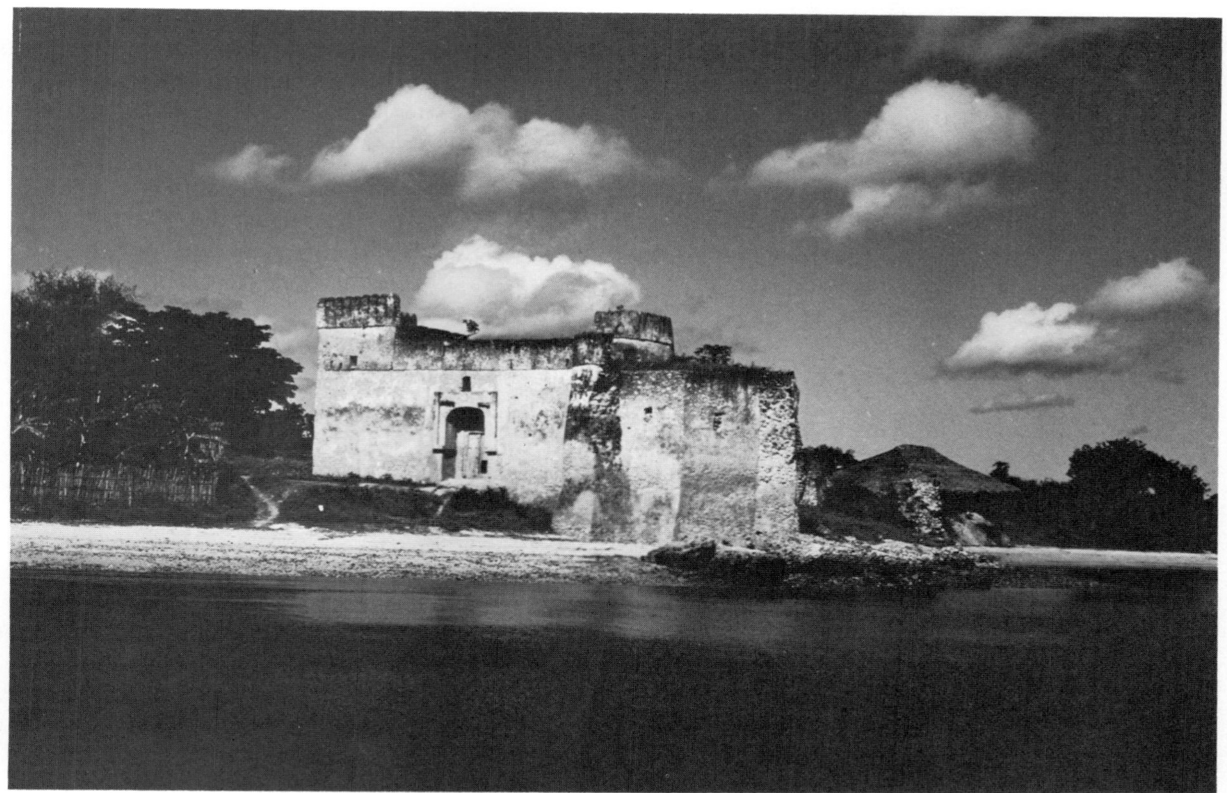

An old fort at Kilwa built by Arabs who settled on the Swahili Coast early in the nineteenth century

Madaka ya nyamba ya zisahani
Sasa walaliye wana wa nyuni . . .

(Where once the porcelain stood in the wall niches
Now wild birds nestle their fledglings . . .)

Yet this was not the end of Swahili civilisation. Though damaged by foreign invasions, it was not destroyed. During our own times Swahili culture has developed in new ways. Swahili cities have become part of the national territories of Kenya and Tanzania and enjoy a new independence together with their neighbours. The Swahili language is nowadays spoken by tens of millions of people. They also read it in Swahili newspapers and in books of poetry and prose, written nowadays with a Latin alphabet that is easier to use than Arabic. The old and gracious monuments of the coast have become a cherished part of the modern heritage of Africa.

SHONA KINGDOMS

For centuries the Swahili were important suppliers of gold and ivory to the Eastern world. Trade, not production, was the secret of their success. Production was the business of the peoples of the inland country. Who, then, were these producers? The answer takes us back to the story of Zimbabwe.

The peoples of the inland country, who included the people of Zimbabwe, provided the gold and ivory. They did business with travelling Swahili merchants and sent their own agents to the coastal ports. The Portuguese in places like Sofala soon heard about these men, and met with some of them. Duarte Barbosa reported:

> They are warlike men and some of them are great traders. The commanders among them wear capes of the skins of wild animals, trailing the tails on the ground, as a sign of their authority and dignity. They carry swords in wooden scabbards that are decorated with much gold and other metals, and these they wear on the left side, as we do. They carry spears and bows, and the iron arrow heads they have are long and finely pointed. Their king is the master of an exceeding great country.

But the true story of Zimbabwe, unknown to Barbosa, was more complicated. By this time there were two strong inland kingdoms, not one, and these already had a long and interesting history behind them.

The empire of Mwana Mutapa

Chapter 2 described how early groups of Africans multiplied in numbers and set up states in wide regions. Those who developed in the high grassland plains of the central-southern interior, between the rivers Zambezi and Limpopo, belonged to the Bantu language family. They afterwards became known by their Bantu language, which is Shona. This language, or group of languages, closely like each other, evolved before AD 1000 among neighbouring peoples in these grassland plains.

The Shona prospered by raising crops and cattle. They became skilled miners and metalworkers. Chapter 6 will have more to say about their skills. Meanwhile we should note that as early as AD 900 they had begun to sell gold and copper to Indian Ocean traders. Indirectly, through the Swahili, they were drawn into the great eastern circuit of long-distance trade. They were the chief providers of its gold. They were like those West Africans who, at the same time, were supplying gold to the western circuit of long-distance trade. And just as the western circuit had political and social effects on the providers of gold as well as on the traders in gold, so also did the eastern circuit. Trade in the west encouraged the growth of inland kingdoms and empires such as Ghana. Trade in the east did the same.

This development among the Shona occurred before any sure details of their history are known. By the fifteenth century, when the Shona embarked on a major period of political expansion, they had already built important states and had completed the towering walls of Great Zimbabwe, residence of their most powerful rulers, in about 1400.

At some early point in that century, perhaps around 1425, they began to reorganise. We still don't know quite why this happened. But one reason seems to have been that they wanted to unite the whole inland country, between the Limpopo and Zambezi rivers and far to the east, into a single area of production and long-distance trade, whether in gold, copper, ivory or other goods. Their strongest ruler at that time, Mutota, moved his capital from Great Zimbabwe far to the northward, near the valley of the Zambezi; there he conquered the Tongo and Tavara peoples and earned from them the royal title of Mwana Mutapa, which means something like 'Lord of the Plundered Lands'. The same title was taken by Shona kings for centuries after that.

The Tongo and Tavara accepted Mutota's overlordship, as did other neighbouring peoples. Mutota established his authority over a wide region before he died and was followed by his son Matope. This second Mwana Mutapa added to the Shona system all the lands of central and eastern Mozambique as far as the Indian Ocean, leaving only the Swahili coastal cities outside its control. By about 1480, when Matope died, the Shona political system consisted of a series of kingdoms reaching from the fringes of the Kalahari Desert, far to the west, right across Middle Africa to the waters of the Indian Ocean. The map below shows how the Shona empire grew.

But the times were not yet ripe for the long endurance of such ambitious schemes. The great system built by Mutota and Matope, and their governors and warriors and traders, was short-lived. After Matope's death, about 1490, lesser kings began to break away. Civil wars broke out, rather like the Wars of the Roses

The Shona states between 1400 and 1600

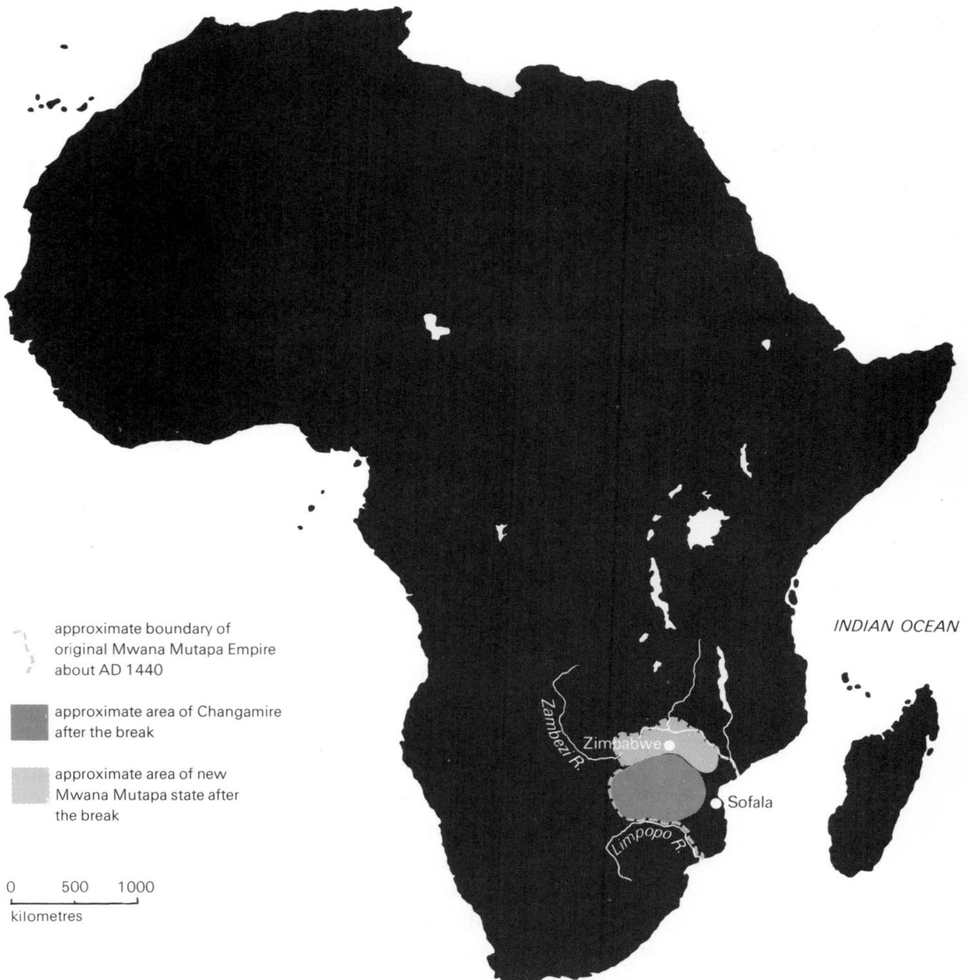

in feudal England a few years earlier. By about 1500, two strong centres of political power had emerged, one in the south under another Shona ruler called Changamire, and the second in the north under the Mwana Mutapa, with his capital on the Dande River.

Although they were rivals at first, these two kingdoms soon developed a tolerant peace. This proved all the easier because the ruling people in both states were all of Shona stock, spoke practically the same language, and shared the same religious beliefs and political methods. Neighbouring states, such as Kiteve on the borders of Mozambique, were of the same type.

Why did all these Shona kingdoms fail to unite into a single political system such as Mutota and Matope had built? The answer is partly that their society, by this time, was no longer a simple one. Here, as elsewhere, division of labour had brought division of society. Some men had much power; others less; many had none at all. Ruling groups, pushing their own interests, competed with each othe for command. At the same time these societies were not so far advanced as to be able to overcome their group rivalries, nor indeed to see any great advantage in doing so. Rearrangements of power 'at the top' meant little to the majority of people: village life continued much as before. Yet changes did come, and for the worse. Once again it was Portuguese intruders who were largely responsible.

Troubles from outside: the coming of the settlers

Settling at a few points along the south-eastern coast, notably on Mozambique Island and at Sofala, the Portuguese arrived when the inland wars were over, and long-distance trade could begin to pick up again. Eager for gold, the Portuguese took by force what they could find in the Swahili ports they seized. But they coul not find enough to satisfy their appetite. They wanted more. To get more, since the Swahili merchants resisted their demands, they had to discover where the gold came from, and, if possible, go and take it there.

They found this a very tough adventure. Not for many years did they have any success in getting gold in the inland country. In 1571 they sent a military expedition westward from Sofala, marching along the old trade route to the Shona lands, and attacked the kingdom of Kiteve, burning down the king's *zimbabwe*, or royal house. This destruction brought them nothing. They were so ignorant of the facts that one of their reports said 'our men expected to find gold in the streets and woods and come home laden with it'. Instead, they found a few of the mine shafts of western Mozambique, but because they were not miners they had no idea of how to extract the metal-bearing ore. The same report says that they spoiled a number of these shafts because, unlike the local Africans, they 'did not know how to work them'. They went back to Sofala empty-handed.

In later years they were able to send traders and missionaries into the southern Shona lands, ruled by the Changamires from Great Zimbabwe; but they were never able to secure any control there. Trying to win this control, they made so much trouble that in 1693 the ruling Changamire, whose name was Dombo, finally got fed up with them, and chased them out of his country.

The Portuguese were more successful in the northern Shona kingdom ruled by the Mwana Mutapas. Here they were able to win strong footholds, and gradually force themselves into a position of control. Soon after 1550, they pushed up the Zambesi river from their base on the coast, and started small settlements at Sena, about 250 kilometres from the ocean, and at Tete, about 500 kilometres from the coast. From these riverside bases they sent out small trading and political missions which were able to establish forward bases in the heartland of the Mwana Mutapas. Pretending to be friends, they offered their military aid to the Mwana Mutapas whenever these rulers were faced with rebellion by subject chiefs.

In 1573 these agents of the king of Portugal were able to persuade King Nogomo, the Mwana Mutapa of that time, to sign a treaty giving them possession of a number of gold mines, as well as permission to look for silver mines which, in fact, did not exist. Nogomo also gave them permission to settle wherever they wished along a strip of riverside land running all the way from Tete to the ocean. In return the Portuguese promised military aid, agreed to pay a yearly tax for the right to trade in the kingdom of the Mwana Mutapa, and undertook to import quantities of cotton cloth, something that was much needed by the Shona and their neighbours, who did not have enough cotton cloth now that they were largely cut off from Swahili trade.

The settlers interfere

Nogomo ruled till about 1589. He seems to have been a sensible monarch who tried to make the best of the fact of Portuguese presence along the river. But once again the Portuguese were not prepared to share in the profits of trade and production. Nogomo's death signalled the opening of a time of troubles. These came chiefly from Portuguese settlers who were now becoming more numerous in the Mwana Mutapa's country. They began to throw their weight around, behave like lords of the land, and force Africans into slavery on their farms. They built small private forts, and raised armed gangs to terrorise the countryside.

The official representatives of the king of Portugal condemned the settlers for their violence and greed, but as they were far away on the coast they were powerless to control them. Soon it was the settlers who were deciding what should be done. In 1607 another Mwana Mutapa renewed the treaty which Nogomo had made some thirty years earlier, giving the Portuguese the right to mine and export gold, and to look for silver. Almost at once the treaty was upset by the settlers who, for reasons of their own, suddenly refused to pay their taxes to the Mwana Mutapa. When he tried to make them pay, they called for soldiers from the coast. Then the settlers combined such forces as they could find, mainly in their settlements of Tete and Sena, and, with the support of a large force of hired African soldiers, declared war on the Mwana Mutapa. In two big battles of 1628 and 1629 they defeated the Mwana Mutapa's forces and killed many of his military commanders. They were then able to set up a new Mwana Mutapa of their own, whose name was Mavura.

Backing up their settlers, Portuguese officials imposed a treaty of surrender. Mavura had to agree to become a Christian and a subject of the king of Portugal, to allow the Portuguese to settle wherever they wished in his lands, and to open whatever mines they wanted. He had to promise to expel from his country all the Swahili traders of Sofala and other coastal towns, because these traders were still, if with great difficulty, competing with the Portuguese for business in the northern Shona kingdom.

This treaty was the forerunner of European colonial domination which was to come nearly three centuries later. The treaty gave the Portuguese control of all t worthwhile trade between the northern Shona kingdom and the coast. It reduce Mavura to little more than a Portuguese puppet. What was worse, at least at the time, it gave a free hand to the Portuguese settlers. Their violence and bullying grew worse. Soon Mavura was protesting, in a letter to the Portuguese senior official on the coast, that the settlers were 'greatly harming my people, killing some of them and wounding others, stealing their sons and daughters and their cattle, so that every day complaints of this are brought to my zimbabwe'.

But complaints were useless. Like other European settlers in later times, the Portuguese behaved as they wished and took what they wanted. Peace and ord gave way to raiding and destruction. The Mwana Mutapas continued to rule, bu they had little real power. Gradually their ancient might and majesty were forgotten.

BUILDING NEW STATES

Many other states emerged in Middle Africa in the same period that saw the mature life of the Shona kingdoms. They were built on the similar achievements of other peoples who, like the Shona, had mastered the techniques of tropical farming, stock raising and metal working, and who now, having thus grown mo numerous in numbers, required new forms of political organisation.

Among these were the Luba and Lunda peoples. Their home area lay in the Congo grasslands in what are now the provinces of Katanga and Kasai (Republi of Zaïre), the ancient area of early Bantu development (see map on p. 103). The peoples began evolving new forms of political organisation in about AD 1500. Such forms became the model for many of their neighbours. Among these were the Bemba and the Lozi in what is Zambia today.

Why had these peoples grown in number to the point of needing new forms o political organisation? The main reason was their successful conquest of the natural difficulties in the lands where they lived: they had studied nature, and made nature their friend and ally. Other reasons came to play their part; one of these, at least after about 1600, was the arrival of new American food plants, especially cassava and maize.

These plants were a valuable addition to Africa's food supply. They had come European sailing ships to the western coasts. There African farmers had eagerly adopted them, finding them unusually resistant to plant diseases and useful item for the cooking pot. The growing of these new plants quickly spread inland, giving valuable new crops. Farmers brought more land under cultivation. Food supplies became larger and populations therefore more numerous. Political reorganisation followed.

The power of long-distance trade

With larger settlements more widely spread apart, there came the development o a larger trade between distant markets. At the same time, these Middle African peoples were now prosperous enough to import foreign cotton cloth and other useful goods from suppliers on the coasts of the Indian and Atlantic Oceans. Another large circuit of long-distance trade came on the scene. By expanding to

The Luba and Lunda kingdoms

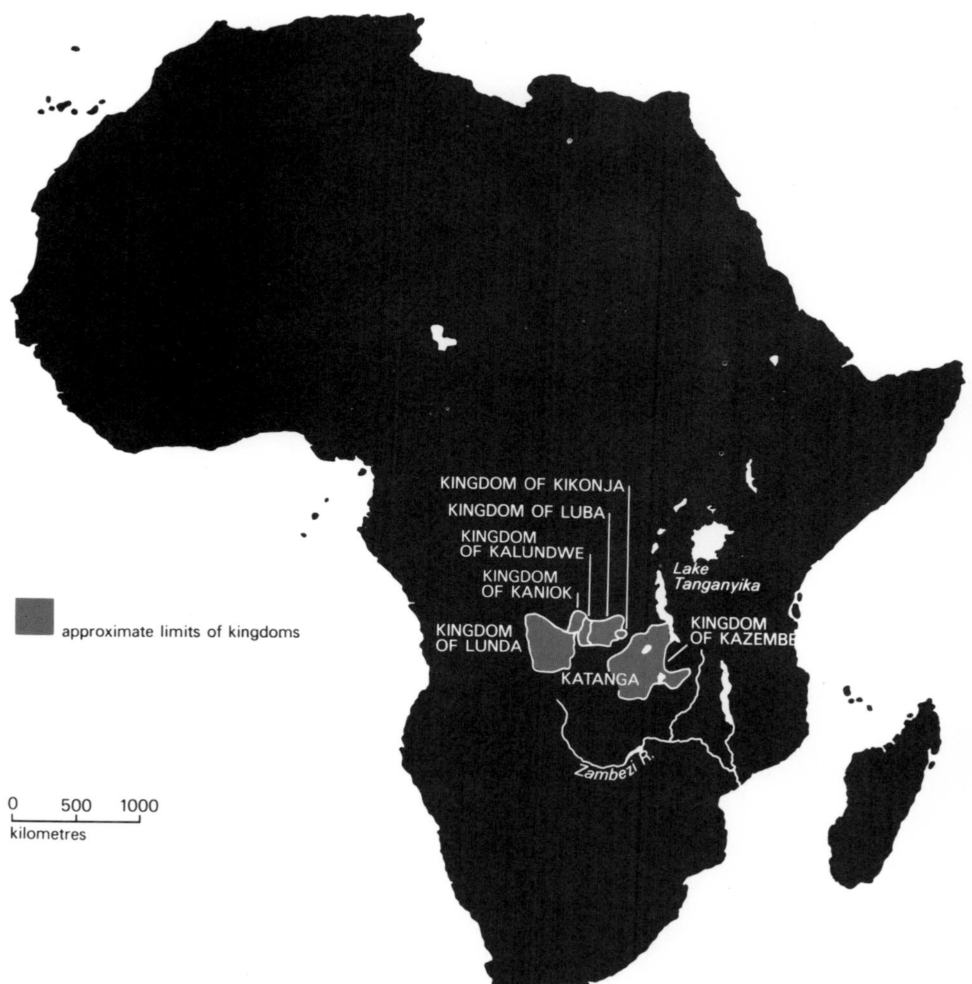

the west as well as to the east the Luba–Lunda group of states were able to join the trade of the eastern ocean with that of the western.

At the centre of this trading system of Middle Africa there stood the strong authority of a Lunda king whose royal title was the Mwata Yamvo, 'Lord of the Viper'. East of him there ruled another powerful monarch called the Kazembe, with other trading neighbours. Little of all this was known to Europeans until long afterwards. They thought that this 'heart of Africa' was 'scarcely beating': in fact it was very much alive. So much can be seen from a brief glimpse of the royal court of the Kazembe, as described by a Portuguese explorer a hundred and fifty years ago. We owe this almost forgotten description to Captain Gamitto, whose journey to the Kazembe took place in 1831.

A visit to King Kazembe

Gamitto and his handful of companions needed many weeks of tough and testing travel to reach the court of Kazembe. They went up the Zambesi and then struck

Gamitto's drawing of King Kazembe seated in royal state to receive his European visitor

northwards through the lands of the Malawi and their neighbours until they reached their distant goal. At this point, Gamitto recorded in his diary:

All five of us whites have let our hair and beards grow; my hair comes down to shoulders and my beard to my chest. I'm wearing a blue and white uniform, an otterskin cap, and a good sword. Dressed like this, and riding on a donkey, I entered what is perhaps the greatest town of Central Africa [the capital of King Kazembe].

We rode into a long street about a mile long, lined on either side by thatched walls to a height of ten or twelve feet, with small gates opening through them i the enclosures of huts. When we reached the King's residence, which they call Musumba, we found a great square filled with a throng of people, and so arranged as to leave empty a small area in front of the eastern gate.

The warriors in the square were the King's army, some five or six thousand m armed with bows and arrows, shields and spears, and standing about without a appearance of military discipline. The King was sitting on the left hand side of t eastern gate of the Musumba. Many leopard skins served him for a carpet, with the tails pointed outward to form a star. Over these there was an enormous lion skin, and on this a stool covered with a big green cloth. On this throne the King was seated in greater elegance and state than any other African king whom I ha seen.

Captain Gamitto went on to describe the king's appearance, and what is eve more useful, he also made a picture of the king on his throne. The king's head w covered by a conical hat with brilliant scarlet feathers, and he wore a cape embroidered with countless little fragments of coloured glass so that 'when stru by the sun's rays it was too bright to look upon'.

From beside the king's seat, two curved lines went out and met some twenty paces in front of him, and along these lines, marked on the ground, there were arranged a number of sculptured figures. Beyond these ceremonial carvings the king's family was seated; beyond these again were his chief officers and ministers. Gamitto recorded that:

The king looks fifty years old but we were told that he is much older. He has a long beard, already turning grey. He is well built and tall. His looks are agreeable and majestic, his style is splendid in its fashion.

Untroubled by the outside world, the farming people ruled by the Kazembe line of kings, in southern Katanga, continued with their quiet lives until struck by great upheavals after about 1850. They belonged to that vivid fabric of inner African history which is only now beginning to be understood or appreciated by the outside world. They developed an important part of the varied and rich heritage of Africa with their customs and beliefs, their fine artistic skills, their love of music, dancing and conversation, their habits of equality and respect for other people's rights. They conserved this heritage through the years.

Other peoples, at the far western end of Middle Africa where the tawny grassland plains tilt down sharply to the Atlantic Ocean, had a less happy fate. Something needs to be said about them, too.

The kingdom of Angola

The rise of the kingdoms of what is now western Angola began in much the same way as that of their inland neighbours to the east. Some time around 1350 bold chiefs began to apply new methods of government. They united village peoples under kings and governors of provinces and headmen of villages.

By 1400, or soon after, two large systems had emerged (see map on left). The more powerful of these was the kingdom of Kongo, so named after the Kongo people who lived, then as now, on either side of the lower Congo River. Their king's title was *Mani*, a Bantu word related to the *Mwana* of the Shona, just as English 'king' is related to the German word *König*. The Mani Kongo, or king of Kongo, ruled over most of modern northern Angola, governing through lesser chiefs who had charge of large provinces.

The kingdoms of Angola

A second important kingdom was that of the Kimbundu to the south of Kongo, lying in what is now west-central Angola. Its name was Ndongo, and its king's title *Ngola*; in 1500 the Portuguese in Kongo mistook the title of the king for the name of the country, and so the name Angola came into use. Other and smaller western kingdoms also took shape in this period and each was organised in much the same way.

The first European expedition to reach this western seaboard of the Congo estuary and Angola was one of Portugal's greatest sea captains, Diogo Cão (pronounced Cahn). He put down anchor in the Congo River in 1483 and was welcomed by the local governor of the king of Kongo. In a later voyage Cão visited the court of the king and for a while the two sides were friendly.

The kings of Portugal and Kongo wrote to each other as 'royal friends and brothers'. Courtesy went hand-in-hand with advice that was at least meant to be helpful. In 1512 the king of Portugal suggested that his African partner adopt the aristocratic titles used in Portugal. The king of Kongo, wanting to please his

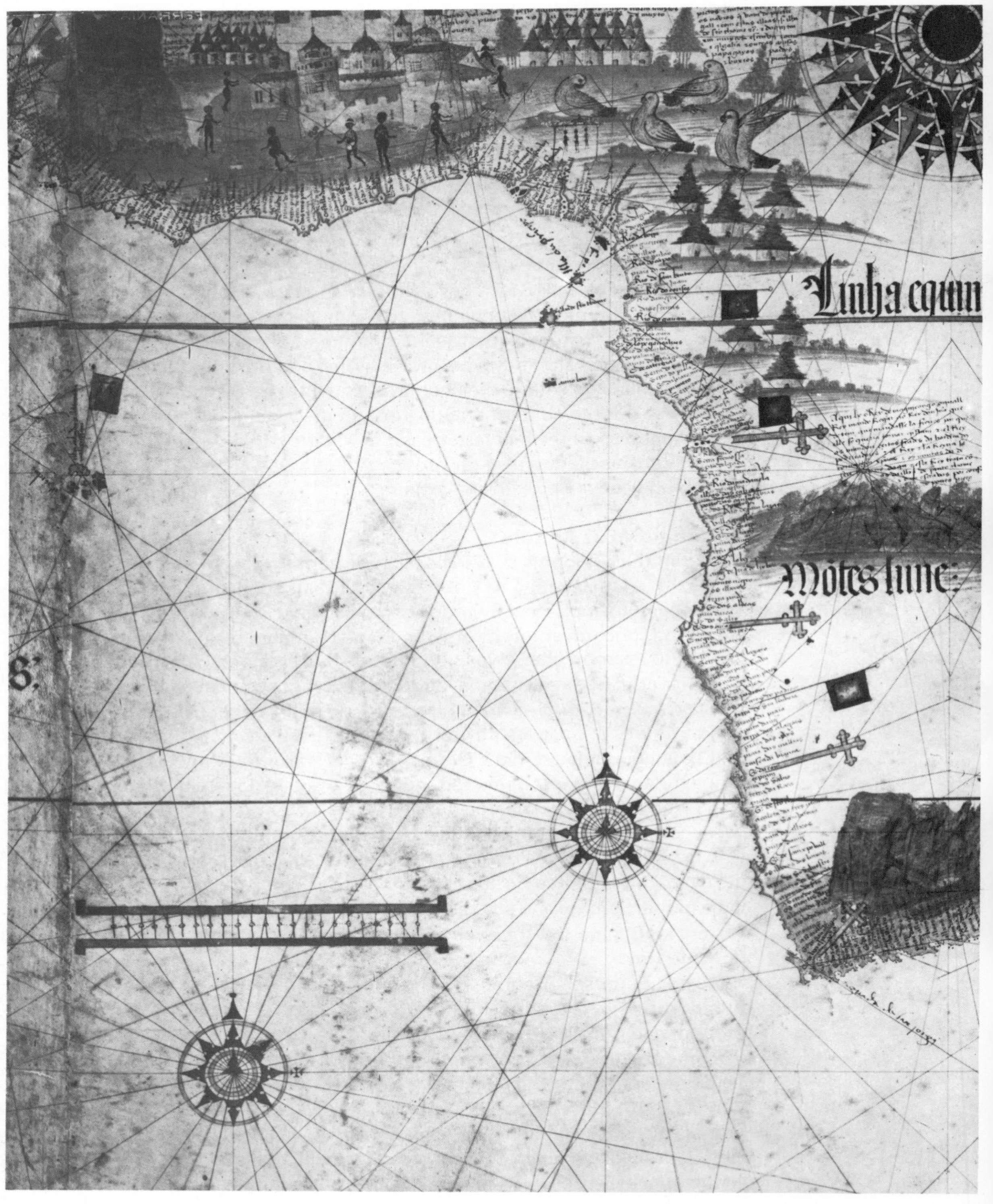
Linha equin
Mõtes lune:

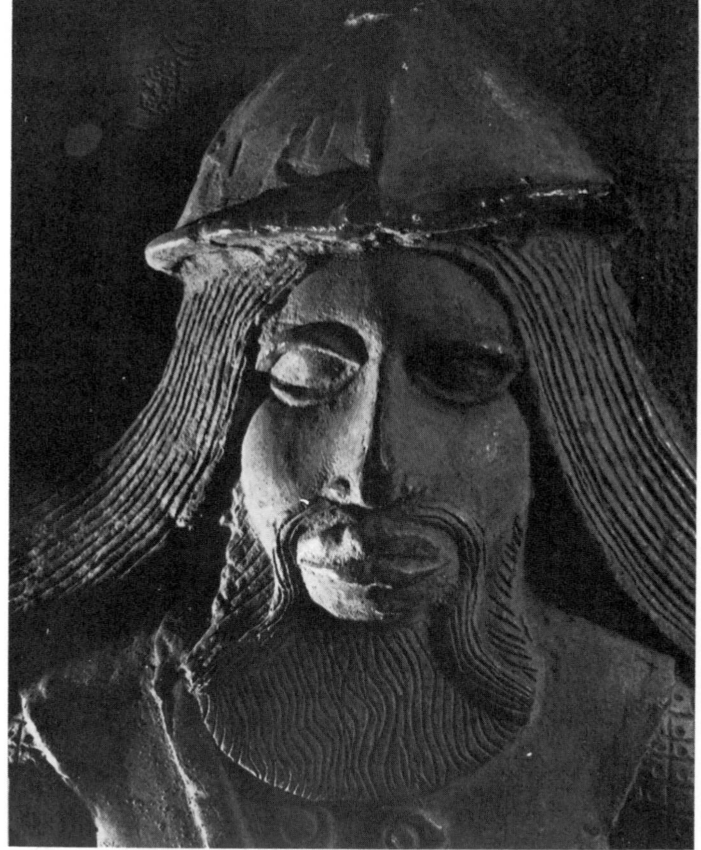

Bronze plaque from Benin dating from the sixteenth century, showing a Portuguese visitor to that kingdom

distant friend, began to bestow European titles such as viscount, marquis, duke, and prince on his governors and chiefs. There was talk of technical aid by the Portuguese as well as Christian missions, and missionaries were sent. They were welcomed at the king's court and given permission to build a church. The king and his governors became Christians, and the name of the capital was changed from Mbanza Kongo to Saint Salvador. The king, on adopting Christianity, changed his name from Nzinga to Affonso. If these relations of mutual respect had continued, the results for Africa, as for Europe, might have been very different.

Opposite: After the 1430s, Portuguese navigators pushed gradually down the coast of western Africa. They got to know a lot about its coastal geography. This famous map called the Cantino Chart showed what they had learned by 1502. They knew nothing about the inland country, but at the top of the map you can see how they imagined the cities of the empires of West Africa. They raised stone crosses where they landed and drew them on the map

A hundred years of invasion

Again, the evils came from settlers' greed for more. This time, to begin with, they were Portuguese settlers on the offshore islands of São Thomé and Principe. These settlers found they could produce highly profitable sugar if only they got hold of enough men to grow it. Having used up the local population, they began importing labour from the mainland of Kongo. They opened a slave trade, using Portuguese dealers and African chiefs. Soon there were other Portuguese, across the ocean in Brazil, who also wanted slaves. From small beginnings this Angolan slave trade grew into a plague.

There were no slaves in Kongo, or in neighbouring kingdoms, when the Europeans arrived. But there were a number of men who had lost their civil rights by capture in war or sentence of the local courts. King Affonso, who ruled between about 1506 and 1540, agreed to sell these 'rightless persons' to the Portuguese. But there were not enough of them. King Affonso blundered. Wishing to please the Portuguese, he embarked on wars with his neighbours in order to get more captives. He soon had cause to regret it. Coastal chiefs began to find that they could do better for themselves by going into this slave trade on their own. In this way, they took no notice of their king. They raided and allowed the Portuguese to raid. The kingdom began to go to pieces.

When King Affonso saw that the demand for slaves was becoming greater, from the offshore islands and from across the Atlantic, he tried to refuse it. He wrote letters to the king of Portugal asking for doctors and teachers, pleading that Portugal should stop its agents from buying captives. In one of these letters, written in 1526, he told the Portuguese king that 'I have decided that there shall be no trade in captives nor any market for slaves in my domains'. It did no good. The slave trade had fastened its grip on the country. Too many people, whether European or African, were now finding a profit in it. The slave trade grew by leaps and bounds. Tens of thousands of Angolans were taken across the Atlantic.

In the early period most of these slaves were captives from wars launched by Kongo against its southern neighbour, the Kimbundu kingdom of Ndongo. This meant that at least the Kimbundu were warned about what they could expect from the Portuguese. And when the Portuguese tried to get a foothold there, believing that Ndongo held rich silver mines, they were forbidden entry or driven out again.

The Portuguese kept on. Their soldiers won a foothold on the coast at Luanda, which afterwards became their main base and capital. From here they dispatched military expeditions which raided for slaves and fought for conquest. In 1579 they launched a large military expedition with the object of destroying the power of Ndongo. The people of Ndongo fought back under their king, the Ngola, and for a time were successful. The Portuguese tried again and again. Their wars of ravage and conquest lasted for nearly a century. By about 1670 Ndongo was a ruined kingdom.

Among African leaders who battled against defeat in those years one of the most courageous was Queen Nzinga. Driven from her homeland of Ndongo she formed a new kingdom to the east. The queen tried diplomacy with the Portuguese, fell back again on military defence, but was defeated in the end.

Kongo suffered much the same fate. For a long time Kongo remained as Portugal's ally, and didn't see that to unite with other kingdoms was the only way to maintain the country's independence. A king of Kongo accepted Portuguese military aid in order to drive out some African invaders. This gave the Portuguese the same strong position in Kongo as they obtained, at about the same time, in the kingdom of the Mwana Mutapa. After the soldiers, once again, came the settlers. In 1665, a Portuguese army of invasion marched inland from the coast.

King Antonio I of Kongo summoned his troops. There followed a desperate battle at Mbwila (Um-bweela), and such were the divided loyalties of those times that Africans and Portuguese fought on each side. This fateful trial of strength began in driving rain with an attack by the Kongo army, led by the king himself,

Queen Nzinga trying to negotiate peace with the Portuguese commander at Luanda in Angola. The commander rudely refused to offer the Queen a chair, so she asked one of her attendants to act as one for her. This drawing is from a Dutch book of that time

which nearly put the Portuguese to flight. Most of the Africans on the Portuguese side withdrew from the field. But the 450 musketeers of the invading army stood firm. Fighting raged for eight hours back and forth until many of King Antonio's commanders had fallen. Deprived of their leading officers, the Kongo regiments gave way and fled. Wounded in the battle, King Antonio fell into Portuguese hands. They killed him and cut off his head, taking it back to their coastal base of Luanda together with his crown.

It was the end of Kongo independence. Gradually the Portuguese penetrated through Angola. Yet it was not until about 1900 that they won control of any large part of the inland country they had done so much to ruin. Even after 1900 the Angolans continued to resist Portuguese rule. This resistance ended successfully only in 1975, after a long war of liberation beginning in 1961.

DEVELOPMENTS ELSEWHERE

But in most parts of Africa, before the nineteenth century, there were no European settlers and no European interference. The Europeans could seldom get far from the coast. Either they met African resistance they could not overcome, or else, when on peaceful missions of discovery, they were stopped by fevers and other natural obstacles to penetration. Through vast inland regions the Africans were left to themselves.

In Middle Africa, besides those groups of kingdoms developed by the Shona, the Luba-Lunda, the Kongo-Kimbundu in Angola and others too numerous to mention, another important group took shape after about 1300 in the green uplands of east-central Africa. Here in hills along the deep rift valleys of this region, there was country well suited to the raising of great herds of cattle, good pockets of soil for growing of food plants and fruit, broad lakes abounding in fish, and pleasant rivers foaming in frequent rapids or opening in long calm reaches where cattle could be watered. Here the kingdoms of Ruandi and Burundi developed in the south, and those of Uganda in the north.

The southern Bantu

A complete picture of the African past, as historians know it today, would have much to say about the southern neighbours of these Middle African peoples. These neighbours, who were also peoples of the Bantu language family, began spreading south from the Limpopo River, into what is now South Africa, around AD 700.

Long before the coming of the first Europeans to South Africa these southern Bantu had made their homes in good farming country as far as the south-eastern tip of Africa, while the south-western tip had been inhabited, since ancient Stone Age times, by the Khoi peoples whom Europeans have called Hottentot and Bushman. The southern Bantu also built some famous kingdoms under strong leaders, notably King Mosheshewe who founded the Basuto nation and King Shaka who built the Zulu empire early in the nineteenth century.

King Mosheshwe, founder of the Basuto nation. Nowadays his country is the republic of Lesotho

The Europeans came as settlers to these southern regions only in 1652, when the Dutch landed a few men at the Cape of Good Hope. A history of the Europeans in Africa would have much to say about them. Here, in a history of the Africans, we should merely note that this little Dutch colony expanded gradually inland, pushing the Africans off their land or else enslaving them, until, some three hundred years after their first settlement, Europeans seized ownership of 88 per cent of all the land south of the Limpopo River in what is South Africa today.

People without kings

Any picture of the African past would still be incomplete if it failed to include the peoples who had no kings and built no kingdoms. There were many such people in every region, and their story is a central part of the record. They used methods of living and working together that strongly emphasised democracy, a subject which you will read about in more detail in Chapter 6. These methods rested on what may be called 'village government'.

For many centuries the central highlands of Kenya, in East Africa, have been the home of the Kikuyu, today the most numerous people in that modern republic. They worked out a type of government well suited to their kind of country. Although closely bound together by language and other cultural ties, the Kikuyu never had a single government which ruled over them all.

Most of their country is good farming land broken by lines of fairly steep hills, one ranged after another, whose well-watered valleys are filled with a dense vegetation of scrub and trees. Long ago the Kikuyu made their homes along these lines of hills, each village occupying a ridge and cultivating its ridge-top and the nearby hillsides. Separated in this way, each village set up its own government of elders; but all these small governments were linked to their neighbours by common beliefs and loyalties. Village courts settled local disputes, or formed legal commissions which could arbitrate on disputes between villages.

This kind of village government, which sometimes spread over a cluster of neighbouring villages, was widespread in Africa. In its time and place, it was stable and efficient. It meant that political power was divided among many rulers, and that those who ruled could never become distant or dictatorial. It expressed a strong African belief in human equality, in the need to respect other peoples' rights and in the duty of every man or woman, boy or girl, to work for the good of the community they lived in.

The Kikuyu were successful in the way of life they had chosen and developed. Other African peoples who chose much the same way – the Ibo of east Nigeria, the Luo of Kenya, the Tallensi of Ghana, to mention only three – were the same. They studied their fertile countries and made the best of them. Developing different forms of village government, they had no kings, no armies, no regular police forces, and felt they needed none. Some of these were more successful than others, but all the peoples without kings were always an important part of the scene. We shall find this again in the rich and varied regions of West Africa.

5 West Africa: forest peoples and powerful states

CENTURIES OF GROWTH

This chapter continues the story of African development in areas lying between the grasslands of the western and central Sudan, to the north, and the Atlantic Ocean to the south.

West Africa was the most densely populated region of the continent in past centuries; to some extent it still is today. Its peoples have a vigorous and creative history, in certain ways the most creative of any part of Africa. And it was West Africa, partly because of its relatively dense population, that suffered the full impact of the Atlantic slave trade, as we shall see, and provided most of the ancestors of the black peoples of the American mainland and the West Indies. It was the civilisations of West Africa that enriched America with the arts, skills, and labour of black people.

These civilisations were formed by varied conditions. Their peoples had to master different types of country, of which there were three main kinds.

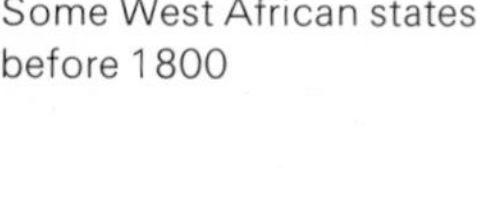

Some West African states before 1800

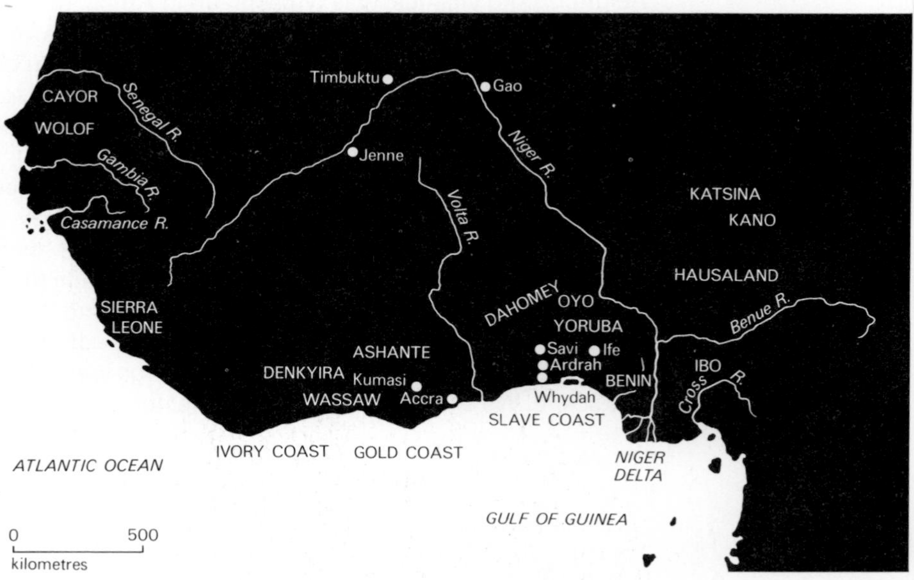

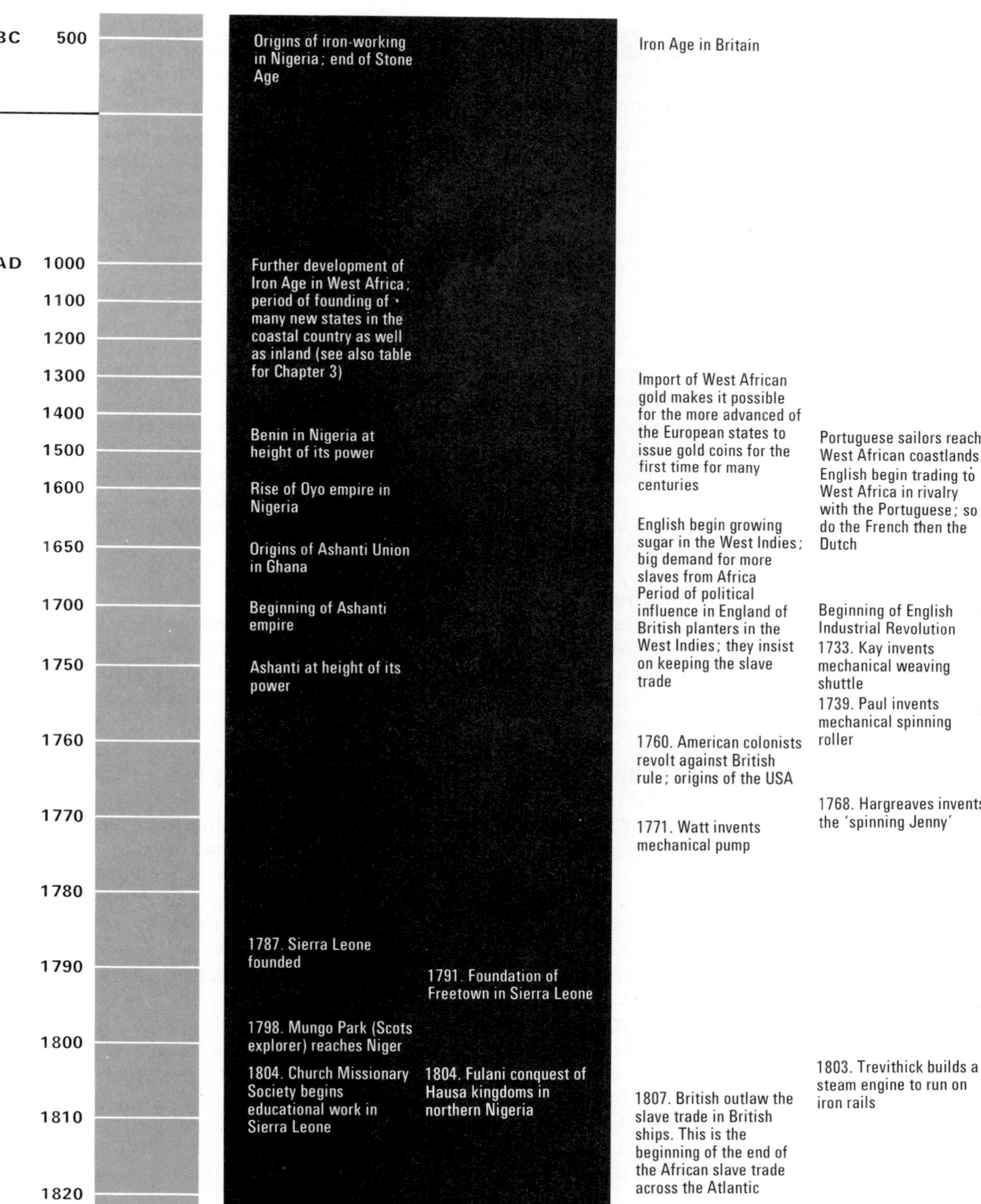
BC 500
Origins of iron-working in Nigeria; end of Stone Age
Iron Age in Britain
AD 1000
1100
1200
1300
1400
Further development of Iron Age in West Africa; period of founding of many new states in the coastal country as well as inland (see also table for Chapter 3)
Import of West African gold makes it possible for the more advanced of the European states to issue gold coins for the first time for many centuries
1500
Benin in Nigeria at height of its power
Portuguese sailors reach West African coastlands
1600
Rise of Oyo empire in Nigeria
English begin trading to West Africa in rivalry with the Portuguese; so do the French then the Dutch
1650
Origins of Ashanti Union in Ghana
English begin growing sugar in the West Indies; big demand for more slaves from Africa
1700
Beginning of Ashanti empire
Period of political influence in England of British planters in the West Indies; they insist on keeping the slave trade
Beginning of English Industrial Revolution
1733. Kay invents mechanical weaving shuttle
1750
Ashanti at height of its power
1739. Paul invents mechanical spinning roller
1760
1760. American colonists revolt against British rule; origins of the USA
1770
1768. Hargreaves invents the 'spinning Jenny'
1771. Watt invents mechanical pump
1780
1790
1787. Sierra Leone founded
1791. Foundation of Freetown in Sierra Leone
1800
1798. Mungo Park (Scots explorer) reaches Niger
1804. Church Missionary Society begins educational work in Sierra Leone
1804. Fulani conquest of Hausa kingdoms in northern Nigeria
1803. Trevithick builds a steam engine to run on iron rails
1810
1807. British outlaw the slave trade in British ships. This is the beginning of the end of the African slave trade across the Atlantic
1820

1. Immediately south of the Sudanese grasslands there is a broad west–east belt of open country covered with grass and clumps of woodland running from the plains of Senegal in the west to the waters of Lake Chad in the east. These plains are sometimes interrupted by ranges of rolling hills.

2. As you move southward across this woodland belt, the trees steadily thicken t the verge of a second west–east belt, this time of dense tropical forest like that of the Congo. Thick forest reaches from the lands near the coast, from the Casamance River of Senegal in the west to the main Congo forests in the east. This forest belt is broken at one point, along the coast of what is now Benin and Togo; here wooded grasslands come right down to the seaboard. This coastal break in the forest belt has been important in history, and is called the Benin Gap

3. Finally, along the coast itself, there is a narrow belt of open land and palm groves. Then you are out on the honey-coloured sands of the West African seaboard, fringed by ocean surf through which canoes push out with flashing paddles or come shooting to the beach.

Several large rivers flow through West Africa. The great Niger flows east and then bends south through Nigeria to the Atlantic. The Volta runs southward alon the eastern side of modern Ghana into the sea. The Gambia flows west to the Atlantic through Senegal. These and other rivers have been useful to West Africans as channels of communication through their successive belts of open woodland, thick forest, and coastal plain.

The picture of the past

Stone Age peoples lived in every part of West Africa from the earliest times of human growth. They developed languages from which the many dozens of existing languages of West Africa gradually evolved. About two thousand years ago they began to work metals. Helped by iron-headed hoes and other tools they began cultivating food in their forest lands, growing West African yams and othe crops native to the region or adopted from the western and central Sudan. Large herds of cattle were raised by the peoples of the grassland. But in many areas the presence of tsetse fly made cattle-raising impossible.

They mastered their woodlands and forests, increased in numbers, learned new skills, began growing cotton and spinning it for cloth, and developed good craftsmanship in metal working. They faced and solved the problems of social an political organisation, as population grew more numerous and villages larger. They evolved early states, moving from one area to another in the splitting up process described in Chapter 2, forming new peoples, developing new languages, meeting new challenges. They wove a rich pattern of social and cultural life.

Little is known of their progress before AD 1000. Oral history for that distant period is wrapped in mystery or legend. We can only guess, from archaeological evidence, at the early growth of small communities and states. After 1000 the evidence of history becomes clearer. Yet it can tell us little in detail before about 1400. After 1400 the records become steadily better. Powerful states emerge. Strong kingdoms are founded. Thriving cities appear.

Towards 1500 ships from Europe reach this dazzling tropical coastland. Often surprised by what they find, visiting Europeans begin to write reports and memoirs. Combined with the oral history of the Africans, and with archaeological evidence, these European reports build into a picture of variety and brilliance.

It is a picture of civilised achievement in the arts of everyday life. Any history book has to say much about kings and battles, because the names and dates of great events and rulers are the 'trail markers' along our journey of discovery. Yet between these markers there lie the daily lives and laughter, sorrows, failures, and triumphs of the people; and it is 'ordinary' people, as the old African proverb insists, who really matter. It is they who have made the real stuff of history, even if their individual names and struggles are seldom or never known.

Another point to keep in mind is that these were not isolated achievements. We consider West Africa as a separate region here only for the convenience of following its history. Many West Africans are closely related to the Africans of the Sudan, at least in their origins. For centuries before the coming of the Europeans, West Africans traded with the north and east. They sold their forest products, gold and the chewing nut that is called *kola*, to the travelling merchants of the Sudan, to the *dyula* of Mali and the men of Hausaland, buying Sudanese and North African and European goods in return. All West Africa was crossed by a network of trade routes linked with the merchant cities such as Jenne, Timbuktu and Kano.

West Africans south of the Sudan also traded much among themselves, building a complex system of regular markets held every four days, or every eight days, or at other regular intervals according to local custom. They used different kinds of money for saving and exchange. Most important of these was the cowrie shell. This became so widely used that a large part of West Africa before 1800 might even be called a 'cowrie area' of trade, in something of the same way one nowadays speaks of a 'dollar' or 'sterling' area. When Europeans first came here, nearly five centuries ago, they were impressed by the business skill of the Africans who went into partnership with them.

This world of West Africa was always an inventive one, restless with the energy of ambitious peoples, eager for new products and new ideas, especially from Europe. But West Africans kept the Europeans safely at arm's length. Until late in the nineteenth century, they remained masters of their region.

THE CHILDREN OF ODUDUWA

We can select here only a few examples of pre-colonial West African development. One of the best known is that of the Yoruba people of Western Nigeria.

Like nearly all peoples everywhere, the Yoruba are the product of intermingling between different groups. Some of their forefathers were undoubtedly living in Yorubaland, a wide and fertile forest country west of the lower Niger River, during the most distant Stone Age. But their modern history begins not long before the year 1000. At that point another section of their forefathers, coming probably from a little to the northward, introduced or invented new forms of government, including kings.

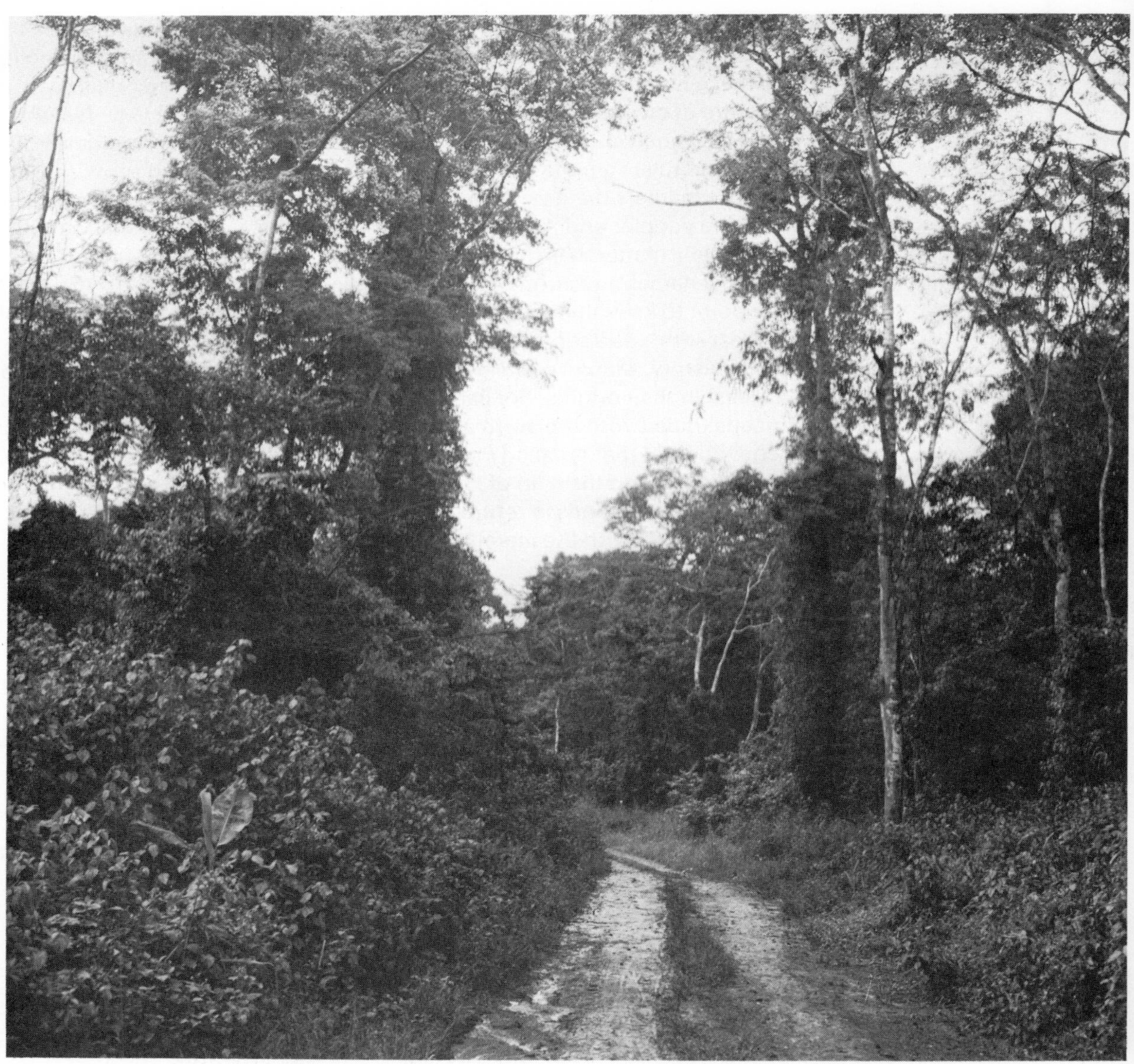

Tropical 'rain forest' in the country of the Yoruba

Yoruba kingdoms

An intensely religious people, the Yoruba explain all this in their beliefs about Go and the making of the world. When God decided to make a home for mankind, they believe, he sent down from Heaven a powerful spirit, or archangel as we might say, to create the Earth. This archangel, Orishanla, managed the work in four days, appointing the fifth for worship and rest. The Yoruba week was five days long. Having created the Earth, God began to people it with mankind, beginning with Yorubaland. And so the first men and women, the Yoruba explai were born at Ife (Ee-fay), most ancient city of their country. They think of Ife as Christians think of the Garden of Eden.

Orishanla the archangel shared the work of ordering the Earth with other spirits. Prominent among these was Oduduwa, a legendary figure whom Yoruba revere as their great 'founding hero'. Oduduwa became the first king of Ife. From Ife his children went out to become kings and queens of other sections of the Yoruba.

Through the Orishanla belief we may glimpse the early existence of Stone Age people in Yorubaland; and through the Oduduwa belief the fact that they were joined by others who introduced government by kings. In the course of time, after about 1000, there came to be many Yoruba kingdoms. Each was centred on a capital town where families of farmers, priests, traders, and craftsmen lived under the rule of local kings, or *obas*, all of whom claimed descent from Oduduwa.

Even today there is nothing more striking in Yorubaland than the size and vigour of these forest towns. Unlike most Africans, the Yoruba prefer living in towns, not villages. Their farmers walk out to till their land, sometimes quite far away, and come home to town in the evening.

Ife remained their chief city, and the king of Ife the most revered figure in the service of Yoruba religion. Ife's great authority can be seen in its ancient art.

Perhaps as early as 1200 there arose at Ife a school of fine sculptors in bronze and in terra cotta, a type of baked clay. They celebrated the majesty of the kings of Ife and of members of the royal family in sculptures now accepted as being among the finest anywhere.

One of the famous bronze sculptures made at Ife about six centuries ago

The town of Ife became the model on which all other Yoruba towns were designed. Each of these towns was divided into neighbourhoods governed by a section chief. Each had its holy shrines, its king's palace, its market squares, its meeting places where city government could settle affairs and people discuss th day's news. Each became famous for its craftsmen, who worked in different ski Some specialised in the spinning and dyeing of cotton cloth, others in metalwo or the training of priests, others again in wood carving or warfare or long-distar trade. In these ways the many kingdoms of the Yoruba were bound together by network of common beliefs and interests.

The empire of Oyo

Many of them were also bound together, after about 1650, by the power of a central government. This was the work of a northern section of the Yoruba, whose capital town was Oyo.

Like other Yoruba, those of Oyo were farmers. They were skilled in the cultivation of the soil of their open woodlands, which lay north of and outside t deep forest. Their craftsmen specialised in spinning and dyeing and were excellent in metalwork, producing a range of goods useful in trade. But they we also traders. They dealt in Sudanese goods coming south to Yorubaland and neighbouring forest areas, and in southern goods going north to the central Sudan. Once again, a circuit of long-distance trade encouraged political chang

High on the list of Oyo imports from the central Sudan were horses. Althoug unable to breed hoofed animals themselves, because of the tsetse fly, the Oyo Yoruba could keep imported horses alive for quite long periods, and they could always bring in more when supplies ran short. Provided with horses, the *alafin*, king of Oyo, was able to maintain a strong force of cavalry. This he used to exte the power of Oyo over neighbouring Yoruba states. By 1700 the empire of Oyo had enclosed much of Nigeria on the west side of the Niger River north of the forest, as well as most of the open woodland of Dahomey (now called Benin) in t Benin Gap. Oyo remained powerful for more than a hundred years, after which i gave way to an invasion from Hausaland and another from Dahomey, together with revolts by some of its subject Yoruba kingdoms. Towards 1900, Yorubalar was invaded by the British and became part of our empire until 1960, when Nigeria became independent.

The children of Oduduwa left their mark at one other place. This was the Nigerian city and state of Benin, among the most renowned of all Africa's old kingdoms.

BENIN AND ITS PEOPLE

The large city and empire of Benin, in southern Nigeria, was founded during the remote past in forest country west of the Niger Delta, about fifty miles from the sea. Its origins belong to the same early period as those of Ife. About a thousanc years ago there developed here, among the Edo people, a system of self-rule by powerful chiefs. These chiefs were the senior members of a ruling council, composed of the heads of leading Edo families. Gradually they won more powe and became *obas* (kings). They borrowed ideas about royal government from If perhaps six hundred years ago, and were able to dominate the ruling council. From that time they called themselves *obas*, using the same title as the Yoruba chiefs.

Empire building

Many *obas* followed the first one, and indeed there is an *oba* of Benin to this day. Little by little, they extended the power of Benin over the Edo villages of the neighbouring countryside. But the main expansion of Benin, and its rise to power and wealth, began with the fourth king, Ewedo (Ay-way-doe). He greatly strengthened royal power over the ruling council, improved the fighting methods of his army, and, perhaps to mark the beginning of a new period, changed the name of his city to Ubini, from which the word Benin later developed. This probably took place between 1300 and 1400.

The next step forward was taken by another powerful king, Ewuare, who came to the throne in about 1440. He again extended the political system of Benin, like Ewedo before him, by creating new orders of chiefs and officials who relied upon the king's command, and who were outside the old network of ruling families. He gave particular attention to the development of his city. During his reign Benin first acquired broad streets and powerful surrounding walls, the ruins of which may still be traced at several points. One small but important incident of this time was the arrival on the shores of Benin, in 1472, of the first ship from Europe, commanded by a Portuguese captain called Ruy de Siqueira.

ronze figure of a king of enin, probably from the eventeenth century

Ewuare and the kings of Benin who came after him were military leaders wh built an empire. But they were also religious leaders. As the heads of Edo religi they were able to increase their power like the great princes of the Christian Church in Europe of the same period. Ritual and ceremony surrounded their liv They were approached on bended knee; nobody, it was believed, could touch their persons without risking divine punishment. They lived in an enormous palace composed of many courtyards, one within the other, and decorated wit superb bronze sculptures which told the story of everyday events, portraying th life of the times. When some Portuguese began living in Benin after 1485 they were pictured in these bronze sculptures.

Early Afro-European friendship

Among the most efficient of the kings of Benin, after Ewuare, was *Oba* Esigie, who ruled from about 1504 to 1550. Portuguese ships were now coming quite often to the shores of his empire. He decided to learn about Portugal. He instructed the governor of the chief port of his empire, a place called Ugwato, t visit Portugal as his ambassador.

'This ambassador,' say the Portuguese records of about 1510, 'was a man of good speech and natural wisdom. Great feasts were held in his honour [after h reached Portugal] and he was shown many of the good things of these kingdo [of Europe]. He returned to his land in a ship of our king's,' taking with him ma gifts for *Oba* Esigie, as well as some Christian missionaries.

Like King Affonso of Kongo, or other kings in Middle Africa, *Oba* Esigie was interested in technical aid. He saw the advantages of keeping up with the times and used Portuguese missionaries as teachers for his sons and the sons of leadi families, who learned to speak and write Portuguese. These men from Portugal were treated well. A letter from a Portuguese royal representative in Benin, written in 1516, says that 'when our missionaries arrived, the King of Benin wa very delighted. He ordered his son and two of his greatest noblemen to become Christians, and built a church in Benin. They learned how to read, and did it ve well.' Portuguese missionaries stayed in Benin for many years, and built severa churches. Yet their attempt to introduce the Christian religion had little result, f the Edo were satisfied with their own. The ocean trade, developing at the same time, proved far more important.

The ocean trade develops

Nothing had previously reached these countries from the Atlantic Ocean. Now, suddenly, there opened the prospect of a new kind of long-distance trade. The people of Benin found that Europeans were eager to buy the pepper they grew quantity, for pepper was then a valuable commodity in Europe, being a spice which Europeans could not produce. They also found that Europeans greatly admired their excellent dyed cottons, and wanted to buy these. Their dyed cottons were in fact better than any produced in Europe until long afterwards, when Europeans were able to learn the secret of high-quality cotton dyeing fro the craftsmen of India. In return, the people of Benin found that the Europeans had useful things to sell them, notably linen stuffs and metalware.

Trade with Europe prospered. Although the rulers of Benin had no idea of wh was happening at the same time in the distant kingdoms of Mwana Mutapa an

A bronze cock from old Benin

Kongo, they had no intention of allowing the Europeans to win the upper hand. The kings of Benin saw to it that all foreign traders paid port taxes and import dues, and entered the Benin empire only as visitors.

If visiting white men thought that they were going into a savage land when they landed at the port of Gwato, they soon learned better. They found themselves dealing with a powerful state organisation whose laws they had to obey. A Dutch report described what happened to the Europeans when they arrived. It referred to the seventeenth century, but what it said was equally true for the Portuguese before 1600:

> Nobody is allowed to buy anything from us Europeans on this coast [of Benin], except the trade commissioners and merchants whom the King of Benin appoints for the purpose. As soon as one of our ships drops anchor, the people of Gwato send messengers to the capital. Then the King appoints two or three royal commissioners, and twenty or thirty merchants who are authorised to deal with us.
>
> The first meeting we have with these commissioners is only for the exchange of greetings and of news. The commissioners come superbly dressed, wearing jasper and coral ornaments, to visit our warehouse [at Ugwato]. They greet our men with the King's good wishes, ask about the news of Europe and our own plans, and give us presents of fruit sent by the King. On our side we Dutch reply with good wishes, and everyone has a drink together.

Once dealing was well under way the visitors were given permission, if they wished, to make the two days' journey to the capital. Those who went there came back with interesting stories of what they had seen.

A large and comfortable city

Not long after 1600 a Dutchman from Amsterdam, Dierick Ruiters, arrived at Gwato, Benin's chief port on the Benin River, as resident agent of the Dutch. After he had paid his respects to the governor of Gwato, he settled down to his work of representing the official Dutch trading corporation. Business soon took him to the capital. Granted permission, he made his way inland along good fores roads, riding his horse past villages and farms on either side. Unsuitably dressed for the tropics, as were most Europeans in those days, he found it an easy but thirsty journey. Fortunately, the officials in charge of the road had the duty of keeping pots filled with drinking water at regular intervals between Gwato and the capital. (For the position of Gwato, see map on p. 168.)

On the second day Ruiters came within sight of the walls of Benin, and saw behind them the outline of an imposing palace pinnacled with metal figures of birds made in copper. Afterwards he recalled Benin for the benefit of his countrymen in Holland:

[It] looks very big when you enter it for you go into a great broad street, which, though not paved, seems to be seven or eight times broader than the Warmoes Street in Amsterdam. This street continues for about four miles and has no bend it.

At the gate where I went in on horseback, I saw a big wall, very thick and mad of earth, with a deep ditch outside. Outside the gate there is a large suburb. Inside, as you go along the main street, you can see other broad streets on either side, and these are also straight.

The houses in this town stand in good order, one close to the other and evenl placed beside the next, like our houses in Holland.

A bronze water-holder in the form of a leopard from old Benin. You poured the water through the nostrils

The largest of them was the palace of the oba.

The King's palace is very large, having within it many square courtyards. These courtyards have gallieries around them where sentries stand. I myself went into the palace far enough to pass through four courtyards. Yet wherever I looked I could still see gate after gate which opened into other courtyards. I went in as far as any Dutchman had ever been: and that was as far as the stables where the king's best horses are kept.

Ruiters and other Dutchmen had much to say about the comfort and courtesy of Benin and its inhabitants. They found the Edo to be good and reliable trading partners. Not long after Ruiters' visit, another Dutchman wrote that 'these people are in no way inferior in cleanliness to the Dutch' – who were at that time probably the cleanest people in Europe; 'and they wash and scrub their houses so well that these are polished and shining like a mirror'.

He spoke of the hospitality of Benin. 'These people have good laws and a well organised police. They live on good terms with us Dutch and with other trading foreigners, and they show us a thousand marks of friendship.' He found that Benin people wore robes of blue and white cotton, while women's fashions included skirts down to the calves of the legs. Women 'like to curl their hair round their heads in garlands, one half coloured black and the other red; and they wear copper bracelets on their arms'.

Occasionally the white visitors could secure the honour of being received by the king. Another Dutchman, about a hundred years after Ruiters, described how he was taken through the palace galleries, passing many fine bronze sculptures, until he reached the royal audience hall. 'There in the presence of three important noblemen I saw and spoke' to the king, who was 'sitting on an ivory couch under a canopy of Indian silk'. At first this Dutchman was obliged, by the rules of court custom, to stand some thirty paces from the king's throne. 'But I asked if I could go nearer so as to see him better, and he laughingly agreed.'

Once back on the high seas, these visiting captains and their official traders might act as they pleased. But so long as they were in port, or on land, they had to mind their tongues and their behaviour. Relations of mutual respect between whites and blacks continued at Benin, just as they did along most of the West African coast, until the opening of the colonial period in the nineteenth century.

THE ASHANTI TRIUMPH

The Ashanti empire

The strong kingdom of Ashanti included most of what is now the Republic of Ghana. It offers another outstanding example of African political and economic development. For nearly two hundred years, after 1700, Ashanti reigned over wide lands. Its armies were irresistible to its rivals. Its trade was a magnet for merchants from many lands. Its capital, Kumase, became the home of ambassadors and diplomatic missions, poets, and priests. Treaties and trade agreements were signed with Britain and other powers.

Origins and early growth

The story of Ashanti development is that of a numerous section of a group of

West African peoples called Akan (Ak-kahn), who speak a language called Twi (Ch-vee). Some of their early ancestors may have come from the southern country of the ancient empire of Ghana. This is why modern Ghana took the nam of that empire when it became independent in 1957. But most of the ancestors o the Ashanti, as of the rest of the Akan, were the descendants of the Stone Age peoples of this country.

These peoples began working iron and cultivating forest crops more than two thousand years ago. Spreading through their forest country, they formed early states after about AD 1200. They developed a rich community culture with a strong emphasis on music and dancing, and they loved stories of folklore and popular wisdom. They had so many proverbs that a missionary in 1879 was able to collect no fewer than 3,600.

By 1400 there were several strong Akan states, including Fante, Akim (Atch-eem) and Denkyira (Den-chee-ra). Towards 1600 their farmers began eagerly adopting the new American food plants brought by Portuguese across the Atlantic, especially maize and cassava. Then it was that the Akan groups who were to become known as the Ashanti became important. These groups became prosperous farmers of the new crops. They also had gold mines and alluvial gold in their country, and as we have seen, they had long traded in this gold with foreign countries. Here was another case where trade, and production for trade, stimulated political change.

Chapter 3 explained how the gold trade of western Africa shifted eastward fro Mali to Songhay, in about 1400, when new supplies of gold began to come northward from the forest country south of the central Sudan. It was the Akan who provided these new supplies of gold. They mined and smelted and worked their country's gold, and welcomed Sudanese merchants. After 1600 the Ashanti took a lead in this. At the same time they began to find another outlet for their gold, and a source of useful manufactured goods, among European mariners and traders who had become established at points along the coast to the south of them. These points were along the seaboard which these Europeans now began to call the Gold Coast.

But the Ashanti groups of the Akan suffered a serious handicap. Disunited among themselves, they had fallen under the overlordship of stronger Akan groups. Around 1650 they began to think about and plan for independence. For long time they made little progress. Though potentially strong, they had not foun a way to unite their forces. In about 1695, a leader called Osei Tutu (O-say Tutu) solved this problem with the help of a priest of Akan religion called Anokye (A-notch-ee). These two men laid the foundations of Ashanti unity. How they did it is told in Ashanti traditions.

The union of the Golden Stool

The answer to the problem of unity among the Ashanti groups, Anokye explaine to Osei Tutu, was to be found in giving all of them a single rule of law, backed by beliefs to hold this firm. In order to do this Anokye would use his religious authority, and Osei Tutu would back him up with hard-headed talk, and then by leadership in politics and war. In this way the Ashanti could throw off their allegiance to other Akan states, and build an independence of their own.

At a favourable moment Osei Tutu called together all the chiefs and leading men of the Ashanti groups. He told them that Anokye, whom they all knew, had an important message for them. Anokye said that he had consulted the wisdom of God, whom the Ashanti called Nyame, and that God wanted the Ashanti to become a great people under one king, not many kings. In proof of this, Anokye would produce for them a holy stool or throne, and Osei Tutu would be their king. Anokye told the assembly of chiefs that this stool or throne must be respected as a sacred symbol to protect and promote the prosperity and welfare of all the Ashanti. No king might ever sit on it, but every king must guard and cherish it. So long as they were loyal to the spirit of the Golden Stool they would find happiness and success. Disloyalty would bring the punishment of God.

The chiefs saw the wisdom of Anokye's message, and agreed that Osei Tutu should be their king. They accepted the Golden Stool as enshrining all their hopes.

The Golden Stool was now the symbol of the Ashanti Union, ruled by King Osei Tutu. In this the Stool was very like the Crown of England, another object made by men but possessing a great and generally accepted symbolic power. No English king or queen could begin to reign till crowned in religious ceremonies by the senior archbishop of the English Church; this indeed is still the case today. The only big difference between the English Crown and the Ashanti Golden Stool, apart from their appearance, was that the Crown had to be worn while the Stool could never be sat on.

From union to empire

After Anokye had opened the way to Ashanti unity, Osei Tutu built towards it without delay. Religious power might be helpful up to a point, but Osei Tutu knew that it would have to be reinforced by law and statesmanship if the newly formed union were to hold firm. He introduced a law which forbade the different Ashanti groups to talk about their former separate loyalties. This law of common citizenship helped to unite these groups.

Next he set about throwing off the overlordship of powerful neighbours. To do this he organised a new army. It was commanded by himself or his own generals, and formed of men from the separate groups of Ashanti. Each group's soldiers had a special place in one or other part of the battle array. Training side by side, these soldiers from different groups forged bonds of unity among themselves.

Soon, King Osei Tutu thought that he was ready to take on his neighbours. In fact, his first battle against Denkyira proved a serious defeat. But Osei Tutu recovered and went on to win. By 1701 the Ashanti Union had achieved its full independence. What was almost as important, Ashanti opened a direct channel of trade to Europeans along the coast. With this, Osei Tutu could now be sure of a regular supply of guns, gunpowder, and ammunition.

In order to keep firm control of trade links with the coast, especially with the Dutch at Elmina Castle and the British at Cape Coast Castle, the Ashanti subdued the coastal Akan states and brought them within the Ashanti system of power. Also, in order to maintain and extend their control of gold and other exports to the Sudan, they embarked on conquest in the open woodlands and grasslands north of their forest, and made subjects of the non-Akan peoples living there. These successes, which were mostly won during the eighteenth century, were especially the work of two warrior kings, Opoku Ware, who ruled from about 1720 to 1750, and Osei Kojo, whose reign fell between about 1764 and 1777.

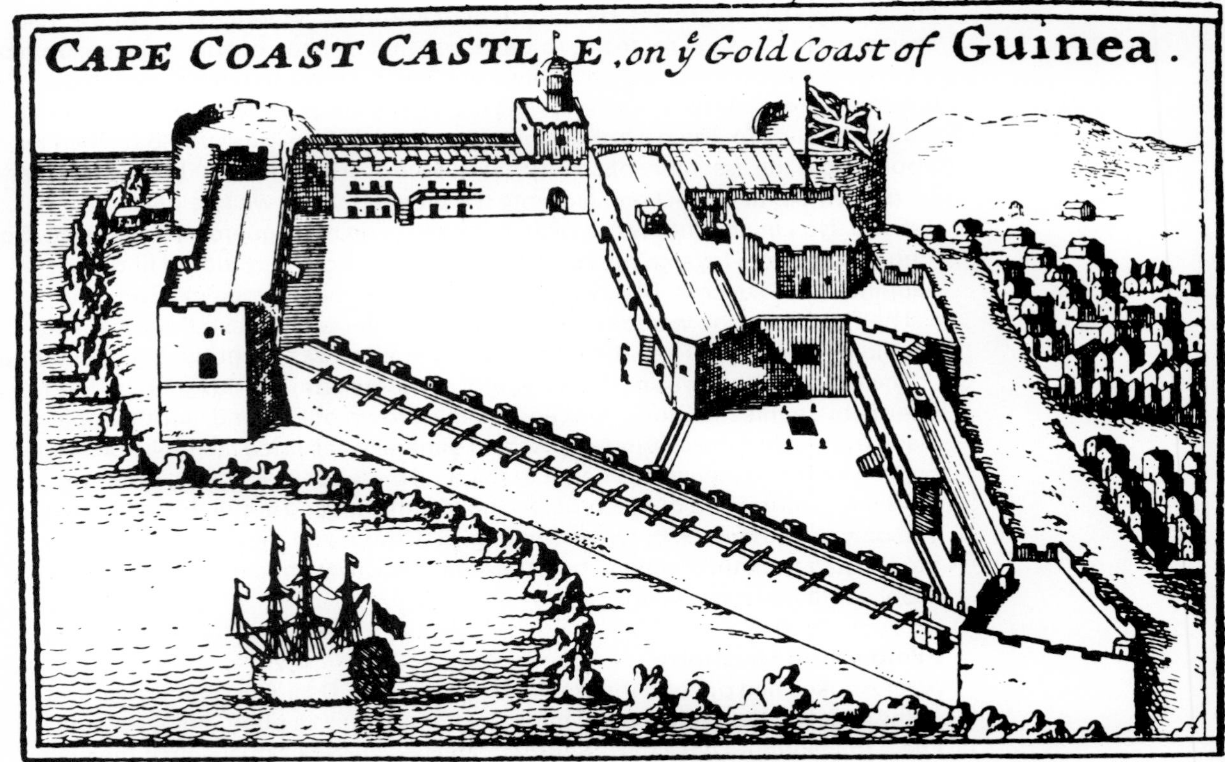

CAPE COAST CASTLE, on ye Gold Coast of Guinea.

Drawing of the old English trading castle at Cape Coast on the Gold Coast, now modern Ghana. The castle is still there, much as you see it in this drawing; but it is no longer used, and the government of Ghana has opened it to tourists

Meeting the needs of the times

Ashanti rulers had to be more than just good generals. As their power grew, these rulers worked out new methods of using and protecting it. They reorganised their system so that it would cope with the problems of a growing empire.

King Osei Kojo (1764–77) was the first important reformer. He found that to rule a wide empire he could no longer govern well by relying only on ministers and officials appointed by right of birth; appointed, that is, simply because they were the heads of leading families. He began to promote men of humble birth, or even 'rightless persons' captured in war. He selected these 'king's men' because of their energy, honesty, and ability. The rulers of Songhay and other Sudanese states had done the same, as you saw in Chapter 3. Like those rulers, Osei Kojo wanted stronger government. He began to form a regular civil service.

What Osei Kojo began, Osei Kwame (1777–1801) and Osei Bonsu (1801–24) continued. These reformers were wise enough to know that peace was always preferable to war: 'Never take to the sword,' Osei Bonsu used to say, 'so long as a path lies open to negotiation.' Strengthening the civil service, Osei Bonsu provided the opportunity for a good career in government for any man of honesty and talent. There is the striking case of Agyei (Adge-ay), King Osei Bonsu's minister for foreign affairs.

Agyei was typical of the 'new men' who owed their careers to their own talents and not to noble birth. He started life as a salt-carrier, carrying salt upon his head along the forest paths, and worked his way up to a responsible job in the service o one of the vassal kings of Ashanti. When his royal employer was charged with misrule by courts in Kumasi, Agyei conducted this local king's defence. He argued for three hours that the charges were groundless, and he argued so well that King Osei Bonsu offered him work in the central government. At Kumase he soon became known as 'the best head for hard palavers', or, as we should say, the best trouble-shooter. In the words of a European eye-witness, Agyei 'continued to advance by his splendid talents, and his firmness in the cause of truth'.

Other reforms also strengthened the power of the king's government. Around 1760 King Osei Kojo started a federal police force, known as the Ankobia, who took orders only from the central government at Kumase, and not from any of the empire's component states. Osei Bonsu improved the status of civil servants by allowing them regular fees for their work and providing them with pensions when they retired. These fees and pensions were paid from the profits of trade or in gifts of farming land.

Life became more complex. As the price of progress in those days, society became more divided. Many 'ordinary' men were able to rise in the world, as officials, farmers or traders. Others were less fortunate. The number of 'rightless persons' became greater. Mostly they were prisoners of war who, once captured, lost their civil rights until they could work their way to freedom. Often they were used as porters, for there were no wheeled vehicles or animals to carry goods. Long convoys of porters went back and forth along the forest trails, carrying the country's export goods, returning with the country's imports.

New ways of government

The main organisation of long-distance trade was in the hands of the state, although there were many private merchants. Nuggets or small bits of gold from the mines, or from goldwashing stations along the rivers, were the property of the king (that is, of the central government) while most gold production was under state control. Traders who did much business had to have government permits. Those who worked for the state were expected to send in detailed accounts, and they were allowed to keep an agreed part of their profits. Many of these official trading agents were 'king's men' who had risen from humble beginnings. Even when they were 'rightless persons' or 'slaves' they often enjoyed great authority.

Europeans along the coast were well aware of the power of these 'slaves' of the king. Whenever one of them came to the Dutch fort at Accra, early in the nineteenth century, to collect the yearly rent which the Dutch had to pay Ashanti for the ground their castle stood on, he was treated with respect. The Dutch used to fire a salute of seven guns in his honour. Of Tando, another royal official, it was noted that he never went anywhere on business unless he was carried in a fine hammock 'covered by a gorgeous umbrella', and surrounded by lesser officials.

This man Tando over-reached himself. He began to make important decisions without first clearing them with Kumase. In 1816 he went to the subject state of Wassaw to negotiate the transfer of some prisoners of war. Then he proceeded to settle a number of other disputes between the king of Wassaw and the king of Ashanti. But Tando had no right to do this. Back in Kumase he was 'at once stripped of all his property, and from being a rich man he became a beggar'. King Osei Bonsu did not disagree with Tando's decisions, which he said were sensible. But he argued that 'no man must dare to do good out of his own head' without

Dutch ambassadors visiting the king of Kongo, in Angola, during the seventeenth century. They are careful to pay him the respect they would show to a king in Europe. This drawing is from a Dutch book of that time

asking for authority from the king because, if that happened, the king would gradually lose power and the system of government would decay.

The big point here is that these reforming kings of Ashanti were changing their government into a more modern type. They looked round for anyone who could do an important job well. They had no objection to employing foreigners if these foreigners could bring useful skills into the country. By the middle of the nineteenth century, the king's government in Kumase was employing quite a large staff of Muslim clerks from the Sudan: men who could read and write in Arabic, or in West African languages using an Arabic script, and so keep departmental records and write diplomatic correspondence for the king.

These kings had no colour prejudice, and sometimes employed white men in leading jobs. As early as 1824 a European ambassador at Kumase noted that the trade controller of the capital (who seems also to have acted as King Osei Bonsu's economic adviser) was a man of Scots-American descent. Later, a Frenchman held another important post. A German was employed in training musketeers from Hausaland to be a special corps that could strengthen the Ashanti army against an expected British invasion. Kumase, the Ashanti capital, became a busy international centre.

A welcome at Kumase

Anyone visiting Kumase in those days found travellers from many West African cities and countries. There were white-gowned merchants from Kano and Katsina in Hausaland; the leaders of *dyula* companies, tall Mandinka businessmen from Jenne and Timbuktu and Gao; envoys from neighbouring kings; Muslim scholars from as far away as Egypt and Tripoli; and visitors from other parts of the Ashanti empire.

In 1817 a group of European officials arrived on a visit from the trading stations on the coast. An Englishman among them, Thomas Bowdich, wrote about this. He and his companions hoped to sign a trading agreement with King Osei Bonsu. They were warmly welcomed. Entering Kumase early one afternoon, they were greeted by the music of more than a hundred military bands equipped with horns, drums and metal gongs, while hundreds of musketeers fired salutes into the air above their heads. 'A confusion of flags – English, Dutch and Danish – were waved and flourished on every side' as they advanced through a throng of warriors, officials and spectators.

Bowdich admired the brilliant scene, especially the uniforms of the war captains. Their gear included a cap with gilded ram's horns and plumes of eagle feathers, fastened under the chin by a chain decorated with cowrie shells, and a red jacket and loose cotton trousers. They had gold and silver charms sewn to their jackets, and wore 'immense boots of dull red leather which come half way up the thigh'. These officers led them slowly through broad streets filled with people, while house-porches on either side were crowded with spectators 'who were curious to see white people'.

At last the visitors reached the palace itself. Here they were received by senior officials and the commanders of King Osei Bonsu's army. All these wore magnificent robes of cloth-of-gold, the dazzling gold-threaded *kente* which is still woven in this country, many fine ornaments, and sandals of red, green or white leather. Then amid the blast of ceremonial horns and the clamour of drums they were introduced to the king, seated on his royal stool. He welcomed them with 'manners that were majestic, yet courteous' and after a while invited the visitors to rest in their rooms.

Bowdich stayed in the capital long enough to see a few of its colourful ceremonies and public spectacles. He found the capital a clean and comfortable town:

> Four of the main streets are half a mile long, and between fifty and a hundred yards wide. Each is in the charge of a senior captain. Every household has to burn its rubbish every morning at the back of the street. The people are as clean and careful about the appearance of their houses as they are about themselves.

THE DIGNITY OF MAN

Each of those states and others like them, near the coastland of West Africa or in other regions, worked out solutions to problems caused by nature, by influences such as the long-distance trade, and by the changes and chances of history.

Visiting Europeans – men like Dierick Ruiters, Bowdich, and many more – were convinced of the importance of these powerful states. But what about the small states, the village communities, the peoples with little power? Most Africans wh had no kings or armies, cities or governments, seemed backward and savage to visitors from Europe. They might have peaceful villages but they had no form of government that visiting whites could see at work. They might have law courts, s much was obvious; but they had no police force. They might have men who claimed wisdom, but none of these could read or write. If they had artists, their dancing and sculpture looked shocking to European eyes. If they believed in Go which Europeans thought was doubtful, they built no temples and altars except i humble thatch and clay.

Exploring into Africa a hundred years ago and less, whites who came from the mechanically advanced societies of western Europe thought that these blacks ha invented nothing. It is not surprising that they thought this, because whites in those days knew little of Africa and next to nothing of its history. There is no excuse for thinking this today.

The study of history makes it clear that *all* these peoples, some more and others less, developed much and invented much in many areas of community life. This is just as true of the peoples without kings or powerful states. They too gradually

A fine wood-carving used in ceremonies by one of the peoples who had 'government without rulers'. It shows two ancestor-figures standing on an elaborate stool

worked out ways by which people could master nature, and could build patterns of community life in face of many obstacles and challenges.

We need to think about these patterns of community. Many peoples of West Africa, as of other regions, were content with little or no government. Often they had few things of their own, scarcely any riches in their sub-soil, no trading wealth with which to buy cotton stuffs for clothing. Their houses continued to be huts of thatch and clay; the weapons they used for hunting were the bows and spears of long ago. Does this mean that they were somehow less intelligent, less able to make progress, than the peoples with powerful states and kings? Does it mean that they had 'stood still in history'?

Behind the seeming simplicity of village life the truth about these 'peoples without rulers' was, in fact, rich and complex. Even the poorest of them, living very close to nature in tiny settlements far off the beaten track, hunting in the wilderness of immense forests, following their cattle from one waterhole to the next, were far from primitive in their beliefs, their ideas about the world, their social customs, even their methods of government.

In their quality of thought and belief these village communities often displayed, more than did the strong kingdoms, a respect for what was good in life and a condemnation of what was evil. They had strong convictions about human equality and the need for peaceful tolerance among neighbours. By reading about them, we may come nearest to the living heart of Africa as it used to be, and, indeed as it sometimes still is.

Chapter 6 therefore turns away from the courts of kings and strong governments, thriving market cities, powerful ministers and men of war, and looks at the ways in which 'ordinary' Africans lived. Then it will be possible to understand many puzzling matters – sorcery and witchcraft, beliefs and superstitions which seem to be primitive – for what they really were: pointers to reason and belief which often had their own good sense and logic.

How Africans lived

GOVERNMENT WITHOUT RULERS

As the Africans built new communities in their plains and forests, they developed technologies and skills to support their growing numbers. This chapter will discuss some of the most important of these skills; farming, metal working, spinning, and other arts of everyday life. First of all, let us take another look at the skills in government which Africans developed.

The last three chapters have described a few examples of African peoples who united their strength in kingdoms or empires. They built armies. They brought wide regions under the power of a central government. They set up civil services people who would carry out the laws made by the central government. These central governments ruled by sending orders to governors, and governors to sub-governors, and sub-governors to headmen of villages. The basic pattern of this kind of government was not in fact very different from that used by kingdoms outside Africa. Yet quite different kinds of government show us a great deal of th hidden truth of African life, and its inventiveness. It is to be found among peoples who were content with 'village government', or with no obvious form of government at all.

Some of these 'peoples without government', or only with 'village government had fertile land. Some of them had plenty of natural wealth, and links with long-distance trade. Others had neither, or they had to survive in particularly tough country. These others, just because they were poor and had no chance of growing rich, are often among the most interesting of all, for they had to find a reliable way of life with the knife of hunger always at their throats. Most years they were threatened by drought that killed their cattle or shrivelled up their crops They were hit repeatedly by pests such as locusts that came in clouds so thick as to darken the sun, and ate up crops and grass leaving desolation behind.

Such peoples could grow in numbers only very slowly. Being so few, they needed little government. Yet they loved their difficult country and wanted to live there in peace, avoiding trouble whenever possible; and so they had to invent some form of government that would give them law and order. As they had no us for kings or governors, and no wealth to support such persons, they invented government without rulers. Not all were equally successful. But often they were able to overcome the natural perils that they faced.

This bronze figure from old Benin shows a hunter coming home with an antelope he has killed

They learned the secret of survival by a thoughtful process of trial and error. As they got to know their land and its climate and its possibilities, so they gradually arrived at the right balance between themselves and nature. They worked out rules to keep this balance, this pattern of community life. They found ways of seeing that such rules were obeyed. Now and then the rules were not sufficient or were broken, and disaster struck. Otherwise these peoples who had government without rulers went on living in much the same way. Change and progress in the world beyond their horizons seldom touched them.

How did these 'small' systems of government really work? What held them together, without anyone to give orders, without a civil service, without a police force, without an army?

The Karimojong homeland

Government by age: 'What set do you belong to?'

Far in the north of Uganda, where good upland pastures give way to thirsty lands along the frontiers of Ethiopia and Kenya, there live a people called the Karimojong. They number today about sixty thousand. Their country, which they call Karimoja, measures about 10,500 square kilometres, about half the size of Wales or a little smaller than Jamaica. It is a harsh country that allows only a little farming. Most Karimojong live by raising cattle driven from place to place in grasslands which are never rich in fodder, and are often ruined by drought.

Settling in this otherwise empty land long ago, the Karimojong found they could survive only by using every blade of grass they could find. They had to study their land in its every detail, above all its water resources and its varying types of grass, so that they knew the grazing value of each square kilometre of it They had to spend much of every year in shifting their herds according to the seasons. Although they were able to maintain fixed villages, where women and elderly folk could grow a little food, the men of Karimoja had to be continually herding their cattle.

This meant, as it still means today, that a man had to spend most of his life in cattle camps, often far from his home village. In these camps he lived and worke alongside men from other villages. So the main problem of government was clearly difficult, for the men in cattle camps were all loyal to different villages or heads of families.

The problem was to work out some way of getting all these men of different villages, of different home loyalties, to recognise the same rules and to apply the rules to settle quarrels. But how to do it? The Karimojong had no wish to solve this problem by setting up a police force, even if the idea had occurred to them. any case they had no government to give orders to a police force, or officials to raise taxes to pay for one. Nor could they rely on general good will, because catt camps were often places where men competed for pastures and so came easily t blows.

Their solution was the *age set*. It was a solution developed by many peoples. Age sets of one kind or another exist among a large number of African peoples, even when these also have other methods of self-rule, including kings and centr governments. But Karimojong age sets are particularly interesting. They are the cement that binds the Karimojong into a single people, and gives them law and order.

Their age sets work like this. In Karimoja, active men are considered to be thos over ten years old but under sixty. Under ten years old you are a boy with no responsibility except to your own family. Over sixty you are an elder who no longer grazes cattle, but stays at home in the village. So a man has fifty years of active life if he is lucky enough to live that long. In this time he passes through a number of age sets, staying in each about five years, together with all other men of about the same age as himself. Each age set has its own name known to all Karimojong, and each has its own duties and responsibilities.

The Karimojong are trained from their boyhood to understand and carry out these duties and responsibilities, which vary with each successive age set. This means that they learn a pattern of behaviour for each period of a man's life; and this is the pattern that conserves their balance with nature. It also solves their community problems. Men who come together in cattle camps, little thatched settlements in Karimoja's plains of grass and thorn, may never have met before. But age set training has told them how every man should behave in every situation. So they know how to work together; they know how to settle dispute

Age set training, which is community training, is obviously vital in any system like this; otherwise the rules will not be known and kept. Like other African peoples, Karimojong give great importance to it. They have no schools like ours, no knowledge of reading and writing. But what they do have is an all-embracin education for everyday life in Karimoja.

Boys begin this education when they are about ten. In different ways, so do girls. Boys go to training camps where, maybe for six months or more, they begi to be taught the laws and customs of their people, the rules that must be obeyed

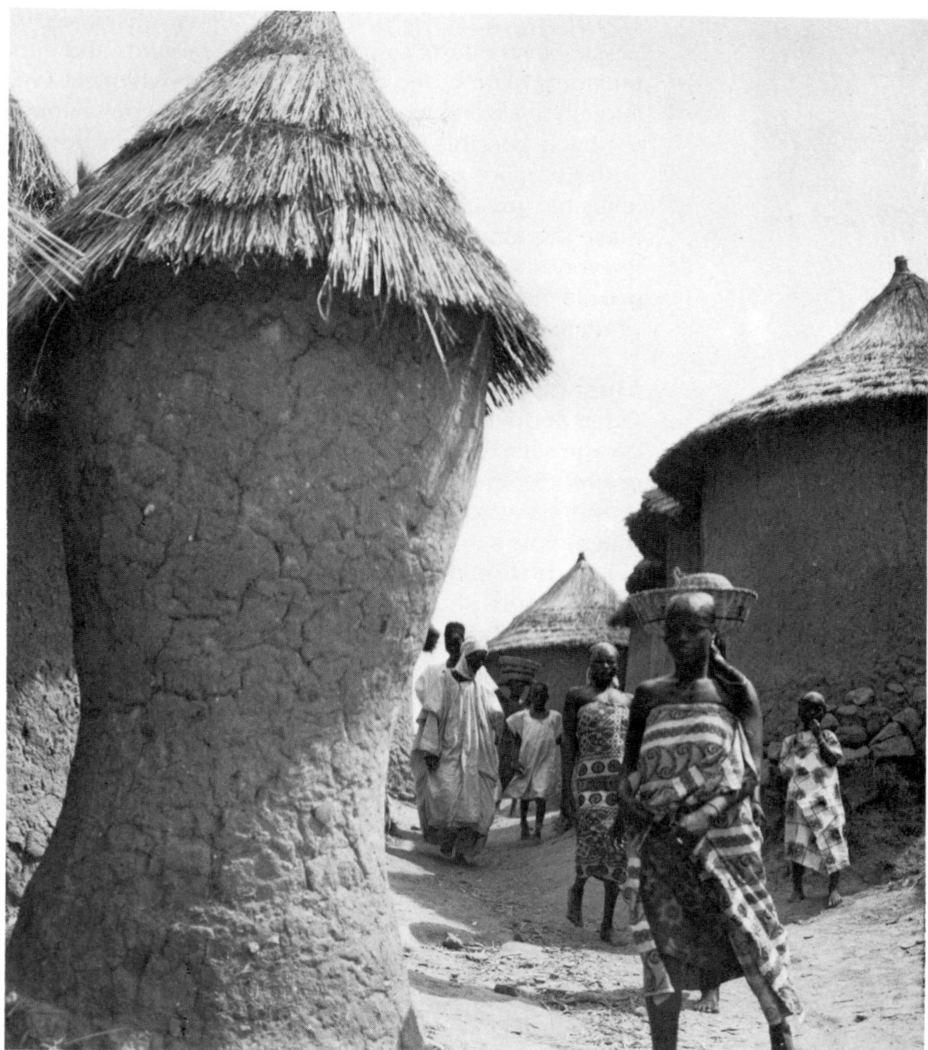

A village scene in northern Nigeria. The construction on the left is a thatched grain-store

the Karimojong are to survive in their difficult land, the religious and other beliefs by which they explain the world they live in. Sometimes this is a hard training when boys have to learn how to face the perils of the wilderness, how to deal with marauding animals, how to develop courage and initiative. But always this is an education for community life: always it is aimed at teaching that the survival of the whole community depends on each man and woman behaving in the right way. The individual is important, but the community comes first.

Back from their first period of training, Karimojong boys are at once treated as grown-ups, but still as youthful grown-ups who cannot yet be given much responsibility. Later, as they enter higher age sets, they learn other things about their country, other duties, other rules concerning right behaviour. Then they undertake greater responsibilities in the settlement of disputes or other community affairs. And when at last they pass into the age set of the elders, at the end of their active lives, it will be their task to act as law-makers and law-givers, preside over courts of justice, to give rewards and punishments, and to act as priests of Karimojong religion, a religion which, as we shall see, undertakes to explain the world as well as to order men's behaviour.

So it is possible for the Karimojong to have a government without rulers, without police or civil service, army or capital city. You might even call this 'invisible government'. For the knowledge, skills, and understandings which make this kind of government possible, and tell each Karimojong how to behave in every situation, are really in the minds and beliefs of the Karimojong. These people may seem poor and primitive. In fact they have a deep and useful understanding of their country and themselves.

Lineage groupings: 'What family group do you belong to?'

Other peoples have found other ways of achieving the same result. Many rely le on age sets, to give social training and keep the peace, and more on *lineage groupings*. We shall see exactly what these are in a moment. Broadly, though, they are a way of organising people to live together, in a community, by linking that people's different family groups. Their rules, their laws and customs, say ho everyone should behave inside his or her family group, but they also say how family groups should behave towards each other.

Now the Karimojong, as you can see, wouldn't have found this kind of arrangement much use to them. Their men meet in cattle camps, away from thei family groups, where rivalry for scarce water and pasture can be a constant danger to peace. Something stronger is needed than rules for keeping peace between family groups. That is why the Karimojong rely on age sets which cut across family loyalties, and help men to settle disputes about matters such as water and pasture.

The Karimojong pattern of life reflects the fact that Karimoja is terribly short of water. But another cattle-raising people, some 800 kilometres to the north of Karimoja, are in the opposite position. These are the million-strong Dinka who live in lands around the Upper Nile. They have too much water. A lot of Dinkaland is flooded every year. This has helped to give the Dinka a way of life, pattern of community, very different from that of the Karimojong.

The Dinka homeland

Because Dinkaland is rich in well-watered pastures, Dinka herdsmen do not have to scatter, but can stay together in quite large groups. But they cannot stay in the same place all the year round, because of the annual floods. They have three regular living places. They have home villages where, as in Karimoja, elder people can grow a little food. These are situated on a few low ridges above reach of the floods. Then they have wet season cattle camps where active people, young and old, as well as their children, live with their herds during the floods from August till December. Thirdly, they have temporary camps in dry season pastures where members of different wet season camps join together for a while.

Wet season camps are pitched on small mounds which rise a few feet above the flooded pastures. Dinka build thatched shelters on these mounds, and tether the cattle to pegs ranged in a ring outside each shelter. Living in these camps is rath boring for young Dinka. They have little to do except to look after their tethered cattle, tell each other stories, make up the smokey fires that keep them warm and cook their food, or watch the rains lashing down outside.

Then springtime comes, the rains stop, the rivers fall, the floods sink into fresh pastures; and this is when young Dinka really enjoy themselves. They leave the cattle camps and help to drive their parents' herds across the fields. There people get together for dances and singing contests, compete in hunting or fishing sports, and stretch their legs after the confinement of the rains. They stay together for a while before going off with their herds to nearby pastures, or visiting their old folks in the permanent villages, where young people help in the garden work.

This looks like a simple way of life. But it is really the product of long experience, of a hard search for the right balance with nature. It is the way the Dinka have mastered their land. Unless they could organise themselves to raise good cattle they would have perished in their watery plains, or been obliged to move elsewhere. But it would have been difficult to move elsewhere because other peoples stood in the way.

And the Dinka may seem 'primitive', for they have very few possessions and wear as few clothes as possible, often none at all. They have no stone houses, at least they had none in the past, because there is no building stone in Dinkaland. They have no obvious form of government. But they have survived, and even prospered. What is the secret of their success?

There are many different ways of life in Africa. Some Africans live on lagoons like this one on the coast of West Africa, where the town is built entirely on stilts

If you saw a Dinka cattle camp during the wet season, just a neighbourhood of thatched huts and tethered cattle on muddy mounds among the floods, you migh think it had no organisation of any sort. Everyone there looks at first sight as if he or she acts pretty much as they like. Yet this is where *lineage groupings* take over where 'invisible government' makes itself felt.

This is an organisation of family life backed by community training, by education in the rules of Dinka life. Every cattle camp consists of a number of 'small families' each consisting of husband and wife with their children, and sometimes their grandparents. When a man can afford it, Dinka custom allows him to have several wives. All these with their children belong to the same 'small family', although, as you can guess, it is often quite a numerous one.

Each of these 'small families' belongs to a 'big family', or *gol*. Which gol a fami belongs to is decided by marriage. Families which are closely related all belong to the same gol. A gol can be several dozen people, or even more. Each gol is responsible for the behaviour of its members. It is governed by a meeting of elder respected for their good sense and character; they form the governing council of their 'big family'. They know the rules of Dinka life thoroughly, and it is their job to see the rules are kept.

But that is not the whole story. All the 'big families' in a cattle camp belong to a still larger organisation of family life. This larger organisation includes everybody in any given cattle camp. It is called a *wut* – a word which also means 'cattle camp' – and each wut is a main section of all the Dinka people. You could even say that all the wuts (or wot, the plural of wut) make up the Dinka nation.

Each wut, like each gol or 'big family' that belongs to it, also has its council of elders. This is the senior body that settles disputes between the 'big families', just as the gol councils settle disputes between the 'small families'. When necessary, wut council, presiding over a whole cattle camp, can call on young warriors to carry out their decisions, and to act as a temporary police force. Things become more difficult if one cattle camp disagrees with another. Then there may be a burs of spear-fighting unless the elders of the two camps can get together, which they generally do, and work out a peaceful solution.

Now all this depends on people knowing what the rules are, and being ready to obey them. And that in turn depends on education, on community training. No Dinka escapes this kind of education. It is supposed to go on all through a person's life – 'elementary' for boys and girls, 'secondary' for young men and women, 'advanced' for people over the age of thirty-five. Practical rules teach the care of cattle and the skills of hunting and fishing. Moral rules teach how people should behave. Religious rules teach what people should believe. Political rules teach Dinka methods of government. Legal rules teach the way to settle disputes punish offenders, keep the peace. The rules are intended to provide for everythin that can happen in Dinkaland.

We shall see more deeply into this when we consider African religion. Meanwhile we should note another aspect of Dinka life. The Dinka are like some other peoples in Africa, though by no means most, in believing that everyone should be as equal as possible in wealth and way of life. They hold that anyone who tries to get more than his or her fair share of wealth or comfort endangers the whole community. In so trying, they argue, he or she upsets the delicate balance that the Dinka have worked out with nature.

Even peoples who have very little respect for the idea of equality, such as the wealthy Yoruba of Nigeria with their many chiefs and privileged persons, teach the dangers of greed and 'go-getting'. A Yoruba saying makes the point:

Let us not run the world hastily:
Let us not grasp at the rope of wealth impatiently;
What should be treated with mature judgement
Let us not treat in a fit of temper.

But Dinka, whose country is a poor one, have had to take the idea of equality very seriously. A 'big family' which got many more cattle than their neighbours would soon cause trouble because they would need more than an ordinary share of space and fodder in wet season camps, or of pastures in the dry season. Therefore Dinka laws are designed to keep an equal balance between groups. If someone steals cattle, for example, the elders will think mainly of forcing the thief either to give back the cattle, or an equal number of other cattle. If anyone kills a man, either by accident or intent, the chief thing, the Dinka believe, is to 'right the balance' by giving the killed man's family the right to kill a member of the killer's family. Better still, because it avoids bloodshed, the killer's family should give cattle or other goods in compensation. In all such cases the elders think most about 'righting the balance'.

'Secret societies': 'Have you paid your entrance fee?'

Peoples everywhere, whether in Africa or not, have worked out their means of government according to their own special problems. The Karimojong found it best to rely on age sets: the Dinka preferred lineage groupings. Yet it is not only peoples living in difficult types of country who have got on all right without strong governments and chiefs.

The Ibo of south-eastern Nigeria have long been one of the most prosperous of all African peoples. Today they number more than six million; even a century ago they may have numbered more than three million. They live in a land of good natural fertility, rich in tall trees. They have plenty of water but are little troubled by floods. From early times they have been energetic traders and travellers, famed for their initiative and skill in producing goods and trading in goods. But, unlike their neighbours of Benin or Yorubaland, the Ibo in the past never tried to come together within a single state. Intensely democratic, mostly believing in equal opportunities for all to have their say, the Ibo have ruled themselves in a multitude of very small village-sized governments.

The Ibo homeland

Tucked away in dense forestlands, these village governments have relied on several methods of self-rule. They have had age sets like the Karimojong, and lineage methods like the Dinka, although these often worked in different ways. They have had village assemblies at which every man could have a share in deciding community affairs. A few Ibo groups in western Iboland even elected kings. Others in eastern Iboland developed another method of self-rule, also fairly common in Africa. It has been called, but misleadingly, rule by 'secret society'. In fact, most 'secret societies' were associations of successful men who governed a town or several towns; their powers came partly from religion, and partly from their go-ahead success. Their meetings were closed to non-members, and their religious ceremonies were held in secret. Otherwise they were, and indeed they

The Efik homeland

had to be, entirely public. For they ran local affairs, made up the local business community, raised the local police force and commanded it.

One such governing association was Ekpe, the Leopard Society of the Efik people of trading towns established long ago on the banks of the Cross River, east of the Niger delta. Ekpe came into existence because the Efik faced special problems. Some of these arose from Efik development of ocean trade with European ships' captains and traders. If the Efik were going to do well in this trade, they had to get organised. They had to be able to act in partnership with Europeans without allowing these Europeans to push them around. They had to be able to close the river to European trade if one or another European trader misbehaved. They had to be able to agree on customs duties, on the prices they were prepared to pay for European goods, and on the prices of their own goods.

They also had to find a way of uniting citizens of different African groups who crowded into these bustling towns from the inland country to the north. Neither age sets nor lineage groupings could be of much use here, because all these incoming groups had their own different customs and beliefs. The Efik leaders accordingly developed their Leopard Society, a governing corporation which wa open to every man, no matter to what group he otherwise belonged.

There was however a third reason which influenced their society's developme This became increasingly important. This third reason was ambition for individu wealth and power. It arose partly from the ocean trade. Turning away from the belief that a good community was one in which all men were more or less equal i wealth, and even in political power as well, these people of south-eastern Nigeri developed a different view. They thought that hard work and shrewd dealing should bring rewards in personal power and wealth.

In theory, every man in the Cross River towns could join the Leopard Society, and have a share in government; but in practice it was not so simple. Entrance fees had to be paid: not just one fee, but a fresh one every time a man went up one grade, or level of power, to the next above. When a man joined Ekpe he wen into the bottom grade and had little power. If he became more successful in business he could go up a grade and the fee would be higher than before. So the men at the top were always the wealthiest citizens. As they were also the most powerful, they could exploit their poorer fellow-citizens. The old equalities of village life disappeared beneath the pressures and opportunities of trade. But in return for this price the townsmen of the Cross River acquired strong governmen and with it a general prosperity for a lot of the people who lived there.

Advance and adjustment

All this illustrates a central point about Africans already mentioned. Facing their varied problems, they found a wide range of solutions. These solutions were revised or adjusted when new changes and chances brought new problems.

Far away in their hills or plains, peoples such as the Karimojong had no reason to change their ways once they had discovered how to master their country and make it yield them a living. Elsewhere, and especially where long-distance trade opened new chances of wealth, other peoples changed their ways. Some developed from small village communities to strong kingdoms and large empires Or, as with the Efik of the Cross River, they evolved corporations of successful men who ruled trading towns.

It would need several long books to examine all this in detail. These pages may be enough to show that every African people found ways of adjusting and advancing its way of government, meeting new opportunities, new dangers, new conditions of life. Some did this better than others. Some had much success; some had none at all. But most were able to solve their particular problems in one way or another. Their solutions had a lot to do with their ideas about morals and religion.

RELIGION IN AFRICAN LIFE

Every people in the past have looked to their religion, to their ideas about spiritual and moral power, for two great benefits. First, their religion explained the world to them, how the world came into existence, how it was put together, how it works. Secondly, religion told them how to behave so as to enjoy the blessings of this world. This means that each people's history is concerned with their religion.

In modern times, by contrast, many people no longer look to religion for an explanation of the world and a guide to behaviour. They do not expect religion to tell them anything important about nature. Instead, they look to science for such an explanation. They think of religion as one thing, and science as quite another.

Africans did not make this separation between science and religion. They thought that their religion could explain everything; for them, their religion was a kind of science. To understand their political history, why they behaved as they did, you therefore have to know something about their beliefs about God and the world of the spirits.

Africa's Garden of Eden

There were many African religions; to some extent, there still are. Each African people has had its own. Yet nearly all these separate religions have been like each other in their basic beliefs. Nearly all African peoples have believed in a single High God who lives in Heaven, and who made the world and all that is in the world. Beyond that they have also believed in lesser gods and spirits. Beyond that again, they have believed in the power of evil. Christians think of evil as the work of the devil. Africans think of it as the work of *witchcraft*. All these religions explained about nature and all its creatures, as well as giving guidance to people on their everyday behaviour.

These religions also tried to answer the same puzzling questions as the religions of other peoples. How and why, for example, did the world begin? The answer Africans have found, usually, is that God made the world by sending down one or other of his spirits, or his children, to do the necessary work: to lay the soil on the ground, to raise the hills and plant the forests and set the rivers flowing, and then, when all was ready, to create mankind. The Yoruba of Nigeria, as we have seen, believe that this was done by two great spirits, Orishanla and Oduduwa. The Ewe (Ev-vay) of Togo and Ghana believe it was done by Nummo, the son of Mawo, their word for God. The Ashanti believe that it was done by powerful spirits, such as Tano, who drew their force from the commands of Nyame, the name by which they call God who rules the Universe.

Why did unhappiness come into this world that God caused to be made? This was another large question asked by Africans, as by other peoples. Their answer has often been rather like the Christian story of Adam and Eve, and the fall of man Long ago, Africans say, there was a blessed time without unhappiness or death. God visited mankind and lived among people. People could visit God if they wished, climbing up to Heaven on a ladder or a rope let down from the sky. Then through someone's fault God became offended with mankind and withdrew his companionship. That is when unhappiness and death came into the world, when the power of evil got its chance.

Africans have told this story in different ways. The Ashanti of Ghana tell about a happy time when 'God used to live on earth, or at least he was very near to us. But there was a certain old woman who pounded her cassava-meal in such a way that the pestle used to knock up against God.' She wielded her long pounding stick so actively that she accidentally hit God with it. Why did she do this? The story does not say: maybe, with a woman's sense of responsibility, she was worried about feeding her family. But in any case, God was upset. 'He said to the old woman, "Why do you always do this to me? Because of what you are doing to me I am going to take myself back into the sky." And of a truth he did that.'

Dinkaland is more than three thousand kilometres from Ashanti. Yet the Dinka and some of their neighbours tell almost the same story about the beginning of unhappiness. They believe that there was once a time when God and people lived together. Then a woman who was too eager in producing food, or wanted more than a fair share for herself and her family, happened to hit God with a hoe. So God went back to Heaven, sent a small blue bird which formed the blue sky, and cut the rope which people had used to reach Heaven when they wanted. 'And since that time,' the Dinka say, 'our country has been spoilt, because people since then have had to work hard for the food they need, and yet often they are hungry.

Finding the Promised Land

Cut off from God's companionship, how were these peoples able to find a way through life? Africans have answered this question in much the same way as did the ancient tribes of Israel, as told in the Old Testament of the Bible. Led by Moses, who enjoyed God's favour, the Jews came to the land of Israel. There, they settled, living by rules that God gave to Moses, and prospered so long as the obeyed the rules. They believed that God had chosen them to live in the land of Israel, and had given them commandments which could solve their problems.

Although in different ways, every African people has believed that its great men of the distant past, its 'founding heroes' or 'founding ancestors', have led them on their ancient wanderings in search of a homeland, have brought them to this homeland, and, once there, have given them rules which could protect them with God's blessing. These beliefs go back to that remote time when African groups were growing in numbers, and were spreading through the solitudes of their continent. Guided by God's will, made known to them through their great leaders each group found its homeland and learned how to live in it.

This explains why there are so many religions in Africa. Each people, like the Israelites, has had its own religion, because each people has had to explain its own origins, its own adventures, and obtain from God its own rules. So that although these religions vary widely from each other in their details, they are alike in basic ways. Each has taught that the will of God was expressed through 'founding heroes' who are linked to living people by the spirits of dead ancestors. African religions have differed in this from that of the Israelites, who believed that the will of God was expressed by God Himself, and that prayers should be said only to God. Africans have generally said their prayers not to God but to the spirits of ancestors who, they believe, draw their power from God.

This shows why the political ideas of Africa, the methods of government, have been inseparable from beliefs about religion. All these different methods of government, it was believed, were worked out by the great ancestors of long ago. These ancestors took their knowledge from God. So the rules by which men could live and prosper were the rules of religion. Let us look at how this worked in practice.

Advice from 'the Bird of Bright Plumage'

A century ago, when white men first followed northward trails out of South Africa across the Limpopo River, and came after days of marching through woods and prairies to the massive walls of Great Zimbabwe, they found there a number of tall stone statues. These were handsome carvings of a bird with folded wings. Admiring these statues for their craftsmanship, white explorers took them down from their stone platforms and carried them away to Cape Town, then the capital city of white South Africa. Here they kept the statues, thinking them another strange mystery of African life.

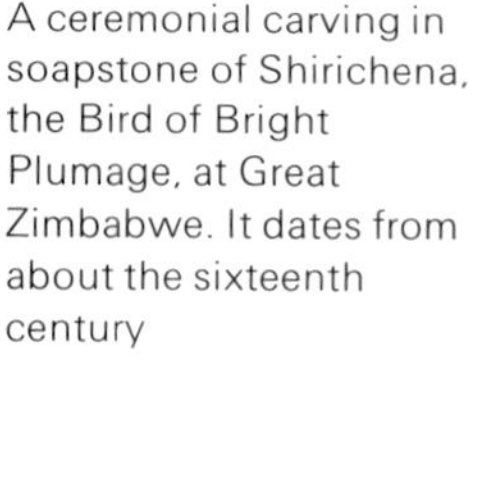

A ceremonial carving in soapstone of Shirichena, the Bird of Bright Plumage, at Great Zimbabwe. It dates from about the sixteenth century

They are no longer a mystery today. The figures taken from Great Zimbabwe were stylised statues of a bird with symbolic religious meaning. The Shona had two names for this bird. One was Shirichena, the Bird of Bright Plumage; the other was Shiri ya Mwari, the Bird of God. To the Shona, in other words, these bird-figures stood for an aspect of their religious beliefs. They believed that their high priests, the wise men who advised their rulers, could find out God's advice by listening to the cries of the Bird of Bright Plumage.

Now this is not to say that the priests of the Shona simply listened to the cries of a bird whose stylised statues stood in a prominent position at Great Zimbabwe, and invented any old thing they happened to think of. The Shona were shrewd farmers who knew their country like the back of their hand. They were not to be taken in by tall stories. They were good cattlemen and metal workers and no fools

The priests of Mwari, as the Shona called God, listened to Shiri ya Mwari and gave advice on practical problems. But the advice they gave was drawn from two sorts of expert knowledge. In the first place, the priests were experts in the rules of Shona life. They it was who had to learn the teachings of the great ancestors, of the 'founding heroes' of the Shona people who, long before – a thousand years ago and more – had led the Shona to their homeland. These great ancestors, such as Chaminuka and his sister Nehanda, the national ancestors of the Shona, were believed to have found the way to this good homeland, taught the Shona how to make iron and grow crops, such as millet, and given the commandments by which the Shona could live and prosper.

The priests of the Bird of Bright Plumage had another sort of expert knowledge. Those who were most respected among them were those who were wisest. They were expected to study the problems of day-to-day life, and give decisions that could help solve these problems. They were the real statesmen of the Shona. No great decisions, such as making war or making peace, could be taken without their advice. This does not mean that the advice was always sensible or right, but it does mean that the advice was the best that could be got. The cries of the Bird of Bright Plumage were turned into words with a lot of careful thought behind them.

In 1890 British settlers and soldiers invaded the lands of the Shona and of their neighbours the Ndebele, or Matabele as the whites called them. These invaders seized about half the cattle of the Africans, and much of their best land. What should be done in this situation? In 1896 the statesmen of the Shona and Ndebele reluctantly decided that invading white men could not be persuaded by peaceful argument to give back land and cattle. They would have to be persuaded by war. Only when the invaders were thrown out could the Shona and Ndebele expect to prosper again.

Following the advice of their leaders, the Ndebele rose in arms against the whites who had taken their land and cattle. A year later the Shona followed suit. Both were defeated by the British. But the interesting point for us is that their war of resistance was commanded by their priests, who, as in the past, were believed to be the men who could give the best advice, and who were therefore the best leaders.

So religion in these old African states was not something set apart from everyday life: on the contrary, it provided a practical guide in every situation. When Africans prayed at their village temples to images of stone or wood, they were not worshipping these objects. They were asking for advice or help from ancestral spirits who, they believed, controlled the workings of the world, and who chose to 'dwell' in this or that object or shrine so that men could get in touch with them.

The duties of kings

The practical side of these beliefs came out repeatedly in important ceremonies. Through such beliefs Africans of small groups could unite in larger groups. We have seen this in the case of the Ashanti Union of 1695, when Osei Tutu and the priest Anokye persuaded the leaders of several small Ashanti states to set aside their loyalties to different lines of ancestors, and to unite in loyalty to a single line symbolised on earth by the Golden Stool.

The same beliefs made it possible to get rid of bad rulers, and in this the kings of Africa had the same position as the kings of Europe. They could expect their people to obey their orders only if they themselves obeyed the rules laid down by the ancestors. If kings failed to obey the rules and tried to be tyrants, people had the right to rise in war against them and remove them from power. This was the 'people's right' that King John of England confirmed to the English barons in his Great Charter of 1215. He promised to accept the old law which laid down that revolt against a bad king was lawful revolt.

African kings had to accept the same 'people's right'. They might try to stretch the rules so as to increase royal power. If they went too far, however, they came up against the rules laid down by the ancestors, and these were stronger than the will of any king. This applied right down the line of political power, from great emperors to local chiefs. In Ashanti every chief had to go through a long and testing ceremony before he could begin to govern. Taking his seat upon his official stool, his *akonnua*, he had to make solemn promises. By these he undertook to set aside his own interests or the interests of his family and relations, and to devote himself to all the people over whom he was chosen to rule. And the chosen representatives of his people, solemnly addressing the official appointed to speak for the chief, gave direct and practical instructions. While lots of local people listened and took note, they said:

Tell him that
We do not wish for greediness
We do not wish that his ears should be hard of hearing
We do not wish that he should call people fools
We do not wish that he should decide matters by himself
We do not wish that it should ever be said 'I have no time, I have no time'
We do not wish for personal violence

Also let the new chief or king act with modesty, with patience, with care for ordinary people. Let him consult his counsellors before taking any important decision. Then he would be acting in line with the good rules laid down by the ancestral spirits, and his reign would prosper. Otherwise it would be better to depose him. Many bad chiefs were deposed. It was more difficult to get rid of a strong king who ruled badly. But this could also be done, and it was done.

Africans were as human as anyone else. Individuals blundered, gave way to greed, believed foolish things, committed crimes. There were ways to correct or

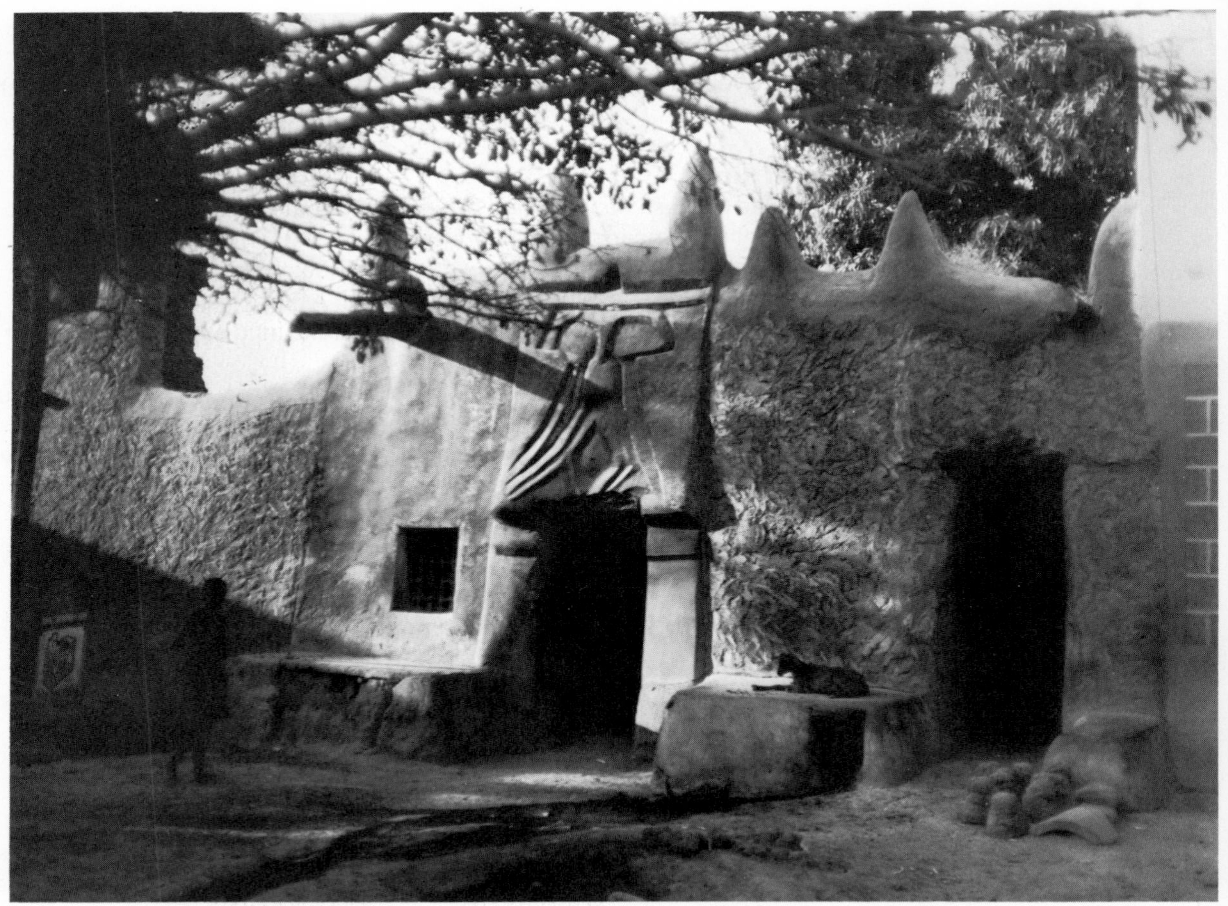

The entrance to a house in the ancient city of Kano in northern Nigeria

punish these failings or faults, and the rules of the ancestors showed how to do it. Their religions were therefore a kind of practical politics.

Christianity and Islam

Two world religions have played their part in African history. Ethiopia became Christian soon after AD 300, and has remained so to this day. The Copts, who were descendants of the ancient Egyptians, embraced Christianity even earlier than that, and have stayed loyal to it. The Nubians of the Middle Nile developed brilliant Christian cultures after 600; these lasted for six centuries before being overwhelmed by Muslim Sudanese from the south and Muslim Egyptians from the north. Missionaries from Europe went to Africa after 1500. They converted kings such as Affonso of Kongo, although it was only much later, in the nineteenth century, that many Africans became Christian.

Islam spread from Egypt through North Africa and southward across the Sahara to the states and empires of the western and central Sudan. It helped towards new achievements, including the development of African schools of learning in cities such as Timbuktu. Islam also spread down the east coast and helped to form the Muslim civilisation of the Swahili.

But most Africans remained loyal to their own beliefs, seeking advice and wisdom from ancestral spirits, and finding it in the words of priests who were also men of practical affairs. These beliefs were about what was good and helpful in life. But they were also about what was damaging and bad.

WITCHCRAFT: THE POWER OF EVIL

Africans believed that the evil in their lives – bad luck, hurtful accidents, whatever caused pain or suffering – was the work of evil powers let loose on the world in the distant past, usually as a result of human failing. These evil powers, they thought, did their work by witchcraft.

Large numbers of people in Europe had much the same beliefs until modern times. Only the rise of modern science enabled Europeans to get rid of their beliefs in witchcraft. Not yet having modern science, Africans continued to believe in witchcraft. They believed that the power of evil chose people in whom to dwell and to do its damaging work. These witches, they thought, were unfortunate people who, because of the power of evil, 'left their bodies' during sleep and flew about the sky, riding owls or other birds, and carrying little balls of fire.

Again like Europeans, Africans believed in the same teaching as that of the Old Testament of the Bible which says, in the Book of Exodus, 'Suffer not a witch to live'. They tested people for witchcraft in a number of painful or fatal ways, and sometimes they killed people whom they believed to be witches. They seldom burned such persons to death, as in Europe, but they used tests or 'ordeals' with the same fatal result. Mankind in every continent, before the rise of modern science, has done much the same at one or other stage of its history.

What 'witch doctors' really were

Africans also thought that no one need be helpless in the face of evil and its witchcraft. They believed that it was always possible to call on good spirits for protection. To do this they turned to priests who were specialists in defeating witchcraft.

When Europeans first went deep into Africa they did not understand what they saw. They thought these specialists in anti-witchcraft, who might be fierce-looking figures wearing masks in strange ceremonies, were in fact 'making' witchcraft, not fighting it, and so they called them 'witch doctors'. Nearly always, in fact, these specialists were 'anti-witchcraft doctors'. Calling on the powers of good, they were working against what they believed to be the powers of evil.

'Anti-witchcraft doctors' have played an important part in African life. They were men or women who had gone through a special training, sometimes lasting several years. Often their calling was handed down from father to son or from mother to daughter. They had various tasks. Always their main responsibility was to work against 'witches', and the damage people thought they caused. This work took many forms because in African belief the power of evil lay behind every mishap or disaster, whether this affected a single person or a community.

Africans generally didn't believe in accident or bad luck. They thought that all misfortunes were caused by the power of evil, usually let loose by someone breaking the rules of right behaviour. They even thought that most deaths were caused by witchcraft. Witches 'flew through the air' at night, and stole away the souls of living persons, thus killing them. In lesser cases, misfortune could come because some offended person was using witchcraft in revenge. So a doctor's task was to 'find the witch', and then advise on how to defeat the witch's plots and schemes. In ordinary cases this led simply to advice on what a person shoul do to protect himself: nothing was done to the suspected witch, to the person acting under the power of evil. But when a people suffered great misfortune, suc as a long period of drought or a pest of locusts, it would be the doctor's task to find the 'witches' who were thought to be responsible for this unleashing of evil, and see that they were punished. Then these unhappy persons would be banished or killed. Often they were worried elderly folk who were pressured by neurotic fears and fancies, and they might even ask for punishment. The records European history are full of such 'confessions' by mentally disturbed people who thought they were witches.

This is not to say that Africans were blind to the obvious causes of misfortune. But they believed that there was always a deeper cause behind the obvious caus They thought that this deeper cause was the work of witchcraft, and that it resulted from some act of wrong or bad behaviour.

A hunter wounded by a lion would know that his foot had slipped at a crucial moment, giving the lion a chance to maul him. But what, he would ask, had caused his foot to slip? What had laid him open to this action of the power of evil? What fault had he committed, so that witchcraft could go to work on him, and cause his foot to slip? Worried in case still worse misfortune should befall him, he would go to his doctor for advice. The doctor, who might be a man or a woman, would consult the good spirits of the ancestors. He or she would do this in a number of ways, and in return for a fee. The doctor might throw bones or some such device. Or he might go into a trance, become 'possessed' by the spirit of his little temple, and then speak with the 'voice' of the spirit, giving explanatio and advice. What he said was not just whatever came into his head. The skilled doctor was more than a priest who knew the rules of right behaviour; he was als someone who had thoroughly studied the habits and lives of the people among whom he lived and practised.

Had the hunter been too greedy? Had he perhaps stolen from a neighbour, wh was therefore 'using witchcraft' against him? Had he failed in his duties to the community? The doctor would look carefully for a deeper cause behind the obvious one; if he got it right the patient would feel better because he would fee that the doctor had reached the heart of his trouble. Then he would put right his wrong behaviour. In putting it right, he would feel protected from witchcraft, fro the power of evil.

Treatment and counsel

All this may seem strange to us. In fact, it was often much the same kind of medical treatment as psychiatric or mental healing in our own country. Its most usual aim was to give comfort to the worried, to relieve mental tensions, to help people through their troubles. When the advice was good the patient felt relief and went away happier, better able to face his or her problems. When it was bad and failed to bring relief, the patient would try another doctor. Like modern doctors, these healers of Africa were judged by their degree of success in treating patients. When this was high, doctors became popular and much visited. Otherwise they were said to lack skill, and their fees were few.

Treatment of illness by herbal medicine was another of their tasks. Good specialists were students of nature who understood the medical value of many kinds of herbs and plants. This knowledge was built up over centuries and taught them which herbs were useful against snake-bite, spear-wounds or certain fevers.

Higher up the scale of responsibility, doctors had to advise on important questions affecting many people. Traders setting out on a dangerous journey, kings deciding to make war, farmers wishing to clear a new stretch of forest for crops would all consult their priest-doctors; and the doctors would give advice according to religious belief and practical wisdom. Then men could start their enterprises with the comforting knowledge that the spirits would approve. So priests like those of the Bird of Bright Plumage, advising the kings of the Shona in their temple at Great Zimbabwe, were also 'anti-witch doctors' in their way. They were concerned with protecting their people from the evil that must follow any serious breaking of the rules of right behaviour and, whenever such a break had occurred, with advising on what should be done to set matters right again.

What, then, should we think of these beliefs in witches and witchcraft? The answer is contradictory. In one way, of course, they were groundless. There can be no such persons as witches. Nobody can 'leave their body', and fly around on owls. A hunter's foot may slip because he has a bad conscience; it is more likely to slip by mere accident. Yet in another way these beliefs were not groundless. They were drawn from African ideas about how the world was put together and held together. They were concerned with the creative power and the destructive power that lie within every human being; with protecting the first and with defeating the second. So they had their own sense and logic according to the ways in which Africans understood the world. In times of great trouble, witchcraft beliefs could lead to cruelty and the sacrifice of harmless people. More often, in everyday life, these beliefs could be a source of help and comfort.

PRACTICAL TECHNOLOGY

African interest in human nature went hand-in-hand with a study of living things and creatures. Most Africans were farmers who knew their land in every detail. They passed on this knowledge from one generation to the next, each new generation adding whatever it could learn from its own experience. They did this in their training schools, where the rules of life were taught. They did it in their practical work, and in their songs and stories.

A kind of science

Each people's knowledge of nature varied with the kind of country they lived in, its climate, its soil and water resources, its special characteristics, but also with that people's chief farming activity.

In Dinkaland, for example, the main activity was raising cattle. So important were cattle to Dinka people that they tended to see their whole world in terms of cattle. They felt about cattle, one can say, as a lot of people today feel about the size of their pay packets. Not only were cattle necessary to life; they were also a

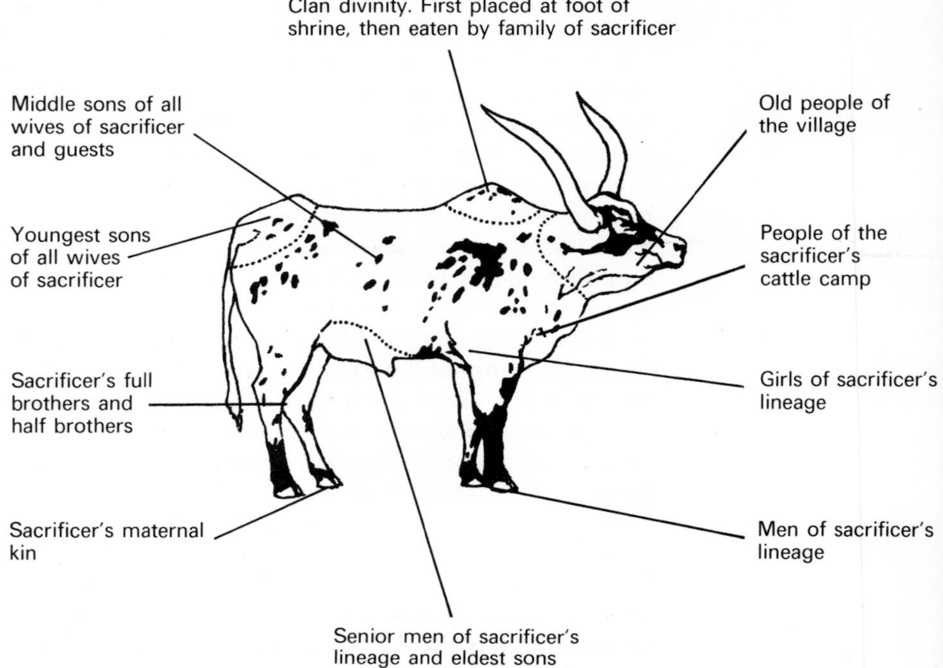

The British scientist Godfrey Lienhardt made this drawing to show how the Dinka people share out the meat of a beast that they have killed as a sacrifice to the spirits in which they believe. As you can see, everyone gets a share

source of pride and rivalry. People in Dinkaland liked to be known by names referring to the cattle they happened to possess. For example, they played singin games where the skill lay in finding new names for themselves.

A man with a fine black ox would begin by being called *ma car*, which means 'black ox' in Dinka language. Then his friends in the cattle camp, whiling away a evening in the season of floods, would start inventing other names for the idea o 'blackness'. Someone would call him *tim atiep* 'shade of a tree'; someone else, going a step further, would think of *kor acom* 'looks for snails', because the blac ibis of Dinkaland does just that. Someone else, still more inventively, would call him *bun anyeer*, referring to the dark undergrowth where the wild buffalo likes t sleep; or even *arec luk*, 'spoils the meeting', because this is what rain does, and rain comes from dark thunder clouds.

These people were playing a game which classified the owner of a black ox with whatever else was black, or could be thought of as black: the shade of a tre a black bird, a dark rain cloud. This ordering of things and creatures into classes, according to their use, appearance, or behaviour, was common to most African peoples. They were persistent classifiers. For them, classifying things and creatures was a kind of practical science. In this way they gathered and sorted useful knowledge, so as to apply it to the problems of everyday life.

The Karimojong, for example, were experts in the quality of pastureland. They studied and named various grasses of their country according to the grazing valu of each type of grass. As they were always short of surface water, they learned to detect those natural features of rock or soil which showed that there was water beneath the surface. They gave a name to each type of rock or soil according to how much water would be beneath its surface. They gave such names to every part of their land. They used these names to draw up grazing plans for every season. Peoples who practised other types of farming did the same. They classified plants, shrubs and trees according to whether these grew or bore fruit in the dry season or the wet season. They studied soils for their crop-bearing values. They listed the habits of animals, insects, and fishes. They were interested in types of cloud formation in order to understand the weather. They knew a great deal about the mineral ores in stones and rocks.

Making the land yield food

As they knew their lands so thoroughly, they were able to invent or develop different methods of raising food.

In the tropical and sub-tropical regions the most important of these methods were for three main types of country: for the use of forest country, of open woodland, and of almost treeless grassland, with lesser variations in between.

African forest farms may look strange to visitors who know nothing of the tropics. Often these forest farms consist of little plots scattered in the shade of high trees. At first sight they may seem to be without any plan or system. In fact, no people in the past ever developed better forest farms. Closer inspection reveals a skilful arrangement of crops so as to give shelter from the burning sun, take advantage of hillslope drainage, benefit from the fertilising compost of fallen leaves. Root crops such as yams or cassava, kinds of African potato, are shaded by broadfronded bananas; while bananas are shaded by the lofty umbrella of tall trees.

Such methods were modified for open woodland farming. Here the main problem, especially in grassland country with very few trees, was the poor quality of the soil, nearly always shallow and soon exhausted. Farming peoples in this type of country relied whenever they could on a mixed agriculture of cultivation and cattle. But the presence of tsetse fly often prevented them from raising stock.

They found they could grow crops in the same fields for two or three years running; then they had to leave their farms, for a period of years, so that the soil could rest and recover its fertility. For this reason they developed what is called 'shifting cultivation'. A village community would 'rotate' from place to place, within its own neighbourhood, during a 'circuit' of some fifteen years. For two or three years, for example, they would farm at Village One. Then they would move to Village Two, leaving the land round Village One to rest. After another two or three years they would move to Village Three; and so on until they came back to Village One again.

When Europeans first began travelling around Africa, they once more misunderstood what they saw. They thought that much of the open farming country was not being used by Africans, when in fact it was only being rested. Europeans took this 'unoccupied' land, and were indignant when Africans told them it was not unoccupied but was only lying fallow.

Even this 'shifting cultivation' could not be carried on without some kind of fertiliser. African farmers used cattle manure when they had any, but in certain areas they found that wood-ash was better. They obtained ash by felling and burning trees and shrubs. Supplies of wood for burning might last for two or three years round a village; then the farmers would make their periodical move, and leave the stumps of trees to grow again for fifteen years or so. Europeans called this 'slash and burn', and thought it a foolish or wasteful way to farm. But European experts nowadays agree that it was probably as good a method of fertilising these poor soils as could be found in times before the development of artificial fertiliser.

These methods were possible because Africans generally suffered from no shortage of land. The size of African populations, at least until the nineteenth century, was about right for these methods. And the fact that the methods were efficient, in their place and time, is shown by the steady growth of African populations. The only peoples who suffered hunger were those whose homelands were particularly poor in natural resources, or those who were struck by severe drought or locust swarms.

Grassland was usually free of the deadly tsetse fly, so it was almost always use for cattle raising, though most grassland peoples managed to grow a little grain and other foods as well. Cattle raising depended on an intensive study of cattle habits, and of grass and water resources. As with the Karimojong and the Dinka, close study of nature was always necessary.

Finding minerals and making metals

To make metals, you have to do four things. First, you have to find the rock that contains the ore of the metal you want to make. Secondly, you then have to dig this ore-bearing rock out of the ground and break it into manageable pieces. Thirdly, you have to pack these bits of rock into a furnace which can melt the ore and so separate it from the rock in which it is contained; this is called smelting. Finally, you have to take the smelted metal and work it into the things you want. This is called smithing or forging.

Goldfields occurred in West Africa in two chief regions. They were found in th land of Wangara which produced gold for the ancient empires of Ghana and Mali: and in the country of Ashanti in the central part of modern Ghana, important for the gold trade after 1350. Experts have calculated that many hundred tons of gold were produced by these West African regions before abou 1500, with perhaps as much again between 1500 and the start of modern gold-mining around 1900. Some of it was panned or washed from rivers; some of it was mined. All the modern gold mines of West Africa are at places where gold-bearing ore was found by Africans in the past, although nowadays machinery ha made it possible to dig much deeper shafts. The same is true of the gold ore-deposits of Middle Africa (mainly Rhodesia, or, as Africans call it, Zimbabwe).

Smelting and smithing

These large amounts of gold, as of other metals, were produced by the labour of many hands. The work was slow and hard. Mine shafts had to be dug with picks of hardened iron. Mineral-bearing ores had to be crushed by hand tools. Smeltir had to be done in small furnaces which could produce only a few pounds of me at each 'smelt'. It is another fact which speaks for African inventive skill that the basic principle of these furnaces was no different from those of modern times.

The furnaces were of varying shapes, from about 50 centimetres to 2 metres high, and made usually of earth taken from anthills. This is a very solid kind of earth, and forms a good material for containing heat. African ants make 'hills' tha can rise to six metres high or more, so there was no shortage of such earth.

Furnaces were packed with alternate layers of charcoal and ore, and a fire was lit beneath the lowest layer of charcoal. But a fire by itself would never have produced enough heat. It was necessary to apply a strong draught. In supplying this draught African furnaces worked on the same principle as modern types. They were 'blast furnaces', if only of simple design: forced-draught furnaces through which air was pumped by bellows. These bellows were worked by hand or foot and made of goat- or sheepskin. They were connected by a little clay pipe to a hole in the bottom of the furnace, where the fire was lit inside.

Working steadily at the bellows the smelter produced an intense heat inside his furnace. When this was at a certain point the layers of ore-bearing rock began to 'melt', and, as they did, the raw metal took shape in a soft red-hot mass. Waste material slid down in half-liquid form to the bottom of the furnace where, when the fire was out, it cooled into solid lumps of 'slag'. Then the smelter broke up his furnace and took out the lumps of metal in it. These he handed to a smith – or did the work himself, if he was also a smith – who worked and hammered these lumps into spearheads, hoe-heads, arrowheads and other things. In these techniques of production, the best African metal-workers had little to learn from any other people till the age of modern machinery began.

Sometimes the job of the smith was to produce pieces of metal that were suitable for trade. For example, a smith might make iron bars for sale. In the lands of old Zimbabwe and Katanga, smiths poured copper into moulds shaped as a cross. These 'cross-ingots' became the standard form in which copper was sold to the Swahili merchants of the East Coast. Smiths also used these ingots to produce fine jewellery. Some of them knew how to harden gold so as to be able to beat it into little sheets no more than five-thousandths of an inch in thickness, and to use this 'gold plate' to cover wooden objects such as the sceptres of kings. Even a gold beater of today, using modern tools, would find it difficult to get his 'plate' as thin as this.

Another of their skills was that of making alloys of copper with tin or other metals to produce brass and occasionally bronze. Much of the fine sculpture of West Africa was made from these alloys. This sculpture was created by a process of 'casting', of transforming liquid metal into hardened objects, which scientists call the 'lost wax' method.

West Africans may have learned this method from the Kushites of Meroë, who may in turn have learned it from Ancient Egypt. However they learned it, they certainly began using it many centuries ago. Some of the rooms of the palace of the kings of Benin, for example, were covered with large plaques or rectangles of brass or bronze which portray a wide range of scenes from everyday life, including figures of visiting Portuguese soldiers and ambassadors. Still earlier, before 1400, the sculptors of Ife, in Yorubaland, used the same 'lost wax' method for their superb metal figures.

It was a method which demanded skill and patience, but it could produce fine art of an extreme delicacy and lightness of metal, and in an endless range of shapes and styles. First the artist modelled his object in a special kind of clay. This 'core' he baked in a furnace till it was hard. Then he covered this model with bees' wax in the exact outward shape that he wanted to create. When the wax was hard he covered the whole object with a mould of clay, leaving little pipes at certain points, some at the top and some at the bottom. Into the top pipes he poured molten brass or bronze. This entered the space between the clay core and the outer covering of clay, melting the wax which flowed out and was 'lost' through the bottom pipes. Once the metal had cooled the artist knocked away the outer covering, removed the clay 'core' from inside the metal shape, and gently hammered the casting so as to smooth any rough edges.

A modern photograph of the cloth market in the city of Kano in northern Nigeria. Kano is a big centre for the manufacture of hand-made textiles, some of which you see here

Spinning, dyeing, weaving

When the Portuguese began trading with West Africans, around 1500, they were impressed by the fineness of African cotton cloth, and by the brilliant 'fast colours' that Africans were able to dye into it, especially blue. 'Fast colours' in dyeing are those that will not 'run' when you wash the cloth. This requires a technique which Europeans did not then possess. The Portuguese, as we saw in

Chapter 5, began importing 'African blue' for sale in their markets at home.

Even three centuries later, around 1800, a British scientist in the West African country of Sierra Leone noted that African cottons were being dyed in several colours which 'are vivid and permanent, especially blue, of a kind equal to or superior to the finest blues of Europe'. Here was another technique which Africans had mastered through their detailed observation of nature. They knew the plants that could yield these 'fast dyes', and they understood how to use them.

Cotton was grown in several parts of Africa, but there was never enough of it for all the people, who often had to go almost naked for want of clothing. There was a great shortage, in other words, of cheap cloth. That is why large quantities of cheap cotton cloth were imported to East Africa, from India, in the days before Europeans sailed into the Indian Ocean in 1498. It is also why, in later times, Europeans sent to Africa large quantities of cheap cloth from India, which they had conquered, and, later again, from their own factories in Europe. Even today, Africans who can afford it prefer to wear their own cloths for important occasions, or for dining with friends, and to use European clothes for ordinary wear.

Another luxury cloth was the famed *kente* of the Ashanti weavers, a glittering material whose brilliant threads of blue and green are inter-woven with gold thread to make rich and heavy robes. Anyone who visits modern Ghana, still the home of kente, will admire the splendour of these garments, worn by men and women with gold ornaments and leather sandals, combining dignity and comfort.

THE ART OF LIVING

The art of living is more than the technology which produces things. It is also concerned with activities which produce ideas, give voice to thoughts and feelings, tell the drama of mankind. These cultural activities are the work of thinkers and poets, to whom Africans have given an honoured place.

Books and writing

Ancient Africa had considerable achievements in the development of writing, notably the picture hieroglyphs of Egypt and the alphabetical script of the Kushites of Meroë. Most other Africans had no knowledge of writing, or any use for it, until the development of long-distance trade or royal government brought new needs. Many of them then learned the use of Arabic script from Muslims, and of Latin (European) script from Christians.

Muslim Africans developed schools of learning, and wrote Arabic books of history, theology and other studies, as well as using Arabic for business and diplomatic correspondence. For them, Arabic was the scholar's language as Latin was in Europe. Then Africans, like Europeans, began to write their own languages, using Arabic letters as Europeans used Latin letters.

We do not know exactly when they began doing this. Historians believe that the change to writing African languages, instead of Arabic, may have begun as early as the sixteenth century. It was certainly in full swing by the eighteenth century among the Swahili along the East African coast, and among some of the peoples of West Africa. There appeared in this way a group of African languages written in Arabic letters, at first for religious purposes. This kind of African literature is known as *ajami*. It includes books written in languages such as Swahili, Hausa, Mandinka, Fulani and Yoruba.

Early Christian missionaries introduced a few coastal peoples to the writing of Portuguese or English. This was a minor development, because Christianity did not become widespread in Africa until after about 1850. But the national library Lisbon still has twenty-two letters written in Portuguese to the kings of Portugal by African secretaries of the King of Kongo, Affonso I, between 1512 and 1540. We also know from Portuguese and English records that King Esigie of Benin, who reigned soon after 1500, and some of his officials could read and write Portuguese, although none of their writings have survived.

Later on, during the nineteenth and twentieth centuries, European missionarie and African Christians began making Latin (European) alphabets for a number o African languages, and these are now widely used. At the same time a small number of Africans were able to get European education. These were to play a leading part, during the colonial period, in the efforts to win back African independence. Of all these languages now being written in one or other forms o European alphabet, among the most important are Swahili in East Africa, and Hausa in West Africa.

Spoken literature

Whether or not they wrote their own languages, Africans possessed an oral, or spoken, literature. They had their popular poets, singers of songs, religious orators. Passed down from one generation to another, much of this spoken literature is very old. Taught in special schools, it tells the story of outstanding men and women, of peace and war, of the triumphs and trials of everyday life, often in fascinating detail.

Proverbs and popular sayings were a branch of this spoken literature. African cultures have been rich in these. Often they illustrate how life used to be. Thus th Ashanti used to say that 'A slave who knows how to serve well will succeed to h master's property', a proverb which shows that the meaning of the word 'slave' i Ashanti was different from the meaning it has acquired in the modern world.

Many of these proverbs are folk wisdom that everyone can recognise. 'A crab,' say the Ashanti, 'does not give birth to a bird', or, as we might say 'You can't mak a silk purse out of a sow's ear'. Or, in reply to someone who is boasting of skills h may not have, 'It is hard to throw a stone at a lizard on a pot' because, if you do, you are more likely to break the pot than hit the lizard. Or, mocking someone wh has said something that is obvious, 'No one following an elephant needs to knoc the dew off the grass'.

Fables were tremendously popular. Often they were about animals and insects whose habits were compared with man's, and were told as shrewd or moralising comments on men's behaviour. Some of them were re-born in America in tales like those about Uncle Remus and Brer Rabbit.

Ashanti children particularly loved stories about Ananse, the Wise Spider. Her is one of them:

Once upon a time, Ananse the Wise Spider thought that the world's wisdom was going to waste; people simply would not use it. So Ananse decided to do something wise about this. He set about collecting all the wisdom in the world. When he thought that he had collected it all, he put it in a pot for safe keeping. But where should he keep the pot? There could be nowhere better, Ananse thought, than the top of a tall palm tree. He tied the pot to himself and began climbing the slender trunk to its tuft of palm-leaves swaying forty feet above the ground.

But he had tied on the pot in front of him, and this of course was not wise. The pot got in Ananse's way. He went on upwards, but when he was half-way to the top, he heard his young son call up to him: 'Father, if you'd really got all the wisdom in the world up there with you, you'd have tied that pot on your back.'

Now this made Ananse very angry because he had to admit to himself that his son was right. Besides, he was tired by all his labour of collecting wisdom and climbing up the palm. He took off the pot and threw it to the ground. It broke and all the wisdom was scattered. Then men came running and picked up what each could find.

And this shows you, says the teller of the story, why some people have a lot of wisdom and others have none at all. But it also shows you that even the wisest person can do a silly thing, just like Ananse.

Proverbs were often used to teach young people about their world and how they should behave. 'A person running by himself,' say the Luyia of Kenya, 'thinks he is the fastest runner.' In other words, a person's opinion of himself should be formed by comparing what he or she can do with what others can do, and boasting will soon be shown up when put to the test of competition. 'Don't laugh at a boat in trouble on the waves of Lake Nyanza,' the wide inland sea beside which the Luyia live, 'because one of your parents may be in it.' No one, that is, should look light-heartedly on the misfortunes of others. Other sayings embodied African attitudes to law and community life. 'The law is blind,' say the Tswana of Botswana in southern Africa, 'it even eats its owner', meaning that judges have to obey the law like anyone else.

This proverbial wisdom and spoken literature can tell us much about the everyday life of Africans. We see them teaching themselves the rules of sensible behaviour and of law, recalling the successes or disasters of the past, learning lessons from these memories, laughing at their own failings or rebuking their own mistakes, weaving their civilisation into a many-coloured fabric of everyday life.

Drums and drama

Many peoples, especially those of West and Middle Africa, had fine sculptors in wood, clay, ivory, and metal. But among the great arts of Africa the most popular were music and dancing. Flutes, guitars, xylophones and sometimes horns were used and enjoyed, but Africans above all loved the drum and excelled in playing it. Drums were for amusement, drama, dancing and for religious and political ceremonies. They were also for sending messages.

Every community, however small, had its drummers. At sundown in the tropics, around six o'clock, they would take their seats in the village 'square', or maybe a clearing in the forest, and tap out their greetings, warnings, or other messages to the next village. Here is a translation from Twi of a New Year's greeting transmitted by the drummers of the Akan of Ghana:

Every community, however small, had its drums and drummers. This drum is from Lesotho

The year has come round:
Long live! Long live! Long live!
Live to a good old age, King:
Earth showers her blessings on you
May years be added to your years.

But drums were mainly used to beat out dance rhythms of great complexity and frequency of change. With a vivid originality of style and musical method, these rhythms were also used for singing. They have since spread across the world in the music of jazz and the blues.

Through their drums, Africans celebrated religious festivals, gave thanks to the gods for good harvests, poked fun at their neighbours, displayed talents for miming and dancing, and generally enjoyed themselves. Many peoples loved these various kinds of drama, often presented with frightening or amazing masks and robes which were applauded when well-made and used, and condemned when not.

Along the creeks of the Niger Delta, for example, there lived and still live a trading people called the Kalabari. They are particularly fond of drama. In the past and still to some extent today, each Kalabari village had its own drama society, and put on as many as twenty or thirty different plays every year. These plays were mainly for fun, though they were also connected with Kalabari religion. Before each year's drama season began, a party of Kalabari would take a canoe and paddle out to a special creek called the 'Beach of the Water Spirits'. There they would hold a religious ceremony and ask the water spirits, who were the spiritual patrons of Kalabari drama, to bless their plays. They asked the spirits to give the drummers the gift of sharp hearing and of speed in tapping the drum, to encourage the dancers to have nimble legs and graceful gestures. Then players would gather before their village audience and start with a play which made fun of some particularly fat warrior, clumsily wielding a spear, or of an idle trader who threw away his money on high living, or of a busy-body 'witch doctor' who was always looking round for bad behaviour.

Nobody could take part in these plays until he or she had gone through much training. Often the training began with boys and girls who were encouraged to join a junior drama society. There they would be coached by the grown-ups, and the best of them would be asked to join the seniors' club as soon as they were old enough.

Confidence and self-respect

All these aspects of the art of living, whether religious beliefs, moral teachings, systems of law, methods of government, skills in using or making materials, and much else besides, made up the cultures of the Africans. These cultures were and often still are very different from our own. Without machines or modern cities, or most of the things we take for granted, they were calm and slow-moving, free of rush and hurry, geared to the changing seasons, interested in little more than local affairs.

Yet if the world they knew was a small one, it could give a lot of amusement and happiness. There might be many wars, but they were brief and did little permanent damage. There might be many times of trouble, but they were mostly of a kind that men could face without despair. Unambitious and easy going, these cultures had no place for big differences in poverty and wealth. Except in some of the large kingdoms, they were cultures in which the members of a community felt direct responsibility for one another, and left nobody in trouble to suffer alone.

These cultures greatly varied from each other in their details and their history. We have seen how this came about, beginning in distant times when Africans were able to multiply in numbers, because of tropical farming and other inventions, and form many different communities and cultures. We have looked at a few of these and seen what they were like. Each of these communities, far more numerous than the few mentioned here, was able to feel at home in its country. Confident in its beliefs and teachings it could boldly face the trials of everyday life. This life was often hard, but it could also be a pleasant one.

This was the civilisation from which the black peoples of the West Indies and the Americas came. And we know that their children and their grandchildren for several generations, and sometimes for many generations, kept warm the memory of their African homeland, and looked back to it as a place they longed to see again. For they had come from cultures that were strong in self-respect, only to find themselves in a trans-Atlantic world where every man's hand seemed turned against them.

STRENGTH BUT ALSO WEAKNESSES

Mankind in Africa created many states, many cultures, many different patterns of everyday life. But all these cultures took shape according to the same basic rules of survival and growth. They all belonged to the same broad process of African development. Shaped by its own problems and solutions this broad development was special to Africa. The result is that Africa's heritage is different from that of other peoples.

Yet from another point of view this black heritage is just the same as that of other peoples. This is because the African heritage, however special its development, arose from the same deep underlying processes as all other cultures and civilisations. Like them, it appeared because men learned how to grow food, work metals, build settlements. Like them, it grew because men learned how to improve food supplies, how to develop groups of craftsmen who specialised in making tools, canoes, music, other useful things; and, with division of labour leading to division of society, how to evolve new patterns of community, new methods of government.

All civilisations, including African civilisation, began and grew according to the same laws of human development. They call for the same respect as any other. Why, then, have people outside Africa so often had contempt for African culture? Why have Africans been called savage and second-rate?

Partly, we know already, because of the ignorance of the outside world, but partly for another reason. This other reason lay in one great difference between the black world and the white. Arising after about 1650, this was a difference in productive power.

Hand versus machine

After about 1650 there began to appear, between the black world and the white, a 'power gap' which had great consequences. The first went on producing wealth in much the same ways as before; the second changed and improved its methods.

Europe became the centre of a progressive revolution in the means of producing wealth. Especially after about 1750 one invention led to another, one improvement in machinery gave rise to a new improvement, one advance in mechanical science opened the path to a further advance. Europeans developed production by machine. Surpassing the Chinese, who had previously led the world in mechanical invention, the more advanced among the Europeans carried everything before them. With each new invention they added to their power. They went to the East and learned its secrets. They went to the West and penetrated the Americas. They went to Africa and took its labour.

For their part, as we have seen, the Africans had mastered their continent and learned to use its natural wealth. But their methods of producing this wealth remained the methods of hand-production. This weakness in methods of production – by hand, while Europeans were producing by machinery – was not because of any natural failing in enterprise or intelligence. It was because the Africans, like many other peoples, lacked the conditions which caused and enabled Europeans to make the shift from hand to machine; conditions that were peculiar to European history.

The 'power gap' widens

When Europeans first sailed to Africa there was no such 'power gap', or little that mattered. If the admirals of Portugal were able to ravage the Swahili cities of East Africa, it was largely because they came as pirates, took the cities by surprise, and were ruthless. Elsewhere they had to sue for trade and friendship with fair words. Coming after them, other Europeans had to do the same. If they could produce some things by machinery, such as guns, there were other kinds of production in which Africans excelled them.

Yet the 'power gap' steadily widened. Muzzle-loading guns might be poor weapons when compared with the rifles of later times, but it was only the Europeans who could make them. Africans bought them in large numbers, and grew skilled in using them, but they had to rely on Europeans for their supply of gunpowder as well as guns. And whenever it came to fighting, as a king of Dahomey said in the nineteenth century, in the end 'he who makes the powder wins the war'.

Ocean-going ships might be small and slow, yet it was the Europeans not the Africans who commanded the oceans.

By 1800 the white civilisations of the western world had become far stronger than the Africans in the power to make goods and wage war. Only towards 1900 did a few African peoples begin to change their methods of production. Trying to defend the western Sudan against French invaders in the 1890s, a famous African leader called Samori Turay employed more than three hundred metal smiths who were able, it was said, to make twelve guns a week and about three hundred cartridges. These guns, the French found, worked well. But the French could make far more, and better. Samori's armies went down in defeat.

. . . and takes effect

Many developments came from this widening gap in productive power. High on the list were European expansion in the Americas, the rise of the Atlantic slave trade to provide labour for the New World, and thus the forced transfer to the Americas of millions of blacks.

Why was it Africa that supplied the labour for American plantations and mines? How was it that so many free men and women from Africa were chained to slavery across the seas? Where lay the menacing trail of events which caused this massive export of Africans? These questions lie at the roots of modern history. They point to the foundations of the world we know today.

There are many detailed answers. They are to be found in a thousand tales of raid and piracy, of deals struck in the creeks and seaways of the African coastland, of courage and resistance as well as cruelty and greed. To find our way through this maze of men and events, we have to go back to the early times of European contact with Africa. We have to watch the wooden ships of Europe, battered by ocean travel, as they thrust their bows towards the African shore. We have to listen to their captains as they land through the surf and speak with the Africans who meet them there. We have to inspect the deals these men made with each other, and the reasons why they made these deals and the consequences of these deals. We have to look at the profit and loss on either side. Then it will be clear why things happened as they did.

7 Africa and the western world: the history of the slave trade

THE EARLY YEARS

The first European ship to reach African tropical waters was little larger than one of the emperor of Mali's middle-sized canoes. But this small ship made history. She cleared from the port of Lisbon in 1441 under Captain Antony Gonsalves, 'a very young man', say the Portuguese records, fired with a nobleman's ambition t win the approval of his royal master, Prince Henry of Portugal. Gonsalves's orde were to sail far down the African coast and, if he could, return from those unknown seas with a cargo of animal skins and the oil of 'sea wolves', or, as we should say, sea lions. Navigational skill and courage would be needed. Success would be praised. But Gonsalves was not satisfied. He was after another cargo.

Raiding from the sea

He took his ship a long way south, using the newly developed sailing rig of the Portuguese that would enable him to sail home against contrary winds. Only on other European vessel, another Portuguese seven years earlier, had taken this route; Gonsalves went farther and probably reached the coast of what is nowadays Mauritania.

Gonsalves's voyage

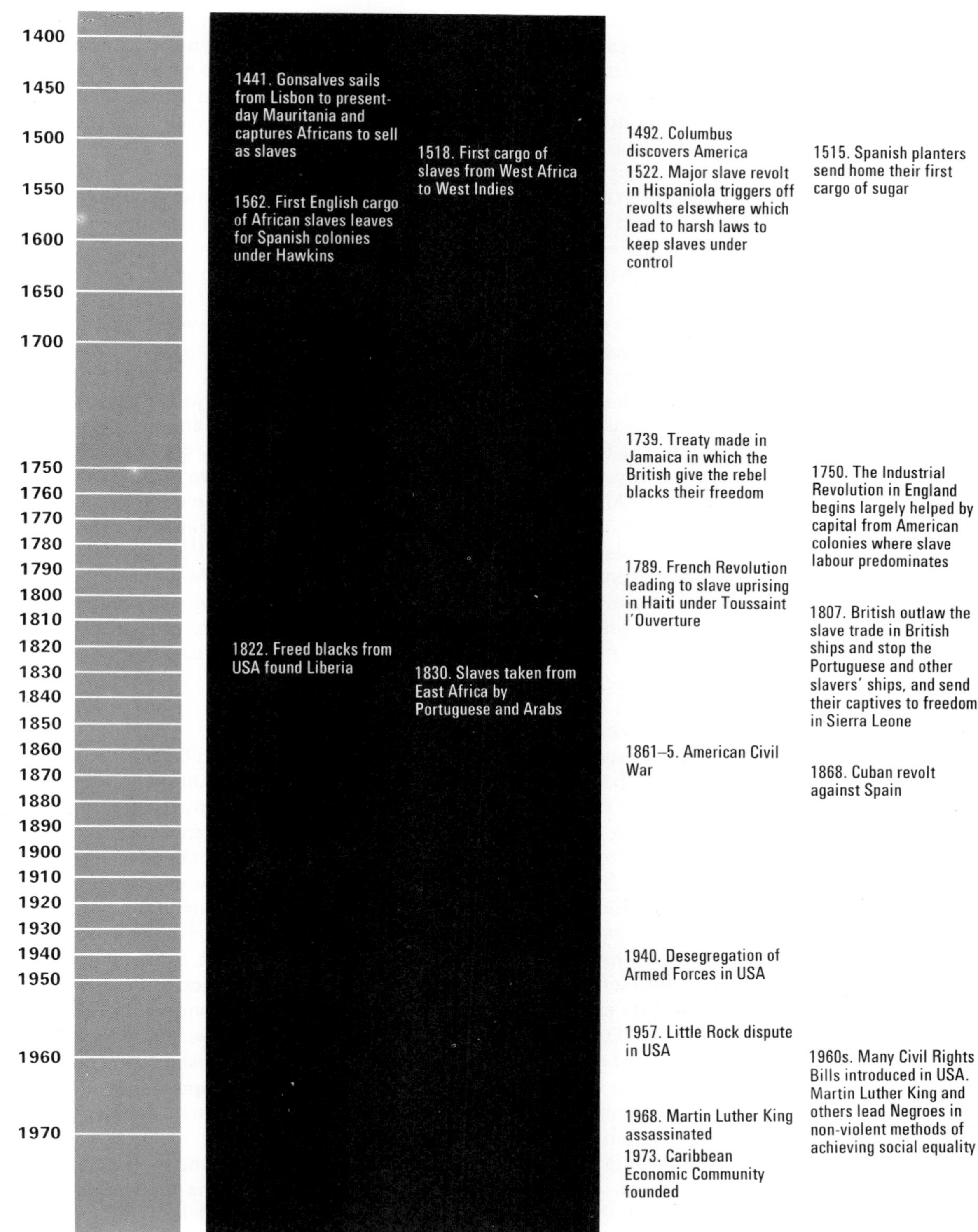
AD 1400
1450
1500
1550
1600
1650
1700
1750
1760
1770
1780
1790
1800
1810
1820
1830
1840
1850
1860
1870
1880
1890
1900
1910
1920
1930
1940
1950
1960
1970
1441. Gonsalves sails from Lisbon to present-day Mauritania and captures Africans to sell as slaves
1518. First cargo of slaves from West Africa to West Indies
1562. First English cargo of African slaves leaves for Spanish colonies under Hawkins
1822. Freed blacks from USA found Liberia
1830. Slaves taken from East Africa by Portuguese and Arabs
1492. Columbus discovers America
1522. Major slave revolt in Hispaniola triggers off revolts elsewhere which lead to harsh laws to keep slaves under control
1739. Treaty made in Jamaica in which the British give the rebel blacks their freedom
1789. French Revolution leading to slave uprising in Haiti under Toussaint l'Ouverture
1861–5. American Civil War
1940. Desegregation of Armed Forces in USA
1957. Little Rock dispute in USA
1968. Martin Luther King assassinated
1973. Caribbean Economic Community founded
1515. Spanish planters send home their first cargo of sugar
1750. The Industrial Revolution in England begins largely helped by capital from American colonies where slave labour predominates
1807. British outlaw the slave trade in British ships and stop the Portuguese and other slavers' ships, and send their captives to freedom in Sierra Leone
1868. Cuban revolt against Spain
1960s. Many Civil Rights Bills introduced in USA. Martin Luther King and others lead Negroes in non-violent methods of achieving social equality

Near the line of ocean surf along that bare seaboard, then a most solitary place, young Gonsalves brought his ship to anchor, and made a speech to his crew. 'How fine a thing it would be,' he told them, 'if we, who have come all this way just for skins and oil, could now have the luck to take our Prince the first captives from this land.' That would be a deed, he said, such as would make their fortunes back in Lisbon.

They went ashore in the night, armed with spears and swords, and at dawn saw footprints in the sand. These they tracked for a while without coming up with anyone, and were about to turn back in disappointment when 'they saw a naked man following a camel, with two spears in his hand'. Shouting with excitement, the Portuguese ran after him. Overtaken, this African turned to meet the Portuguese 'right worthily, and began to defend himself as best he could, and bravely'. But one of the Portuguese threw a spear. This wounded the African, and the Portuguese got hold of him. Then 'as they were going on their way, they saw a black woman', and they grabbed her too.

Back at their ship again with two captives, they were joined by another Portuguese vessel, likewise commanded by 'a youthful knight very keen and valiant'. The two captains decided on a joint raid. If they could take two prisoners why not more? They led their men ashore and raided two unsuspecting camps, killing four Africans and snatching ten more prisoners, 'men, women, and boys'.

Two years later the same 'youthful knight' who had joined Gonsalves came down the coast a second time. This time he returned to Portugal with twenty-nine men and women taken from canoes along the shore of Mauritania. Lisbon investors grew interested. They got together and financed a bigger expedition. It rewarded them by bringing back 235 prisoners for sale in Portuguese slave markets. In this way the business in African slaves opened a tragic new chapter in history.

White slaves and black

These early raids for black captives who could be sold in Europe have to be seen against the background of their times. By 1441, when Antony Gonsalves sailed out from the Portuguese coast and swung his helm boldly to the southward, the slave trade in Europe was already very old. It went back to Roman times, and beyond that to ancient Greece before the Romans. It remained an important part of everyday life in Europe until the close of the Middle Ages, and even later.

This was mostly a trade in European slaves. These usually came from the Slav countries of eastern Europe because Slav peoples were converted to Christianity later than other Europeans; and Christians, like Muslims, saw nothing wrong about enslaving non-believers. It was a trade not confined to Europe. Christian states, especially the city-states of Italy such as Genoa and Venice, sold large numbers of European slaves to the kings of Egypt and western Asia. And when the supply of non-Christians ran short, they bought Christians and sold them too. The Genoese were so active in selling Christians that Pope Martin V, as late as 1425, launched an order of excommunication against them, expelling the Genoese from the Church.

But the fate of these captives was very different from the trans-Atlantic slaves of later times. As in Africa, they became 'rightless persons' who could be bought and sold, or given as gifts, to serve as domestic staff or skilled craftsmen. They could rise to positions of authority, marry into their masters' families, work themselves to freedom. They were well cared for because they were expensive. Only the rich could afford them. So Gonsalves and his fellow-captains, bringing back African prisoners to Lisbon, saw no crime in what they had done, and knew they had valuable cargoes.

Like the white slaves of Europe, the black slaves of that period suffered from homesickness and loss of civil rights, but generally they had little else to fear. Lisbon records of the time claim that Portuguese buyers

> made no difference between them and the free servants born in Portugal. They trained young blacks in skilled crafts. Those whom they considered able to manage property they set free and married to Portuguese women, treating them as members of the family.

No doubt many captured Africans were less fortunate. The point is that so long as the slave trade stayed in Europe and Africa it was little more than a traffic in household servants and craftsmen, while the living conditions of the slaves were much the same as the majority of poor people in those times.

Besides this, raiding soon gave way to peaceful trade along the coast. Awakened to their new danger from the sea, Africans could and did defend themselves. Then their kings and chiefs, already used to giving or exchanging their own 'rightless persons', began selling some of these for European goods. An African–European partnership began. It was a fairly small business. So long as things remained as they were, it stayed small. But things did not remain as they were.

The rush for Eldorado

European discovery of the Americas changed everything. Financed by the king and queen of Spain, Columbus sailed from Europe on 3 August 1492, and made his first landfall in the Caribbean sixty-nine days later. Being the first European captain to cross the Atlantic since the forgotten days of the Vikings, Columbus had no idea where he was. He thought that he had reached the eastern outskirts of India, and that the Carib peoples whom he found were Indians.

Pushing on, Columbus came to a 'very large island which the Indians call Cuba'. But beyond that, they told him, was a much bigger island 'which I believe to be Cipango [Japan]'. Of course, he failed to find Japan. But east of Cuba he found the large island which he named Hispaniola, nowadays divided between Haiti and the Dominican Republic.

This 'Spanish Indies' soon received another name: Eldorado, the Golden Land. Columbus had little luck in finding gold, though he looked for it in every island that he reached. But he did find some. He found enough to whet the appetite of adventurers back in Spain. The consequences were great and terrible. Out from Spain, westward across the ocean, there poured a tumultuous flood of settlers and prospectors. This was the gold rush that swept away, in the years that followed, most of all that the native peoples of these lands had built and cherished, as well as destroying countless lives.

The adventurers stole and burned and killed; but above all else they stole. In 1503 the king of Spain's income from the 'Indies' was only 8,000 ducats, Spain's golden pounds of that time. Nine years later, in 1512, it had increased to 90,000 ducats. Then came the Spanish conquest of the rich civilisations of Mexico and Peru, turning the dream of Eldorado into a new nightmare of violence. Spain became a gold and silver warehouse stuffed with the wealth of the Americas, an the king was its owner. But the king's subjects who had emigrated to the 'Indies fared less well. Most of them found little gold or silver; many turned to farming. And since these colonists considered work beneath their dignity, they hunted 'Indians' and forced them into plantation slavery. Enslaved 'Indians' died in hug numbers; soon the supply of them ran short. The king and his financiers in Spai began sending out European slaves, but there were not enough of these either. The rocketing demand for labour in the 'Indies' would therefore have to be met from some other source. Where else to find slaves? The answer was not long in coming. Spanish planters in the Caribbean sent home their first cargo of sugar ir 1515. Three years later they received their first delivery of slaves brought direct from West Africa.

From then on and for centuries, 'King Sugar' and afterwards his no less grim companions, 'King Tobacco' and 'King Cotton', presided over something that history had never seen before. This was the enforced transfer of millions of peop from one continent to another. To meet the settlers' need for labour, a new slave trade was brought into being, the slave trade with Africa. And with some early exceptions, this was no longer the tolerant slavery of the past, but a new slavery without relief or comfort, often a slavery without hope.

Ways to get slaves

After Spain and Portugal, other European nations competed for their share in th spoils of discovery and conquest. The lure of the 'Indies' soon drew the English and the French after the Spaniards and the Portuguese. In 1562 an English captain took the first English cargo of African slaves across the Atlantic for sale t Spanish colonists. It was an incident that can also tell us something about the early involvement of Africans in the business of exporting other Africans.

John Hawkins sailed from England to the small coastal kingdoms of Sierra Leone, now a modern republic. Rather surprisingly in the circumstances, his shi was called the *Jesus*. Like Gonsalves more than a century earlier, Hawkins planned to get other goods than gold and ivory. He knew that African captives were selling for a high price in Hispaniola.

Reaching Sierra Leone, he began by attacking a Portuguese ship and seizing two hundred African captives intended for Portuguese planters in Brazil. Next h found that two of the kings of Sierra Leone were at war with a third king. These two kings asked Hawkins for military aid. Hawkins led a party of English soldiers to battle alongside the troops of the two kings. They attacked a well-defended town and took it after a sharp fight. In return for this aid the two kings gave Hawkins 260 prisoners of war. With the *Jesus* full of captives, Hawkins sailed fo the slave markets of Hispaniola.

In ways such as this the early Atlantic trade in slaves, or rather in captives, developed from outright piracy to a partnership. Slaving captains still fell back o piracy now and then, sending their crews ashore to kidnap men and women, bu usually they bought the captives they wanted. African rulers sold their 'rightless persons' in the ordinary run of everyday life, just as Europeans had done for centuries. Later, when the demand for captives grew by leaps and bounds, some of these kings realised what they had done and tried to draw back. But the trade proved too strong for them. African slave labour had become the sinews of the western world. And the western world was not to be denied.

'KING SUGAR' AND HIS PROFITS

Where the Spaniards and Portuguese had led, the British and French, Dutch, Danes and others followed after 1600. Their colonists settled in Caribbean islands captured from the 'Indians' or the Spaniards, and began growing sugar for sale in Europe. Their exports boomed. It seemed there was no limit to the sugar Europe wanted.

But the sugar was grown by black slaves, not white colonists. As they expanded their plantations, the colonists called for more labour. Under 'King Sugar's' tyranny, year after year for more than a century and a half, the West Indies consumed black slaves in millions. It seemed there could never be enough of them to fill the ranks of those who toiled, and of those who died.

The slave trade became very big business. In 1658 the Jamaica whites had 1,400 black slaves; forty years later, growing sugar, they had 40,000. By 1787 there were more than 450,000 black slaves in the British West Indies. The great French sugar colony of Saint Domingue (Haiti) had more than 200,000 slaves in 1763; during the next twenty years its colonists brought in another 100,000.

This vast and unceasing demand for black labour was swollen by the needs of North American colonists. Tobacco as well as sugar became a prized commodity in Europe. But it was sugar that made the great fortunes. The sugar dealers of England and France became the richest men in the world, outshining even kings and princes. They owed their wealth to black labour that was organised for a new system of long-distance trade. Thanks to black labour in the Americas, this new system helped to make Britain and France the strongest trading nations. But the system did more than that. It helped to accumulate capital wealth in Britain and France. And this piling up of capital helped to bring about the revolutionary advance in methods of machine-production, after 1750, which is called the 'industrial revolution'. This was the technological revolution which made it possible for our nation, and then other European nations, to lead the world. It was a leadership gained partly from using the profits of slave labour.

Wealth to Europe

The new system or circuit of trade came to be called the 'triangular trade', because it had three 'sides', and each side yielded a profit.

British and French manufacturers sold their goods to shippers in big Atlantic ports such as Liverpool in England, Glasgow in Scotland, and Nantes in France; metalware, woollen stuffs, cheap cottons, guns and gunpowder. These goods were taken to Africa, mostly to West Africa, where they were exchanged for captives. That was the first side of the trade. It gave a profit to the manufacturers, who sold their goods for more than these goods had cost to make.

The captives were taken across the Atlantic and auctioned in the slave markets. That was the second side of the trade. It gave a profit to the slave-dealers. Every captain aimed to get more money for his captives than he had bought them for.

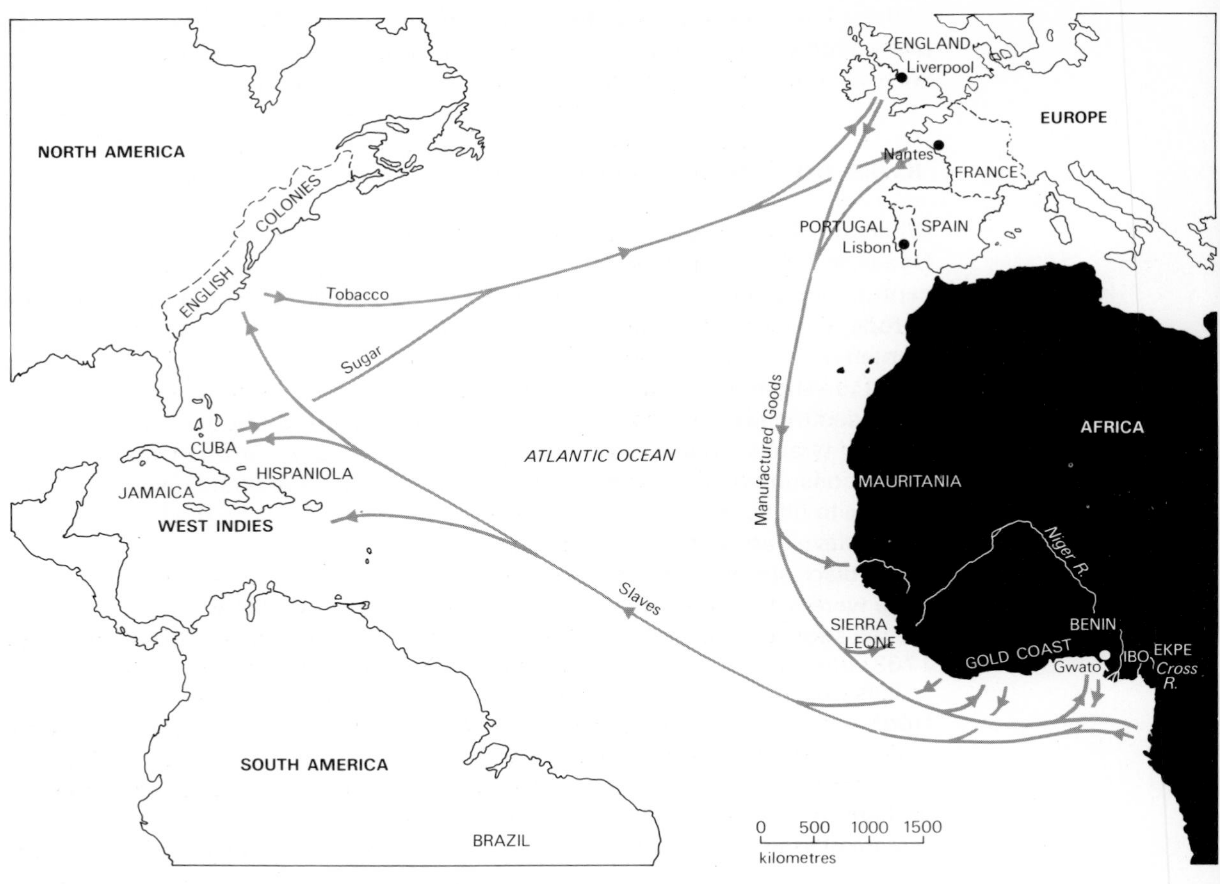

The 'Triangular Trade

With the money they got from slave auctions, the captains bought cargoes of slave-grown sugar and tobacco for sale in Britain and France. This gave a profit the sugar planters as well as to the owners of these cargo ships.

Every ambitious businessman thrust his hand into this sugar barrel. It was not long before new tycoons were operating along all three 'sides' of the trade, whil 'little men', dealing in small quantities, invested their savings in the triangular trade rather as people do today when they buy shares in companies. During the 1720s Britain was importing about half a million tons of sugar every year. By 1800 the figure had climbed to two and a half million tons a year. In 1719 the great slaving port of Liverpool had only 18,000 tons of registered shipping. By 1792 this had grown to 260,000 tons.

With an expanding home market, there came a demand for large quantities of cheap everyday goods, also for sale abroad. This set men to inventing machines which could make more goods, but could also make them at lower cost. In 1733 Kay invented a mechanical shuttle for rapid weaving. In 1738 Paul added a mechanical roller for rapid spinning. In 1768 Hargreaves made 'the prince of inventions' of those days, and gave Britain a worldwide lead in the manufacture of cheap cottons for sale at home and abroad. This was the 'spinning jenny', a machine with which a cotton-operator could work many spindles at the same time. And so it went on. In 1803 Trevithick built the first steam locomotive and opened the way for another 'revolution', this time in transport.

These were the years when the 'power gap' between the white world and the black world began widening to a gulf. The power of the white world forged ahead; that of the black world, indeed of all other parts of the world, fell far behind.

Yet it was not a case of all gain on one side and all loss on the other. History is not as simple as that. Once again we have to see these developments against their wider background. Black workers suffered on the plantations of America, but it is doubtful whether they suffered much more than white workers in the new factories and 'sweat shops' of early industrial Britain. These factory workers were supposed to be free, but for a long time they were little better than slaves. Sugar merchants and cotton barons in England and France, bankers and plantation owners, got benefits from the trade; but so also, in a smaller way, did their partners in Africa. The records make this very clear.

Why did Africans sell Africans?

'The trade in slaves,' wrote a French slave trader in the 1680s, referring to his African partners, 'is the business of kings, rich men, and leading merchants.'

We have seen how African leaders got into the slave trade. They entered into friendly agreements with the agents of the kings of Portugal. They accepted occasional military help from pirates or adventurers like John Hawkins. They were glad to buy European goods. In exchange for these gains, or possible gains, they sold their gold, ivory, pepper and foodstuffs to the crews of European ships. And they sold some of the 'rightless persons' in their kingdoms – prisoners of war or persons sentenced for serious offences in the courts.

Then the whites asked for more and more captives, and began offering more and more guns and gunpowder in exchange. Africa's 'kings, rich men, and leading merchants' accepted the trade and its advantages to themselves. Some accepted eagerly, others with reluctance; but all found it hard to refuse. Each knew that if one refused to sell captives, another would agree; and then the one who had refused would lose his chance of buying guns and other European goods. When they ran out of 'rightless persons' in their own countries, they began buying such persons from their neighbours. When their neighbours would not sell, they made war for captives.

They can be blamed for this. But history's task is to explain *why* people behaved as they did. And the explanation shows that the position of these rulers was difficult. It was made more difficult because the slave trade did not grow suddenly into big business. It grew slowly, edging its way into daily life, thrusting its foot in the door and gradually pushing the door wide open. A few kings saw the danger and tried to stop it. As they failed, they blamed themselves. 'It is a disgrace to us and to rulers before us,' wrote King Garcia V of Kongo in 1641, 'that we, in our simplicity, should have opened the way for many evils in our kingdoms.' One of these evils was the slave trade.

It was not just 'simplicity'. It was also self-defence. Once the buying of guns became common, there was not a single coastal ruler who could feel safe without a supply of them. But to buy guns and gunpowder he had to sell captives. Only a

At the court of the King of Dahomey in the eighteenth century. On the right, inside the royal tent, sits the King smoking a long pipe. In the middle of the picture are ladies of the court, some of whom also served as soldiers. On the left are some British visitors

united African agreement to stop the trade could have succeeded; and no such agreement was possible.

The African position with regard to the sale of captives can be seen in another way: in the position of the Europeans and their attitude to the sale of guns. Many Europeans were against the sale of guns to Africans. They knew that Africans with guns were better able to resist European pressure than Africans without guns. Yet the sale of guns went on, and greatly increased, because the European could not agree among themselves to stop it. Unity among the white nations was no more possible than unity among the black nations.

A Dutch government official on the West African coast explained all this when writing home to his friends in Amsterdam in 1700.

Perhaps you will wonder how it happens that the Negroes get supplies of firearms? The reason is simply that we sell them incredible quantities, so handing them a knife with which to cut our throats [a weapon, he meant, with which to defend themselves against European demands]. But we are forced to do this. For if we Dutch refused to sell guns, then the blacks would still get them from the English, or the Danes, or the Germans. And even if all of us officials could agree to stop selling guns, the private merchants from England and Holland would still sell them in abundance. Besides, guns and gunpowder are the easiest goods to sell here, and without them we should do a poor trade.

The last point was no minor one, and had several aspects. It was not only the trading companies who needed to sell guns if they were to prosper. So did the gun-makers of Europe. Gun-making became a large export business. By about 1750 the gunsmiths of England alone were selling tens of thousands of guns to the African market every year.

African disunity and African needs in self-defence were two important reasons for the growth of the slave trade. There was also a third: African self-interest. Like guns in Europe, captives in Africa became a valuable export business. Many African peoples suffered grievous damage from the trade in captives; some of them suffered disaster. But others gained.

How did the trade work?

None of those who gained from the trade were more successful than the people of the Cross River towns, east of the Niger delta, whose methods of self-rule were mentioned in Chapter 6. Under the skilful government of the leaders of Ekpe, the Leopard Society, the Cross River towns became a thriving centre for the export of captives.

A nineteenth-century engraving of captives being marched to the coast for export across the Atlantic

The area of the Cross River towns

Ekpe chiefs developed a new type of trading corporation to meet the needs of the trade. They called this a 'canoe corporation'. Each merchant of any wealth in these towns possessed at least one large canoe capable of carrying up to eighty men, and armed with one or two small brass cannon mounted on swivels at bow or stern. With these canoes they paddled up their inland creeks to the densely populated country of the Ibo. There they bought captives from Ibo merchants who, in turn, had obtained them from farther inland. If the 'canoe company' foun no captives for sale, they went ashore and seized them from defenceless villages.

Having assembled their captives, they kept these under guard while they bargained with the captains and supercargoes of European ships anchored in the Cross River. The Europeans had to pay a regular scale of fees for permission to anchor in the river, to buy yams and other foodstuffs for their crews and for the captives they would take across the Atlantic, and generally to ensure African goodwill. If any European trader was found cheating or trying to bully his Africa partners, the Leopard Society declared a boycott on dealings with him. Then the trader had to make amends or haul up anchor and depart without a cargo.

Each side tried to get the best price it could. This meant long bargaining. The price was seldom reckoned in money: usually it was reckoned in goods. These goods might be tobacco, iron bars, copper bracelets, rolls of cotton, or cowrie shells. Pricing these things called for skill and experience.

The logbook of an English slaver, the *Albion-Frigate*, trading in the Cross Rive in 1699, records the following transaction:

> On the morning of the 25th we went ashore so as to pay our respects to the King [of one of the Cross River towns] and suggest a deal. He told us that he expectec for every slave he sold us, one bar of iron more than Edwards [a rival English captain] had paid. He also said that the metal basins and mugs, yellow beads anc other of our goods, were in no demand at the time.

Ready to deal, this African king was not going to make it easy for the English. Th English knew this, and tried again. The next day they went ashore and had another conference with the king and other African traders. 'This lasted from thre in the afternoon until night, but without any result.' The African traders held out for a price the English thought too high.

Four days later they had a third conference, again with no agreement. The king's spokesmen told the English that the king was 'sorry we could not accept his proposals. It was not his fault, for he had a great esteem for the whites, who had much enriched him by trade.' But the price for captives in the inland country had gone up, and so he had to insist on thirteen iron bars for a man captive, and ten bars for a woman. Still, to show goodwill, he was ready to take thirteen bars for a man and nine bars for a woman, together with two brass rings. Haggling in this way, the two sides finally agreed.

Having agreed, both sides met on board ship and drank to each other's health and prosperity. There was no room here for any discrimination or lack of mutual respect. Africans and Europeans were careful to entertain each other at feasts anc suppers. As time went by, one or two white traders in the Cross River were even allowed to join the Leopard Society and take part in its decisions on trade. Strong in their own country, the blacks had no objection to the whites so long as the whites obeyed local laws and trading customs.

In this drawing made in 1844 you can see a boatload of captives being rowed out to a ship that will take them across the Atlantic to be sold as slaves

Though generally peaceful, the trade was brutal to its victims. Some of our sailors who had made a first slaving voyage refused to make a second, because they were so horrified by what they had seen. Captives were treated like animals. Once sold, they were paraded before their white buyers. These gave each captive a detailed examination, accepting only the healthy and the young. Those passed as 'good' were often branded on the breast with a hot iron, to distinguish one buyer's property from another's. 'Care is taken,' says one account of the 1680s, 'not to burn the women too hard.' Stripped of such clothing as they had, the captives were then taken to the ships. It is hard to imagine their feelings of anger or despair.

Ending it at last

No matter what suffering it caused, the slave trade went on for centuries. Too many rulers and investors drew profit from it; too few, on both sides, wished to stop it. Even when the Europeans tried to stop it, they found this extremely difficult. The British, who for long were among the worst slavers of all, began trying in 1807. By then the new manufacturers of the industrial revolution were far more interested in the profits of wage labour in Britain itself. At the same time there arose in Britain, and soon afterwards in France, a powerful wave of disgust at the whole institution of slavery.

In 1807 the British government outlawed the slave trade in British ships. They set our navy, then the strongest in the world, to preventing it in the ships of other nations. Our warships stopped Portuguese and other slavers on the high seas, and took their cargoes of captives to Sierra Leone, where these were set free. Then the French government outlawed the slave trade, but some other governments refused to stop it. At the same time, beginning in the 1830s, a new slave trade developed in East Africa. This was partly the work of Portuguese settlers in Mozambique, raiding far and wide for captives whom they could send to Brazil. Even more, it was the work of Arabs who now began to rule in Zanzibar and some other East Coast places.

In partnership with Swahili traders, the Zanzibar Arabs raided for captives as far as the Congo Basin. They used their captives for slave labour in new plantations of cloves which they opened on Zanzibar and Pemba Islands. Other captives they sold to Arabian dealers, or to French colonists who now began growing sugar on Indian Ocean islands such as Mauritius, or to slave ships from North America, or to anyone else who would buy them. In this way they exported tens of thousands of captives. But, gradually, in the 1880s, the whole grim business came to an end. Almost four and a half centuries after Captain Antony Gonsalves snatched his first captives on the shore of Mauritania, the last slave ship crossed the Atlantic.

The consequences of the slave trade reached far outside Africa. The sufferings of the slaves are part of this story; so is their bravery.

SLAVE VICTORS AND SLAVE HEROES

Slaving captains could often buy Africans without using force. But they always had to use force to keep them. Having examined, selected, bought and branded his cargo of captives, every slaving captain sent them aboard his ship in boats guarded by sailors armed with swords and guns. Usually he sent them aboard in chains.

Such precautions were not enough. As the captain went up over the side of his ship and climbed the steps to his quarter-deck, to his place of command, another but unseen passenger went with him. And this invisible passenger whom nobody saw, yet nobody ever forgot, was fear. Not fear of the perils of the sea, of storms, hidden reefs, hunger, shipwreck; these captains and their crews were hard men who took all such dangers in their stride. What haunted them was the fear of slave revolt.

Many captains described it. Thomas Phillips was one of them.

Resistance at sea

Captain Phillips wrote of a voyage, in 1693–94, that was typical of other slaving voyages, whether in British ships or those of other nations. He brought his captives aboard under armed guard and in chains. Generally he had them chained in pairs; sometimes five or six captives were linked together with a length of chain shackled to each of them. And, until the voyage was over, Captain Phillips kept them in chains.

The slave trade in British ships was finally banned by the British parliament in 1807 after a long campaign of popular protest against it. One of the leaders of this campaign was the African Olaudah Equiano, whom you see here. He came from Iboland (in eastern Nigeria)

Chains alone could not banish his fear of a revolt. Although the captives were thrust down into holds beneath the deck, he always kept sentries at the hatchway openings of the holds. There they stood, by day or night, ready to shoot down at any captives who should threaten to break free. For other members of the crew, he had 'a chest full of small arms, ready loaded and primed [with gunpowder], constantly lying at hand on the quarter-deck'. Also on the quarter-deck, he had two cannon aimed at the main deck, and two pointing through port holes in the wooden wall below.

Twice a day, unless storms were blowing, the captives were brought up from the holds to have their food in the open air. Then Phillips ordered some of his crew, guns in hand, to surround the captives while other crewmen stood with matches lit to fire the cannon loaded with grapeshot, in case of any trouble. Only when the captives had finished eating, and 'gone down to their kennels between decks', were these precautions relaxed.

Such precautions were common to all slavers, whether British or French, Dutch, Spanish, Portuguese, or American. But they did not prevent revolts. The history of the 'Middle Passage' is one of suffering and loss of life through bad treatment. But it is also one of brave bids for freedom. Captives revolted against their enslavement before the ships they were in had weighed anchor. They rose against their captors while ships were steering out of sight of land. They revolted on the high seas, far from land, although none of the slaves knew how to navigate and so get back to Africa again. Many men and women preferred to die rather than endure their fate.

Precautions against revolt added to the tortures of Africans aboard ship. But so did other things. As time went by, the tortures grew worse.

Grim weeks or months

Slaveship owners back in Europe, counting their profits and losses, began calling for 'tighter packing' of captives aboard their vessels. The more captives that a ship could carry across the Atlantic to slave markets eager for black labour, the higher would be the profits of its voyage. Slavers began to stow captives below decks on shelves built across the holds, allowing so little headroom that a man or woman could barely kneel upright, let alone stand.

Slaveship owners began to reduce their costs by cutting down the size of crews. This meant that captains increased their security precautions. In earlier days captives were often released from their chains when brought up on deck for food and fresh air. Now it became the rule to chain captives throughout the voyage. To give them a little exercise, they were brought on deck every day and forced to jump up and down in their chains. This was called 'dancing the slaves'.

If a voyage prospered, it could be made in three or four weeks from the West African coast to the Americas. But many voyages ran into storms and contrary winds, or were lengthened by errors of navigation and the wretched condition of the ships. Then voyages stretched grimly to two months or even three, ships ran short of food, or fevers broke out among the crew or the captives. Many died of hunger or sickness or of both.

Long voyages led to appalling cruelties. Not a few cases are on record of slaving captains who threw sick and dying captives overboard to drown.

The pick of Africa's people

Only the healthiest of men and women could hope to survive the 'Middle Passage'. If many millions did in fact survive, this was in no small measure because they were selected for their health and strength. Those who reached the New World were among the pick of Africa's people.

Loaded with their chains, cramped and tortured, sick and hungry, the Africans were delivered to the slave markets. Sometimes they were auctioned straight away, while still on board, or as soon as they were taken ashore. This kind of auction was called a 'scramble'. Planters eager for labour scrambled for the slaves they wanted, rushing at them and tying handkerchiefs to those they fancied most, sometimes fighting with each other for particularly strong or handsome men and women. Or else the captives were kept in prisons until the market authorities were ready to sell them. In any case they were treated like cattle, and sometimes worse. Yet they remained men and women conscious of their humanity and of their human rights. They remained people who wanted to regain their freedom in these strange lands to which the 'Middle Passage' had delivered them.

RESISTANCE IN THE AMERICAS

Just as Africans rebelled against their captors in the slave ships, so also did they rebel against slavery in the Americas. Far from quietly accepting slavery, many strove to win back freedom. Almost as soon as the Spaniards began importing

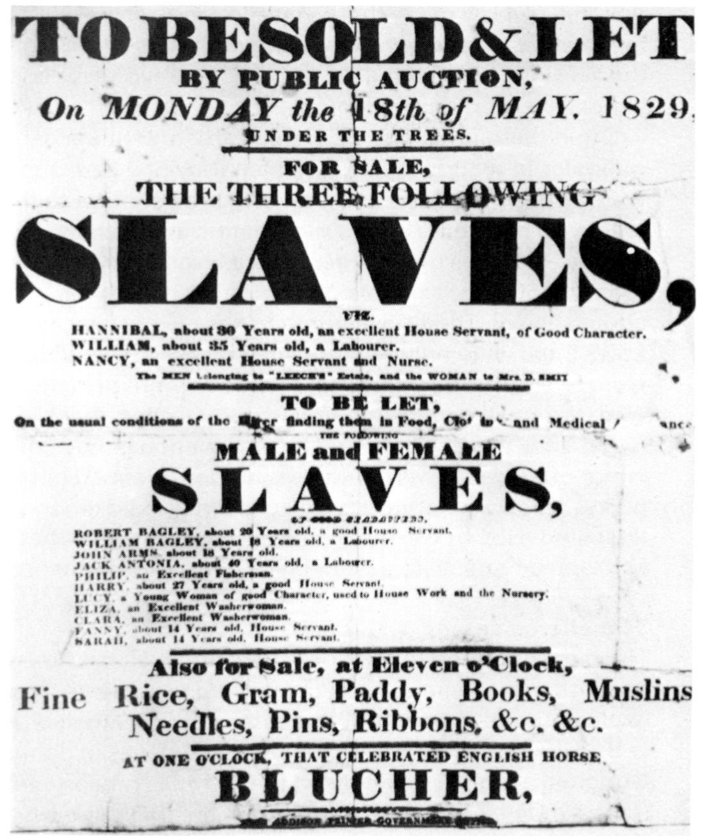

TO BE SOLD & LET
BY PUBLIC AUCTION,
On MONDAY the 18th of MAY, 1829,
UNDER THE TREES.

FOR SALE,
THE THREE FOLLOWING
SLAVES,
VIZ.
HANNIBAL, about 30 Years old, an excellent House Servant, of Good Character.
WILLIAM, about 35 Years old, a Labourer.
NANCY, an excellent House Servant and Nurse.
The MEN belonging to "LEECH'S" Estate, and the WOMAN to Mrs. D. SMIT

TO BE LET,
On the usual conditions of the [illegible] finding them in Food, [illegible] and Medical [illegible]
MALE and FEMALE
SLAVES,
ROBERT BAGLEY, about 20 Years old, a good House Servant.
WILLIAM BAGLEY, about 18 Years old, a Labourer.
JOHN ARMS, about 18 Years old.
JACK ANTONIA, about 40 Years old, a Labourer.
PHILIP, an Excellent Fisherman.
HARRY, about 27 Years old, a good House Servant.
LUCY, a Young Woman of good Character, used to House Work and the Nursery.
ELIZA, an Excellent Washerwoman.
CLARA, an Excellent Washerwoman.
FANNY, about 14 Years old, House Servant.
SARAH, about 14 Years old, House Servant.

Also for Sale, at Eleven o'Clock,
Fine Rice, Gram, Paddy, Books, Muslins,
Needles, Pins, Ribbons, &c. &c.

AT ONE O'CLOCK, THAT CELEBRATED ENGLISH HORSE
BLUCHER,

In those harsh days it was common for slaves in England, France, America, and the Caribbean to be put up for sale at auction

Africans to solve their labour problems, they met with trouble. 'Pray send no more', was the message sent back to Spain by the governor of Hispaniola as early as 1503. Black slaves in the islands were running away and spreading ideas of revolt among the 'Indians'. It was hard to catch them, the governor complained, and often it was impossible. The message fell on deaf ears. Spanish need for slave labour overcame all fear of using it. More Africans were poured into the island from across the Atlantic. Nineteen years after that governor's message, Hispaniola was shaken by a major slave revolt.

Other Caribbean islands erupted in the same way; so did colonies on the neighbouring mainland of Central and South America. New messages of warning were sent back to Spain. Nothing availed: the flow of slaves continued, and the revolts as well.

Repressive laws

The system of production based on the slave trade and slavery ignored all warnings, protests and precautions. Plantation slavery might have its risks and dangers to those who managed it: but these seemed small beside the profits that were drawn from it. So it came about that slave revolts were seen as part of the price that had to be paid for the rise of European New World civilisation, whether in North or Central or South America, just as the labour of the slaves was part of the effort which made this civilisation possible. After about 1650 there were so many black slaves in the mainland countries of the Americas, and in the islands of the West Indies, that the threat or fact of revolt was felt, and was accepted, in almost every colonised region.

Often these uprisings were small affairs of a few determined men, operating as guerrillas in woods or hills to which they had fled, and were soon over. Yet they were enough to give a home among the colonists to that old passenger, named fear, who had come across the Atlantic in the ships. Fear grew stronger as the number of slaves grew larger. And as fear grew stronger, laws became harsher.

Until 1661, for example, the colonists of Virginia in North America had no laws about slavery. Then slave numbers rose every year as plantations developed. In 1625 there were only twenty-three blacks in the whole colony. By 1715 there were twenty-three thousand. And such were the fears of the colonists, so many were the small revolts and runaways of slaves, that slave laws were brought into force. They were severe; and as time went by, they became more severe. Even for minor offences slaves could be whipped, maimed or branded. This was also the period when new attitudes of racism took hold among plantation owners and their kind. Now it was not just fear of slave revolts that ruled men's minds, but a widespread refusal to accept black people into American civilisation.

The slaves resist

The big risings and revolutions were not in North America, where slaves were fewer than elsewhere, or were grouped together in smaller numbers. The big explosions were in the Caribbean and South America.

By 1700 there were so many runaway slaves in Jamaica that white colonists launched a regular war against them. These rebels were called 'maroons'. Taking their stand in wild inland country, where they built villages and began farming for themselves, the maroons held their ground against repeated military expeditions. Fighting back under a leader named Cudjoe, they burned planters' houses and freed more slaves. In the end the British had to make peace with them, signing a treaty in 1739 which declared that the maroons were free 'for ever', and recognising Cudjoe as their leader.

Another great revolt led to the foundation of the free black settlement of Palmares (Pal-ma-race), in north-eastern Brazil. Ruled by kings of its own, this state held out for nearly a century against repeated white military attacks. Yet another revolt shattered the Dutch colony of Surinam, on the northern coast of South America. Large numbers of black slaves took refuge in deep jungle where they formed a state of their own, and held it against the Dutch army. Like the British in Jamaica a little earlier, in 1761, the Dutch were obliged to make peace with these Africans, whose leader was Captain Adu.

The largest of all these revolutions took place in the Caribbean country of Haiti during the French Revolution of 1789 and after. For more than a century the western half of Hispaniola, as the Spaniards had named the island, had been the most profitable of all the colonies of France, an important homeland of 'King Sugar'. Its slave-grown produce had brought wealth to merchants, and nourished the growth of the French nation. Then in 1789 the French people rose against their kings and nobles under the banner of 'Liberty, Equality, Fraternity'.

Far away in Haiti the slaves heard the echoes of the French Revolution and

Toussaint L'Ouverture, the man who led the fight for liberty in the French sugar colony of Saint Domingue, afterwards called Haiti

hoped for their share of its freedom. But this was not at all to the taste of the French colonists, or of their partners in France. Soon the slaves found there was to be one law for them and another for the French. They were to remain slaves. They rose in revolt under a leader called Toussaint L'Ouverture, the son of an African chief who had been brought to Haiti as a slave. They made their own revolution, and took possession of the country. Bitter struggles followed, in which French armies and then British armies both failed to beat Toussaint and his men.

Afterwards Haiti fell on evil times. Yet the memory of those wars lived on. 'What men these blacks are!' recalled a French eye-witness, years after the armies of Toussaint had defeated all their enemies. 'How they fight and how they die! You need to have made war on them to know their reckless courage. I have seen a single column, torn by grapeshot from four cannon, continue to advance without a backward step.'

Many of these slave wars came to seem like 'race wars'. This was because the slave-owners were of one colour, the slaves of another. In reality they were not wars about 'race'. They were wars about freedom. The slaves understood this, even if the slave-owners did not. In 1868 the people of Cuba rose in revolution against their overlords of the Spanish Empire. Men of every colour fought in the Cuban independence army. One of their generals, Antonio Maceo, happened to be black. At a certain point in the war some white Cubans came to General Mace and suggested that blacks and whites should be organised in separate regiments Maceo would have none of it. 'If you were not white,' he told them, 'I would hav you shot. But I don't want to be accused of being a racist, like you are. So I will l you off, but next time I shall not be so patient. The revolution has no colour.'

NEW WORLD PIONEERS

The records of protest and revolt are important for several reasons. Through them we may see that Africa's descendants were far from being 'natural slaves', people who had no notion of freedom, as owners often liked to think. These records sho that those who came from Africa were repeatedly able to keep their heads above the tide of misery into which slavery had plunged them. This in turn helps to explain why so many of them, in becoming Americans, were able to survive the evils of enslavement, and play their part in laying foundations for American growth and expansion.

The first way in which black Americans helped to build the new civilisations o the Americas was by sheer weight of numbers. For a long while whites were few while the 'Indians' were either killed off or pushed away into the wilderness.

By 1756, after about a century of the triangular trade, Virginia had 120,156 blacks and 173,316 whites. By 1765 the Carolinas had about 90,000 blacks and 40,000 whites. By 1773 Georgia had about 15,000 blacks and 18,000 whites. Elsewhere in North America there were fewer blacks, but still there were many. I 1771 the black population of the state of New York stood at about 20,000.

Black numbers were far greater in the Caribbean and in Central and South America. In 1787 the British West Indies had more than 450,000 blacks, Saint Domingue (Haiti) not far short of 300,000; Brazil nearly 2,000,000. Other colonies had large numbers; Venezuela, for example, had some 500,000 blacks out of a total population, including 'Indians', of 900,000. Scarcely a single land c Central and South America was without its large black population; sometimes, a in Brazil, the blacks were many more than the whites.

The vast majority of all these blacks were slaves. Their conditions of life varied. Some suffered much in slavery, others less. The main point to notice here is that all of them *worked*. In most American countries, the blacks were the main working force. Little or nothing could be grown, built, or made without them. They supplied the 'raw labour' of conquering the wilderness. But they supplied more than that: they also helped to shape the Americas with their skills. At certai decisive points their skills were more important than their numbers or their capacity for toil.

Miners, farmers, cattlemen

The colonists were well aware of this. Every time a black slave was offered for sale, his or her skills were listed by the seller. In South America, and to some extent in Central America, the skill most valued among all the skills brought by Africans across the Atlantic was that of mining and metal-working. For a long time after 1500, when the slave trade began delivering Africans to the Americas, European methods of mining and metal-production were, with some exceptions, not much more advanced than those of Africa. African mining skills played a big part in developing these lands.

Between 1700 and 1800, Brazil is estimated to have had about 600,000 black miners. Most of them, or their parents, were born in Africa. Around 1800 the vast inland region of Brazil called Minas Gerais had about 15,000 whites and 200,000 blacks. Writing at that time, a Swedish mining engineer with long experience of the country explained that smelting and smithing there were learned from the blacks. He described the methods of iron production then in use throughout the region. His description shows that the methods used were those of Africa. This began to change only after 1800 with the introduction of machinery from Europe. What was true of the iron industry in Brazil, and in other parts of South America, was also true of a variety of metals. New World Africans took over a host of other skilled jobs. Much the same story of African skills is true of the plantations. Just as in their mines and workshops, the Portuguese and Spaniards had little or no machinery on their farms. They relied on the tools and toughness of the Africans, partly because the whites refused to do hard work themselves, partly because the blacks had developed some immunity to certain tropical diseases, such as malaria.

With their knowledge of tropical farming, the Africans understood how to farm this foreign soil and make it fruitful. They produced the sugar and other crops that fed the triangular trade. They supplied the colonists' towns with food that the colonists could not or would not grow for themselves. Brazil again offers a startling example. By 1800 there were about a million Africans growing sugar in Brazil: another 250,000 were producing coffee there; others grew bananas, cotton, and other crops. They also went into cattle breeding, another African skill, and their cattlemen rode the plains of South America wherever ranching was possible.

Shortage of white skilled labour was less acute in the North American colonies. This was because most of the North American colonists had come from European countries less backward in methods of production than Portugal or Spain. Yet even in the North American colonies it was often the blacks, whether as slaves or freemen, who supplied the labour for workshops as well as for plantations. This workshop labour was vital to the development of the southern colonies of North America. Without it, the southern whites would have found it hard even to market their produce, let alone grow and harvest it. Blacks were fewer in the northern colonies of North America, but here too it was often black labour that made white enterprises possible. In 1775, for example, the state of New York had as many as 8,000 black farm workers.

So we see that the chief black contribution to American civilisation was to create wealth, the result of their labour in plantations, mines and workshops. But it was more than that. It was also a contribution that wove new strands, whether of music or dancing or language, into the broadening cultures of the Americas. In the loom of life that made these cultures, black strands were there from the first, along with all the others. They have given to the fabric of New World civilisation a great deal of its diversity and strength. That is why the heritage of Africa stands together with the heritage of Europe in the making of the Americas.

WHAT IT MEANT TO AFRICA

The slave trade's consequences for Africa were, for the most part, painful and destructive. A few peoples gained from it; most sorely lost. The total number of captives who reached the Americas and the West Indies and were sold into slavery there is not known. Research into the records suggests that this total was nine or ten million, though it may have been more. Yet the total who reached the West Indies, or the mainland countries of North and Central and South America, was not the total of those who were taken from Africa. Many died during the horrible 'Middle Passage' across the ocean.

Again, the total who began the voyage was not the total of those who were the victims of the trade. Others died in slaving raids or wars, in famines or upheavals which followed on such wars, or during the violent invasions of the Portuguese in Angola and Mozambique. Perhaps the true total of those who died in Africa because of the slave trade was as much as double the number of those who were landed alive across the Atlantic. This means that Africa may have lost twenty or thirty million people, because of the trade, during the four and a half centuries that it lasted. Some African peoples were entirely crippled by this loss of population. But most were not, and the growth of their populations was able to make up for their losses.

This remains true even when one takes account of the other slave trade to which Africa was subject: the export of captives overland to North Africa, Egypt, and the Middle East. All the evidence suggests that this overland trade was much smaller than the Atlantic slave trade, at least after about AD 1650. Though painful like the other, the overland trade was less important in its consequences.

Widening the power gap

But Africa suffered other kinds of damage. Some of these were of a political and social nature. Going into the slave trade as junior partners of the Europeans and white Americans, African kings and traders often ceased to be the responsible representatives of ordinary people, and became the active enemies of ordinary people. They shovelled Africans into the slave ships, but also, as time went by, they developed their own patterns of slavery modelled on those of the Europeans. The slave trade brought about a steady degradation in African political life wherever its influence was strongly felt.

There were vast inland areas, of course, where its influence was felt little or not at all. Perhaps one half or even two thirds of all the Africans taken across the Atlantic came from West Africa, and most of the others from Angola and the Congo. Only in the nineteenth century did large numbers of East Africans become victims of the trade.

Another kind of damage was suffered in the economic field. This related to the growing 'power gap' between Africa and Europe. After about 1700 the British, followed later by the French and some of the other peoples of western Europe, actively developed a new system of society, known as capitalism. This system is based on the private profit got from employing wage labour. It led to much suffering, but it also led to continued and important advances in methods of production. Precisely at this time, after about 1700, the slave trade with Africa grew to its greatest size. For England and France, the slave trade became an important means of accumulating the capital that came from private profit.

While this new capitalism in England and elsewhere stimulated the invention and organisation of new methods of production, Africa's kings and traders went on with an economic activity, the sale of captives into slavery, that led to no progress for them at all. True enough, the captives were sold for imported goods. But these imported goods were nearly all of the 'consumer' type, adding nothing to the productive capacity of the Africans. Or else they were guns and ammunition for the making of more wars and raids.

Instead of moving ahead into new forms of production, forms that could have kept them level with the Europeans in the command of wealth and new technology, African rulers were content with the export of large quantities of able-bodied workers, and often of skilled workers. This helped to develop western Europe and America, but it could bring no development in Africa. On the contrary, Africa's export of a work force, millions strong, undoubtedly helped to widen the 'power gap' between Africans and Europeans or white Americans, and always to the disadvantage of the Africans. While Britain and France pushed on with their industrial revolutions, partly through the profits of slavery, Africa continued to rely on production by hand methods.

Could it have been different? This is the kind of question that history cannot answer. What history can explain is that the slave trade and slavery helped Britain to lead the way to a productive revolution, in Europe and afterwards in America, that is called industrialization or industrial capitalism.

This new productive system, based on machinery and factory-labour, proved much stronger than any previous system. Grown powerful in this way, we and then other Europeans began to use our new power for conquest in Africa. Both north and south of the Sahara, the century that began in 1800 was the starting of a time of new needs and new opportunities. Africa's old ways of community life had served well for a long period. Now they were breaking down under a variety of new pressures. Fresh developments were called for.

In some parts of Africa the steady growth of population, during earlier centuries, was reaching a point where people felt a shortage of land for crops and cattle. This led to rivalries for land and sometimes to wars; that is what happened far in the south-east where the Zulu kingdom emerged in the 1820s. In those south-eastern regions, too, land shortage was worsened by the arrival of European or Afrikaner settlers. Afrikaner is the name of South African whites of Dutch origin.

Kings got more power, whether for reasons of security or rivalry between ruling groups. Elsewhere, new types of government began to appear, backed by public services in which ordinary people could make careers not open to them before. That was the case, for example, in the Ashanti kingdom of what is Ghana today. The Africans, in fact, were beginning to experiment with new ways of community living that could better meet the challenges of the modern world. Such experiments took place especially among coastal peoples involved in trade with Europe or the Americas.

In 1807 the British began to stop the slave trade. Our parliament prohibited the carrying of captives or slaves in British ships, and set the Royal Navy, then the master of the seas, to stop the ships of other nations from carrying captives or slaves. The French followed us a little later, and then, more or less unwillingly, the

Portuguese and North Americans. By 1850 the slave trade was almost ended, even though the last slaving ships sailed the Atlantic as late as the 1880s.

Those African states along the coast which had carried on the slave trade were thus faced with the need to find another form of trading. Some of the most successful in doing this were the small states of the Niger Delta, for long a big slaving centre. Their kings and merchants now went into other kinds of export. They began producing the palm oil that an industrialised Europe greatly needed for making soap. But this sort of independent African adjustment to changing times was not allowed to continue. Colonial invasion cut it short.

Towards modern Africa: colonialism and after

THE COLONIAL ERA

Half a dozen European powers, with Britain and France in the lead, invaded Africa and divided almost the whole of it into several dozen colonies. Only Ethiopia kept its independence, apart from Liberia, originally a colony of black American emigrants from the United States. All other African countries were subjected to one or other form of European rule. Under European laws of varying harshness and rigidity, all their peoples lost their rights of citizenship and freedom.

The reasons for this extraordinary invasion of a whole continent were of several kinds, but all of them, in the end, boiled down to a wish to gain political and economic advantage. At the beginning of the enterprise, in the second half of the nineteenth century when most of the invasions had not yet begun or were still in their early stages, leading European governments and big capitalist companies were reluctant to embark on a business that looked as though it must be very costly, but could promise little profit. Yet the governments, if not the big capitalist companies, were rushed along by the growing strength of an inflamed nationalist public opinion.

Each country's traders persuaded their own governments to clear the way into Africa by force of arms. Explorers and adventurers came home to Europe with colourful and sometimes fantastic tales of the African wealth that was waiting to be taken. Missionaries and churchmen spoke of Europe's duty to 'civilise the Dark Continent'. Nationalist newspapers thumped the drums of military glory.

So the enterprise to conquer Africa got under way, and then European rivalries drove it further and faster, especially rivalries between the British and the French. These powers each strove for 'the best bits', while lesser powers, like the Italians or Portuguese, did what they could to 'keep up'. Getting hold of African colonies, whether by trickery or outright force, was turned into a matter of European nationalist prestige.

Economic reasons were also on the scene, though these were less important at the beginning than they became later. Industrialised countries such as Britain and France needed secure sources of cheap raw materials for their factories: they also wanted 'captive markets' in which they could sell their goods abroad. Africa, they argued, could provide both the raw materials and the captive markets.

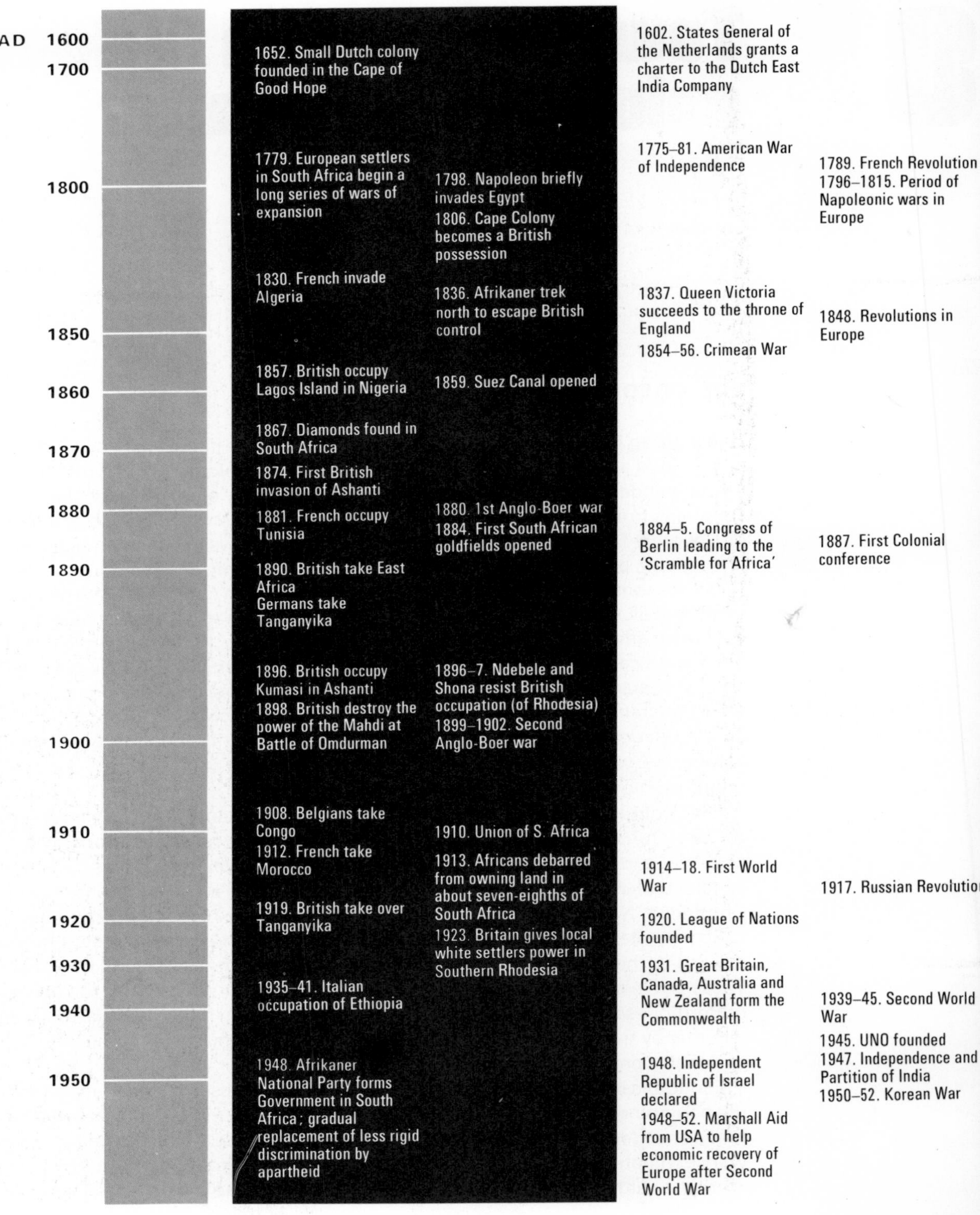
AD 1600
1700
1800
1850
1860
1870
1880
1890
1900
1910
1920
1930
1940
1950
1652. Small Dutch colony founded in the Cape of Good Hope
1779. European settlers in South Africa begin a long series of wars of expansion
1830. French invade Algeria
1857. British occupy Lagos Island in Nigeria
1867. Diamonds found in South Africa
1874. First British invasion of Ashanti
1881. French occupy Tunisia
1890. British take East Africa
Germans take Tanganyika
1896. British occupy Kumasi in Ashanti
1898. British destroy the power of the Mahdi at Battle of Omdurman
1908. Belgians take Congo
1912. French take Morocco
1919. British take over Tanganyika
1935–41. Italian occupation of Ethiopia
1948. Afrikaner National Party forms Government in South Africa; gradual replacement of less rigid discrimination by apartheid
1798. Napoleon briefly invades Egypt
1806. Cape Colony becomes a British possession
1836. Afrikaner trek north to escape British control
1859. Suez Canal opened
1880. 1st Anglo-Boer war
1884. First South African goldfields opened
1896–7. Ndebele and Shona resist British occupation (of Rhodesia)
1899–1902. Second Anglo-Boer war
1910. Union of S. Africa
1913. Africans debarred from owning land in about seven-eighths of South Africa
1923. Britain gives local white settlers power in Southern Rhodesia
1602. States General of the Netherlands grants a charter to the Dutch East India Company
1775–81. American War of Independence
1837. Queen Victoria succeeds to the throne of England
1854–56. Crimean War
1884–5. Congress of Berlin leading to the 'Scramble for Africa'
1914–18. First World War
1920. League of Nations founded
1931. Great Britain, Canada, Australia and New Zealand form the Commonwealth
1948. Independent Republic of Israel declared
1948–52. Marshall Aid from USA to help economic recovery of Europe after Second World War
1789. French Revolution
1796–1815. Period of Napoleonic wars in Europe
1848. Revolutions in Europe
1887. First Colonial conference
1917. Russian Revolutio
1939–45. Second World War
1945. UNO founded
1947. Independence and Partition of India
1950–52. Korean War

AD				
1948				
1949				1949. North Atlantic Treaty Organization (NATO) founded 1949. Birth of Communist China
1950	1950. Guinea becomes independent			
1951	1951. Libya becomes independent			
1952	1952. Rise of new nationalism in Egypt			
1953				
1954				1954. South East Asia Treaty Organization founded (SEATO)
1955	1955. Tunisia becomes independent			
1956	1956. Morocco becomes independent Suez crisis Sudan becomes independent			
1957		1957. Ghana becomes independent		
1958				1958. European Economic Community founded United Arab Republic founded
1959				
1960	1960. Belgians withdraw from the Congo Nigeria and many French colonies become independent			1960. European Free Trade Association founded
1961		1961. Republic of South Africa formed outside British Commonwealth Sierra Leone and Tanganyika become independent	1961–74. Angolan war of independence against Portugal	
1962	1962. Uganda and Algeria become independent			1962. 1st Commonwealth Immigrants Act Cuba crisis
1963	1963. Kenya becomes independent Organization of African Unity formed	1963–74. Guinea-Bissau war of independence against Portugal		1963. President Kennedy of USA assassinated
1964		1964–65. Zambia, Malawi and The Gambia become independent. Rhodesian settlers rebel against Britain and declare 'unilateral independence'		
1965				
1966	1966. Basutoland becomes independent as Lesotho, Bechuanaland as Botswana			1966. Commonwealth conference in Lagos, Nigeria
1967		1967–69. Nigerian Civil War	1968. Swaziland becomes independent	1967. Arab-Israeli Six Days War
1972				1972. Pakistan leaves the Commonwealth
1973				1973. Britain joins the European Economic Community 1973. Arab-Israeli 'Yom Kippur' War
1974	1974. Haile Sellassie, Emperor of Ethiopia deposed			
1975		1975. Mozambique and Angola become independent		

Springboards for invasion

Now it was that Africans paid an extra price for their kings' and merchants' involvement in the slave trade. During that trade they had agreed to let the Europeans have a number of useful castles and trading posts along their coasts. These small trading footholds got a new importance when invasion became Europe's aim. They became the springboards from which invasions could be launched.

And that is what happened. After about 1850 the French invaded the African kingdoms of the western Sudan from their posts along the shores of Senegal. A little later the British invaded Ashanti from their forts along the Ghana coast. Aft about 1880 the British began pushing into Nigeria from their base on Lagos Island. Then they moved into East Africa from bases along the Swahili coast, an thrust northward from their southern colonies of the Cape of Good Hope and Natal. And where the British and the French led, the Germans and the Portuguese, the Italians and the Spanish, and finally the Belgians, duly followe

None of them found it easy. There was much armed resistance. Yet many Africans found it difficult to see what was really happening to them and their lands. This difficulty is understandable. Often the invaders came with fair words and good promises, and as friends. Only later did they show that they meant to masters.

This is how a West African poet wrote in 1900 about the way the colonial system came into existence:

At the start of the affair, they came
Peacefully,
With soft sweet talk.
'We've come to trade,' they said,
'To reform the beliefs of the people,'
'To stop oppression here below and theft,'
'To clean up and overthrow corruption.'

Not all of us saw what they were up to:
So now we've become their inferiors.
They fooled us with little gifts
And fed us tasty bait . . .
But lately they've changed their tune . . .

(Umar of Kete Krache)

Others were not fooled. 'I know the trick of those people,' declared the Ethiopian emperor Theodore after being attacked by a British army: 'First they send the merchants and the missionaries. And then the ambassadors. And after them the cannon. It's better to cut it short and go straight to the cannon.' There were many who agreed with him.

The growth of racism

Racism is the idea that some peoples are naturally better or more civilised than others – that whites, for instance, are better than blacks. This idea is as old as it i false. But the nineteenth century was the period when modern racism took shap 'White people' were then taught to believe they were the world's 'master race',

Afrikaner (Boer) farmers of South Africa about eighty years ago. They believed that whites were born to be the masters of blacks. Today, their descendants have used this racist idea to set up a system of wholesale discrimination called apartheid. In this system the blacks are exploited by the whites in every field of life

and that their 'mission' was to dominate and 'civilise' all other peoples, especially 'black people'. This belief in 'natural white superiority' marked a new form of racism, based on so-called 'scientific principles'.

There had been plenty of white racism during the time of the slave trade. The slave trade itself helped to stir it up; that was another way in which the trade did its damaging work. For a long time Europeans in Europe, or white Americans across the Atlantic, saw Africans only as slaves. Many came to believe that Africans were 'natural slaves' who scarcely minded their sufferings. These Europeans conveniently forgot Europe's own history of slavery in the past. They also forgot that it was the Europeans who had started the slave trade with Africa.

Even during the slave trade there was no such systematic contempt for Africans as infected Europeans later on. The European traders knew that they depended on the goodwill of their African partners. They also knew that many of these partners were the rulers of strong and well-ordered kingdoms. These rulers were widely respected. But leaders of European opinion now began to assure their listeners, whether in Britain or France or other countries, that the Africans were no better than 'grown-up children'. The Africans, it was said, were helpless to help themselves, had no history, possessed no civilisations of their own. The new racists argued that Africans must be ruled with Europe's 'firm hand'. This, they said, was Europe's 'sacred mission'.

These false ideas about one 'race' being naturally better than another 'race', especially the 'black race', grew stronger during the colonial period in each European country which invaded Africa, and not least in Britain. Such ideas spread a deep infection of anxiety and strife. Though less widespread than it used to be, this racist sickness is with us still.

Some key dates

In North Africa, it was the French who took the lead by a brief invasion of Egypt in 1798 with an army under Napoleon, who was soon to be French emperor. This was cut short when Admiral Nelson destroyed Napoleon's fleet, and the French invaders of Egypt were cut off from France. After that Egypt continued to be part of the Ottoman Empire of the Turks. But it was ruled by half-independent Turkish governors, and the British, intense rivals of the French then as later, gradually won a dominating influence there.

Smarting from their defeats in Napoleon's wars in Europe, the French looked for conquests elsewhere. In 1830 they invaded the great North African city-port of Algiers, and went on, though against stiff Algerian resistance, to make the whole country into a French colony. Many Frenchmen settled in Algeria's fertile coastal regions, and these regions were afterwards governed as part of France itself. Some twenty years later, around 1850, the French began pushing eastward from the coast of Senegal, in West Africa, and from then until the end of the century their soldiers fought to bring the whole of the western Sudan under their control. In 1881 they established a 'protectorate' in Tunisia.

At the other end of Africa, thousands of miles away in the far south, the little Dutch colony founded in 1652 gradually got bigger. Dutch settlers spread into the countryside to north and east of the Cape of Good Hope. Cut off from Holland, these farmers and their descendants formed a language of their own, Afrikaans, and began to think of themselves as a separate people and then as a nation, the Afrikaners or, as the British called them, the Boers. (Boer is a Dutch word meaning farmer.)

Origins of South Africa

During Napoleon's wars the French had designs on the Cape of Good Hope, at least as a useful fuelling station for their ships and crews. Having the same idea, the British gained the upper hand in 1806, and the Cape Colony became a British possession. Then the British pushed their rule gradually northward from the Cape although they were repeatedly opposed by the Africans and also, from time to time, by the Afrikaner settlers. Modern South Africa began to take shape. Its history was greatly changed in 1867, when rich deposits of diamonds were discovered, and again in 1884, when prospectors found the great goldfields of the Witwatersrand in the Transvaal, South Africa's most northerly region and at that time an independent Afrikaner republic.

A long and violent struggle for power followed between the British and the Afrikaners. This came to a head in a ferocious war that broke out in 1899, chiefly by British provocation, and lasted three years. The Afrikaners, formed in highly mobile 'commandos' of mounted men, proved a hard enemy to beat. In the end, after several disasters, the British had to send nearly 450,000 men to overcome Afrikaner resistance. This was also the first war in the 'Third World' – the world outside Europe and North America – where concentration camps were used. The British Army formed these concentration camps, as they were called at the time, so as to round up Afrikaner civilians who might otherwise help their commandos with food and information. Terrible epidemics struck the prisoners. By the end of the war some twenty-five thousand Afrikaner women and children had died in the camps.

The Afrikaners called this war their 'War for Freedom', but it was very much a 'white man's war'. By tacit agreement, neither side tried to use African soldiers. On the contrary, both sides agreed that whoever won it was not going to be of any help to the Africans. Their fate was to be the servants of the whites. This fate was confirmed in 1902, when the finally victorious British, after losing 22,000 men and spending more than £200 million, made peace with the defeated Afrikaners on terms which also provided for African servitude. And those terms were confirmed again in 1910, when the imperial partliament in London agreed to hand over the government of South Africa to the local whites, and to let these whites have a free hand in treating the Africans as they wished.

Africans had lived in South African lands since the most distant time of human settlement. In 1910 they vastly outnumbered the whites. Yet within three years of the Act of Union, the law of 1910 which united the provinces of South Africa into a single country, the local whites passed a law denying Africans all right to ownership of land in seven-eighths of the country. Only one-eighth was 'reserved' for African farmers. Other racist laws quickly followed. These laws were the foundations on which the South Africa of today was built. Only a few South African peoples escaped this fate, either by skilful resistance or good luck. These included the Africans of Lesotho (Basutoland), Botswana (Bechuanaland), and Swaziland.

British explorers and settlers, and then British soldiers, had meanwhile moved further north into African lands beyond the Limpopo river, South Africa's northern frontier. By force or else by something very like trickery, two more British colonies came into existence, those of Southern Rhodesia (Zimbabwe) and Northern Rhodesia (Zambia). Nyasaland (Malawi) also became a British colony at this time, though mostly by peaceful agreement. The vast territories of Angola and Mozambique were enclosed by the Portuguese. King Leopold of the Belgians, a clever business operator, 'claimed' and 'was given' the whole of the Congo basin: this became a direct Belgian colony in 1908.

Carving up a continent

By this time the European powers had long decided to carve up Africa without serious quarrelling among themselves. This decision was prepared at an international 'carve-up' conference in Berlin in 1884–85. The European powers then accepted the results of the invasions that had already taken place, and drew

How Africa was divided into colonies

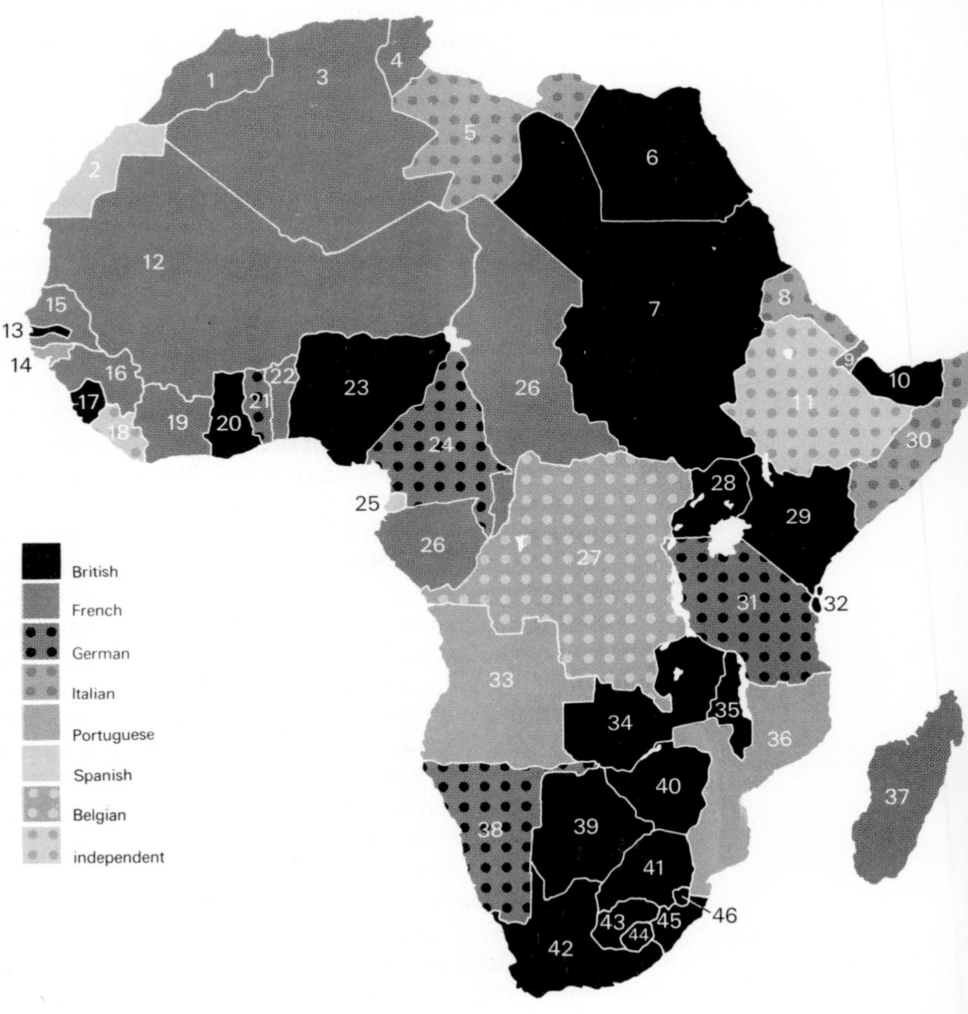

1 French Morocco
2 Rio de Oro
3 Algeria
4 Tunisia
5 Libya
6 Egypt
7 Anglo-Egyptian Sudan
8 Eritrea
9 French Somaliland
10 British Somaliland
11 Ethiopia
12 French West Africa
13 The Gambia
14 Portuguese Guinea
15 Senegal
16 French Guinea
17 Sierra Leone
18 Liberia
19 Ivory Coast
20 Gold Coast
21 Togo
22 Dahomey
23 Nigeria
24 Cameroons
25 Spanish Guinea
26 French Equatorial Africa
27 Belgian Congo
28 Uganda
29 British East Africa (Kenya)
30 Italian Somaliland
31 German East Africa (Tanganyika)
32 Zanzibar
33 Angola
34 N. Rhodesia
35 Nyasaland
36 Mozambique
37 Madagascar
38 German South-West Africa
39 Bechuanaland
40 S. Rhodesia
41 Transvaal
42 Cape Colony
43 Orange Free State
44 Basutoland
45 Natal
46 Swaziland

agreed lines on the map of Africa to provide for the invasions that were to follow. The various powers then began 'occupying' the colonies they had thus given themselves. Then, after 1890, most of the colonial frontiers were fixed in detail.

In West Africa the British set about completing their occupation of Nigeria, the Gold Coast (Ghana), Sierra Leone, and the Gambia, while the French did the same in the rest of West Africa, except for Togo and Cameroun, which were 'awarded' to the Germans, and for Guinea-Bissau, 'awarded' to the Portuguese. In East Africa, the British were again first in the field, except for the Portuguese in Mozambique. Britain 'took' Kenya, Zanzibar (now federated with Tanganyika in the Union of Tanzania), and Uganda, but left Tanganyika to the Germans, who by this time had also seized Namibia (South West Africa). The French took and kept the great island of Madagascar.

By 1900 the 'carve-up' was mostly complete, at least on the map, but late-comers such as Italy were still trying to get a foothold. The Italians had managed to win European agreement to their possession of Eritrea, north of Ethiopia, but wanted more. Somalia was declared an Italian colony in 1908. In 1912 the French added Morocco to their empire. Tripolitania and Cirenaica in North Africa were declared Italian colonies in 1913, and united into the single colony of Libya in 1934. In 1935 the Italian Fascist armies of the dictator Mussolini launched a particularly savage invasion of Ethiopia, which also became an Italian colony until our armies defeated the Fascists there in 1941, during the Second World War.

Four main periods

How did the colonial system work? What did it mean for Africans? The answers to such questions can be found by looking at what happened between about 1880 and 1960. Four main periods can be distinguished.

First, the period of invasion and conquest before and after the conference of Berlin, 1884–85. This lasted till about 1900, although, as we have seen, there were some exceptions.

Second, the period of setting up the colonial system and destroying the last remnants of African armed resistance. This went on till about 1920, or later in some colonies.

Third, the central period of colonial rule. In most cases, this ran from about 1920 till about 1950, though again with exceptions.

Fourth, the period when a new and steadily successful form of African political resistance to foreign rule took the centre of the stage. This began to happen in about 1950. The new form of political resistance was called *nationalism*. It was a nationalism aimed not at the conquest of others, but at the winning back of African independence within colonial frontiers, which Africans now accepted as the frontiers of the new and independent nations they wanted to build.

Invasion and conquest

'The most horrible war I ever took part in.' So remarked, after it was over, the commander of Britain's invasion in 1874 of the ancient and powerful kingdom of Ashanti (modern Ghana). He was General Sir Garnet Wolseley, a veteran commander of Britain's imperial armies in the reign of Queen Victoria when the British Empire covered half the world. Sir Garnet knew what he was talking about.

His regiments met with stiff military resistance all the way along their hard-fought march to Kumase, the Ashanti capital in the forests of what is now centra Ghana; and even then their success was not decisive. They occupied the Ashant king's palace and looted its treasures, but they failed to find the king: and then they had to march back again to the coast, leaving a still independent Ashanti behind them. Not until another British invasion, more than twenty years later, wa Ashanti resistance finally broken.

The story was much the same in every part of Africa where the invaders came against strong African states that were ready and able to defend themselves. Many in Britain and other imperial countries opposed these invasions, and questioned whether they were wise and right. But ruling opinion thirsted for national glory, as well as for the profits that glory might make possible. And so the invasions continued. In the western Sudan the French fought many battles over nearly half a century before they could say that they had won. The Portuguese needed almost as long to complete their occupation of Angola, Mozambique and Guinea-Bissau. In South Africa the Africans of the Cape Colony fought nine wars of resistance, chiefly against the British, while the armi of the Zulu kingdom, formed by a remarkable military leader called Shaka during the 1820s, destroyed both Afrikaner and British attacking forces before being overcome in 1879.

These European invasions were harsh. Not many people today would think them right if they were to happen now. But in those days they were pushed on b flag-waving careerists and profiteers. Many liberal-minded people in Europe, as well as some leaders of Christian opinion, also believed that the invasions shoul go on. They thought that Europeans had a 'duty' to govern Africans. They were 'do-gooders' who were ready to 'do good' by force if they must.

Reasons for African defeat

The invasions succeeded. But the reasons for African defeat had nothing to do with any human inferiority, and seldom with any lack of individual courage or good sense. The chief reason for African defeat was that African civilisations wer still at a low technological level: in other words, they made goods by hand and not by machine. But the strongest nations of Europe were far advanced, by now, in the development of machine-production, made possible by the invention and the growth of industrial capitalism.

This industrial power and new wealth gave Europeans a desire to expand their power overseas to find new markets for their goods, and new sources for raw materials. And they were able to do this because their new technological power and scientific knowledge meant that they could equip their armies with weapons which were far superior to the Africans', even though their armies might be quite small. They had more guns than the Africans and these were far better, including early types of artillery and machine-guns, such as the Maxim and the Gatling. Even so on many occasions the European invading armies were beaten up by African defenders, or forced to retreat. But in the end they always had the edge.

There was another large reason for the defeat of the Africans. They had no unit among themselves, and their many independent states could therefore be picked off one by one. Often, too, the invaders found that this or that African state was ready to fight with them against another African state.

The British empire-builder Cecil Rhodes. He made a fortune out of cheap black labour in the gold and diamond mines of South Africa, and founded the colonies of Southern Rhodesia (Zimbabwe) and Northern Rhodesia (Zambia) at the end of the nineteenth century

There was also disunity inside African states. Some of the largest were made up of a number of different African peoples, with one people among them ruling and often oppressing some or all of the others. This made it easy for the European invaders to recruit a lot of African soldiers for their invading armies. These African mercenaries or conscripts played an important part in making the invasions successful.

The Europeans took possession of nearly all of Africa, but of course they did not unite the continent. The many hundreds of independent states were compressed into about fifty colonies. These colonies were collected into two large empires, those of Britain and France, and into several smaller empires, such as that of the Portuguese.

Enclosed like this, African countries became part of the history of their European 'mother countries', as these were now often called. For the time being, the fate of Europe became their own fate. This being so, they were duly drawn into the wars of Europe. Hundreds of thousands of Africans were conscripted during the First World War, either as fighters or as porters, and suffered heavy losses. Of 134,000 West Africans called up by France for the fearful battles of the Western Front in that war, some 24,000 were killed or died of sickness. On a smaller scale, the same thing happened again during the Second World War.

How the system worked

Once the invasions were completed, and later African resistance quelled, the colonial system entered on its central period between about 1920 and 1950. It was in fact several different systems because each European power had its own methods and approaches to the problems of colonial rule. Yet all these systems added up to a single system which relied on two basic rules. The first was that

European interests always came before African interests, whenever a choice had to be made. The second rule was that the colonies were there to make profits for their European possessors. The Europeans did not always succeed in making profits, but this was not for want of trying.

When profits were made they went largely to European investors, and, later on, to American investors as well. But they also went to local white settlers wherever these could find a colony with suitable land and climate. The main colonies of white settlement were South Africa, Kenya, Rhodesia, and Algeria. Pockets of white settlement also developed in other colonies, such as Mozambique, Angola, Tanganyika (Tanzania), and the Belgian Congo (Zaïre today). All the colonies were ruled on racist principles, but racist rule was generally much harsher in the colonies where white settlers ruled or had a big say in running affairs.

There were two chief ways of making profits. One of these was to force or persuade Africans to work in European-owned mines, or in the growing of products such as cocoa, coffee, sisal and groundnuts, nearly always for low rates of pay or price. The Europeans then sold these products on the 'world market'. A second way to make profits was by selling European-made goods to Africans, while taking care that such goods were not made in Africa. In both these ways the Africans were enclosed within the economic systems of their colonial rulers, and had little or no means of defending their own interests.

All this brought many changes to African life. A few of these, as we shall see, were for the good. But most were not. Among the painful changes, one of the worst was caused by Africans having to work for Europeans. Few of them wanted to do so. Nearly all the Africans of the central colonial period were country people, farmers and stock raisers, and preferred to go on working for themselves. But the Europeans had to have African workers, and as cheaply as possible, if they were going to get the minerals and export crops from which profits could be made.

Ways of using African labour

At first, Africans in large numbers were made to work for Europeans simply by sheer force. Chiefs were told to provide a certain number of their able-bodied people, women as well as men, and were punished if they refused: when necessary, the colonial police forces did the job of rounding up the victims. Most of the early colonial roads were built by forced labour, as well as the few railways, and sometimes the cost in human life was high. The practice of directly forcing Africans to work continued in the French empire till after the end of the Second World War in 1945 and in the Portuguese colonies till 1974.

The British also used forced labour in the early colonial years, but later switched to a different system which was one of indirect pressure. This consisted in making Africans pay taxes in money. As money was little used in African village life, this meant that Africans could pay their taxes only by earning money; and earning money, for the most part, meant going to work for Europeans. Usually, African farmers had to do this by leaving their village homes, and working, often very far away, on 'contracts' that lasted six or twelve months or longer.

Then these 'migrant workers', as they were called because they usually had to go and stay a long way from their homes to work for Europeans, could at least earn enough to pay their taxes in money. Perhaps, at the end of a long contract, they might even be able to afford a couple of blankets or an item as expensive as a bicycle. But they had to be very thrifty in order to do that. For the employers worked out their wages on the basis of the bare weekly needs of a single man, no matter whether he had a family or not. The families of these 'migrant workers', left behind in distant villages, were supposed to provide for themselves while their men were away: the men were paid nothing for the upkeep of their families. The 'migrant labour' system was therefore an unusually severe form of colonial exploitation, and was really a modified form of slavery.

In fact, of course, it was hard and sometimes impossible for wives and young children to work their village farms without their menfolk. In time, the long and repeated absences from home of large numbers of able-bodied men, working on 'labour contracts' far away, had a disastrous effect on many rural communities. By the end of the colonial period after the Second World War, millions of village Africans were flooding to the towns, hoping to find relief from the poverty of their village life, brought about by the war.

eep down in a South rican gold mine. The ack miners do the work r very low wages, the hite miners supervise for ry high wages

Colonial education

In return for this profound and often painful upheaval in African society, the Africans were supposed to receive the blessings of European civilisation. Some such blessings did come their way. The great process of change, which the colonial system involved, did have some constructive consequences. African civilisations needed to modernise themselves if they were going to be able to stand up to the pressures of the twentieth century: and the colonial system, eve if in a disruptive or unplanned way, sometimes did a little towards that. Many of the European colonial officials worked with a sincere devotion for the benefit of their 'subjects'. And Africans often came to prefer the impartial justice of the better-governed colonies to the sometimes wayward or abusive practices of the own former rulers. The colonial system was often a prison for Africans, but sometimes it also could be a means of entering the modern world. At least in those colonies where there were few or no white settlers, there was a steady eff to introduce the foundations of a modern system of education. This was eagerly welcomed by Africans, especially by those who lived in towns and cities.

Mostly, this colonial education was at the primary level, and reflected the attitudes of ruling classes in Europe towards the working classes in Europe. It wa carried out largely by Christian churches, helped financially by the colonial governments by money from taxes paid by Africans. Only a handful of Africans managed to get any higher education, and often this only turned them into 'second class Europeans'.

Of all the tropical colonies, those of West Africa fared less badly than the other There were no white settlers there to insist on large quantities of government money being spent on the expensive education of their own children, and in any case the colonial system of West Africa was generally less rigid and racist than in other parts of the continent. By 1938, towards the middle of the central colonial period, about 76,000 children were at primary school in the Gold Coast (Ghana) and more than 26,000 in Nigeria, while French West Africa had founded primary schools for more than 25,000 children. In all three regions, as well as Sierra Leone and the Gambia, there were several thousand children in secondary schoo by this time, while Sierra Leone had long possessed a College of Higher Education at Fourah Bay, near the Sierra Leone capital of Freetown. The Belgian in the Congo also opened a lot of primary schools for African children. In the Portuguese colonies there were practically none at all.

Even this small amount of education was given in lessons which taught Africans that they were inferior to Europeans. This was bad for African self-respect, and tended to make Africans think they were helpless without European guidance.

The second major handicap was lack of money for other social services as well as schools. The Europeans who ruled Africa said that each colony must pay for a its own expenses, whether hospitals or whatever it might be, even though the cheap labour of its people meant that foreign companies made big profits and took these profits away to Europe or North America. The colonies, in short, were able to spend only a small part of the money that was made from their labour and natural resources; the rest of the money was taken abroad.

Even though some colonies produced great wealth, their peoples could still no benefit from it. After 1930, for example, the discovery of rich copper mines in

Northern Rhodesia (Zambia) yielded huge profits every year to the foreign companies who owned the mines, and worked them with a small European labour-force and a large African labour-force. Yet when Zambia became independent, in 1964, the country possessed only one secondary school where Africans could study up to 'O' level. The colonial rulers said there was no money for more and better schools. In fact, there was plenty of money. But it was taken abroad every year by foreign companies. This kind of thing happened in many colonies, and to some extent in all colonies.

For this and other such reasons, the blessings of European civilisation that were given to Africans during the colonial period were few and far between: and they were paid for at a high price.

NEW WAYS OF AFRICAN RESISTANCE

The Africans bitterly resisted the conquest of their countries, as we have seen, and their armed resistance continued for a long while. Many colonies were shaken by African revolts, large or small, right into the central colonial period (1920–50).

New forms of resistance began to take shape after the First World War (1914–18). Defeated in war, Africans turned to the making of new weapons of self-defence. These were the weapons of political organisation. Far-seeing leaders began to realise that they would have to develop modern forms of political

The medical doctor James Africanus Horton, of Sierra Leone, who was born in 1835, made a fine career during which he defended the cause of African progress, and died in 1883. He was the author of important books about Africa

Born in the Caribbean island of St Thomas, Edward Blyden became a Liberian diplomat and a leader of black progress. This photo shows him in old age, a year before he died in 1912

struggle. For the most part, these were men who had managed to get modern education in spite of many obstacles, and because of it they now understood th world of their foreign rulers as well as their own African world. Such leaders ha emerged long before the First World War. Some of the most important were J. L Dube and Sol Plaatje of South Africa, J. Africanus Horton of Sierra Leone, Casely Hayford of the Gold Coast (Ghana), and such men as Herbert Macaulay of Lagos, Nigeria. Several were black men from the West Indies who, returning the West African lands of their forefathers, made distinguished careers there. Among these was Edward Blyden who became a Liberian, and had great influence on progressive African thought.

These pioneers were followed by many others in the central colonial period after the First World War. They studied the political ideas and history of their foreign rulers in Europe, and began to apply these ideas to the cause of African progress. The idea of nationalism was perhaps the most important of these. Basically, this was the European idea that each European people or group of peoples, organised in a nation, had the right to rule itself. African leaders began argue with their foreign rulers that what was right for Europeans must also be right for Africans. They argued that the peoples of each colony should form themselves into a new nation, and that these new nations should strive for their freedom.

The influence of this African nationalism grew steadily, but slowly. It was stil only an idea which was held by the 'educated few'; most Africans knew nothin about it, or could not see how it might help them. Little or no progress could be made till after the Second World War (1939–45). After that the situation chang and the cause of African freedom went rapidly ahead in nearly all the colonies.

There were four chief reasons for this improvement in the African situation af the Second World War.

Influence of the Second World War

One reason was that the ideas of African nationalism, especially the idea that Africans had as much right to national freedom as anyone else, became a rallying call for masses of ordinary people in every part of the continent. Thousands of Africans had fought with the Allied armies against the racist dictatorships of Nazi Germany and Fascist Italy, or against the armies of imperialist Japan, which was in its own way as racist as Germany or Italy. These ex-servicemen now came home to their colonies, and added their voices to the rising chorus of political protest against colonial rule that was also racist rule. Thousands of young men and women who had also had the beginnings of a modern education, especially in West Africa, now joined the ranks of political struggle. From being an idea of the few, African nationalism grew into a popular cause.

A second reason was that the Second World War, fought against the extremely racist governments of Germany, Italy and Japan, also became to some extent an anti-racist war. It led among other things to the foundation of the United Nations, a world-wide organisation of states which promised, at least in theory, to defend every people's right to freedom. This also had some influence on the African situation, not least because the United States government, for reasons of its own advantage, had an interest in the weakening of the British and French empires.

A third reason was that the British and the French, the greatest colonial powers in Africa, were in different ways greatly damaged by the Second World War. The French had been defeated. We in Britain could only win at very great cost. One important result was that we had to withdraw from our empire in India; other Asian countries also won their freedom from Britain or other colonial powers. These advances in Asia were encouraging to Africans. They began to press harder for their own freedom.

A fourth reason was that the British, who had the lion's share of colonies in Africa and were also, partly for that reason, the most developed of the colony-holding nations, now began to change their minds about the colonial system. Important sections of our people began to press for an end to the British colonial system. Even those who did not agree with this began to understand that their economic interests need not necessarily suffer if the colonial system was ended.

British governments after the war were pushed hard by the demands of African nationalism, as well as by anti-colonial groups in Britain itself. They began to make carefully-controlled political concessions. Much the same thing happened in France and the French colonies. African nationalists saw their chance, and pressed still harder for political change. All this opened the way for an end to the old colonial system.

INDEPENDENCE

Winning political freedom

The leaders of Africa's struggle for independence from colonial rule, men such as Kwame Nkrumah of Ghana, Houphouët-Boigny of (French) Ivory Coast, Jomo Kenyatta of Kenya, Sékou Touré of (French) Guinea, became the planners and spokesmen for the new nationalist parties and 'congresses' (as such movements were often called). With others like them in Africa north of the Sahara, these men

Three important leaders of modern Africa:

Kwame Nkrumah, of Ghana (died 1972). He led Ghana to independence in 1957 and was one of the great pioneers of the modern idea of all-African unity

Julius Nyerere, of Tanzania, founder of the country's nationalist movement and president of Tanganyika and then of the Union of Tanganyika with Zanzibar, the Union of Tanzania

Jomo Kenyatta, of Kenya, became the country's president when Kenya won its independence in 1963

led the way to colonial freedom along a political road that was never easy to follow, and was often difficult and dangerous.

North of the Sahara the first breakthrough came in 1955 when France, reeling from a major defeat in Vietnam where the French had been fighting to keep their colonial power, gave independence to Tunisia, and then, in 1956, to Morocco. Meanwhile the Egyptians had formed a strong nationalist movement under Gamal Abdul Nasser. This soon brought an end to British military bases in Egypt and the beginning of a new Egyptian independence. Following that, the British also left the Sudan in 1956. Libya, once a colony of defeated Italy, had already become independent in 1951. Only in Algeria was the fight for freedom a long and bloody one. But in 1962, after nearly seven years of harsh colonial warfare, the Algerians were at last able to get rid of French rule.

Most Europeans thought that the pace of Africa's march to political independence would be much slower south of the Sahara. Yet it proved otherwise. In 1957 Kwame Nkrumah led the Gold Coast to independence as Ghana, and in 1958 Sékou Touné achieved the same in Guinea. Then it was only a matter of time before all the other British and French colonies in West Africa became independent states, most of them in 1960 or soon after.

In East and Middle Africa the struggle was longer and more difficult. The Belgians withdrew their political power from the vast Congo in 1960, but in conditions which ensured a great deal of trouble which duly followed. Elsewhere the local white settler communities strongly opposed any political advance for Africans. This opposition was toughest of all in Kenya. Only a great African farmers' rebellion there, the so called 'Mau Mau' of the middle 1950s, in which some 10,000 Africans lost their lives in fighting against the British army and white-settler soldiers, was able to open the gate to African independence. This came in 1963, two years after the independence of Tanganyika (federated with Zanzibar in 1964, as Tanzania), and one year after the independence of Uganda.

Zambia (Northern Rhodesia) and Malawi (Nyasaland) became independent in 1964, but the case was different in Zimbabwe (Southern Rhodesia). Southern Rhodesia was formally a British crown colony. In fact, the local white settlers had been given the right to rule the country in 1923. They ruled it on racist principles. In 1961 these settlers agreed to some political advances for Africans, which would give the Africans majority rule, but only after many years. Most of the Rhodesian settlers thought these small concessions far too great. In 1965 they rebelled against the British Crown, and declared their 'unilateral independence' under a white settler government which at once made racist rule far stricter than before. This settler government brought in racist laws modelled on those of South Africa, where local whites had possessed all the political power since 1910, when

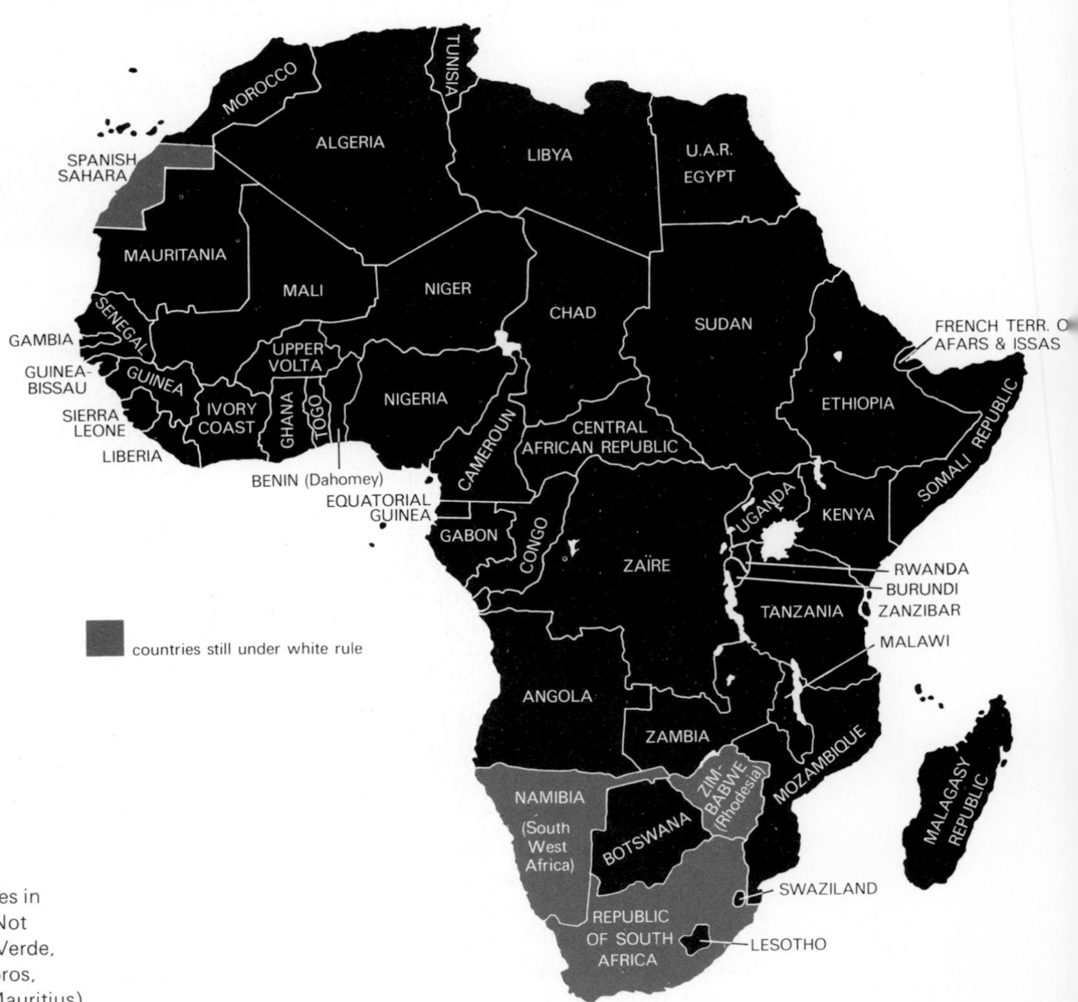

Independent states in Africa in 1977. (Not shown are Cape Verde, São Tomé, Comoros, Seychelles and Mauritius)

South Africa had become an independent country. Zimbabwe Africans began to press for majority rule, since they outnumbered the local whites by a proportion of at least sixteen to one. But the local whites would not agree, and tried to maintain their dictatorship. A long struggle began.

In 1968 the last of the African colonies became independent, except for Djibouti (a small French colony in north-eastern Africa); Rhodesia; the three mainland colonies of Portugal (Angola, Guinea-Bissau, and Mozambique); and the Portuguese-ruled offshore islands of the Cape Verde archipelago, as well as the small islands of São Tomé and Principe; and some very thinly populated Spanish colonies, mostly in the western Sahara.

But in these remaining colonies the situation was also changing fast. In Rhodesia, African political resistance began to gather strength again after the settlers' rebellion in 1965, and was joined early in the 1970s by a new armed resistance. Meanwhile full-scale colonial wars were being fought by the Portuguese against armed independence movements in Angola, Guinea-Bissau and Mozambique.

These Portuguese wars were extremely painful, but by 1970 African resistance was generally gaining the upper hand. This resistance led to big African political advances as well as military gains. In 1974 the Portuguese army finally threw in the sponge, and the political organisations of African resistance formed independent governments. Guinea-Bissau became independent in 1974; Cape Verde, Mozambique, the two islands of São Tomé and Principe, and Angola, in 1975. These victories ended the Portuguese empire in Africa.

The gains of political independence

Africans emerged from all these struggles with a fresh hope and confidence in their own future and in themselves. They had regained a large measure of freedom. The progress they had made could now open the way to further advances.

Independence enabled the Africans to build a new basis of equality, and therefore of friendship, with other peoples in the world, including those of the former empire-holding countries in Europe. Africans were now free to move around their own continent and get to know each other properly. They sent out travellers and representatives to visit their neighbours near and far. Their newly independent governments despatched spokesmen to the United Nations in New York, and to other world assemblies. Increasingly, Africans became aware of belonging to a single 'great community' of people in every part of their continent, whether north or south of the Sahara. They began to see that all the peoples of Africa had large interests in common. These interests could best be served if they acted together. The idea of African unity won new ground. In 1963 the governments of all the former colonial states joined together in forming a 'united nations' organisation of their own. This is called the Organisation of African Unity, or OAU for short. At the same time, the British colonies which became independent countries decided to stay inside the British Commonwealth. Nowadays they play a part in all the joint affairs of the Commonwealth.

The new governments set to work at providing the kind of social services which a modern way of life expects. They began to tackle the everyday problems that the foreign rulers of the colonial system had largely ignored or pushed aside. They got some control of the wealth of their own countries, and began using it for education, medical services, better communications, and much else. They tried to make these improvements on the basis of African needs, and not on the basis of European ideas about African needs. Young men and women began to take courses in science and engineering at new universities and technical colleges, subjects which the colonial rulers had not thought 'necessary' for Africans. The care and treatment of disease were accepted as national responsibilities.

Now that they were free to move into jobs and posts previously kept for Europeans, Africans entered a whole range of new professions. Having their own governments, they built up their own civil services. They used European experts when they had to, but quickly started to train their own men and women for the jobs. As trained people became available, Africans began to manage every aspect of their countries' governments, to plan how their countries' money should be collected and spent, to consider and decide how their countries should develop.

Good for Africans, this was also good for Europeans and others who had previously tended to despise black people. The fact of African independence helped such Europeans and others to free themselves from their racist beliefs about 'black inferiority'. They could learn now that Africa was not a 'savage backwoods' but a continent full of human beings whose hopes and fears, joys and problems, were much the same as those of everyone else. Not all Europeans have learned this yet; but many have. Even the Europeans of Kenya, those who fought most bitterly against African progress in that country, have come to see that their racist beliefs were wrong and foolish.

Independence and its gains solved many problems for the Africans. It gave the whole continent a fresh start. It improved everyday life in a multitude of ways. It lifted away a lot of persecution and annoyance. Not least, it provided a chance to face and deal with other problems, left over from the past, which independence and its gains were not enough to solve.

These other problems, left over from the past, are not about getting rid of foreign rulers and foreign police forces and foreign armies, or about stopping racism, or about giving Africans the opportunity to speak and act for themselves. All that is being dealt with, at least in most of Africa. The unsolved problems which remain are different, and they are also harder. They are about overcoming the limits of nationalism, and the dangers of nationalism. They are about finding new and better ways of political and economic organisation. They are about closing the gap between the few rich and the many poor.

After independence: new problems

Let us have a look at some of these new problems of today. One of them is about the frontiers of the new nations.

The European idea of a state, taken over by the Africans, is that it should consist of a single nation with a frontier round it. Beyond the frontier are other and different nations. Yet this tidy idea of what a state should be was not the idea that the Europeans actually applied in Africa. As these pages have shown, they carved up Africa into fifty colonies according to the push and pull of European interests and rivalries, and not at all according to the interests of the peoples whose countries they invaded. Often, the Europeans simply drew lines on maps, even when they had only the vaguest notion about the peoples and the countries through which the lines were drawn. One European nation said: 'That bit's ours.' Another said: 'All right, then this bit is for us.'

The result was that few of the colonial frontiers made much sense to the people who lived within them. Often the frontiers cut right through this or that people's territory, leaving some under one colonial power and some under another. The Yoruba of western Nigeria, which became a British colony, were cut off from their fellow-Yoruba in Dahomey, which became a French colony. The Makonde of Tanganyika, which became a German and then a British colony, were cut off in the same way from the Makonde of Mozambique, a Portuguese colony. The Kongo people of the Belgian Congo were similarly divided from the Kongo people of Angola. There were many such cases.

Some regions of Africa were enclosed within vast colonies inhabited by many different peoples who had formerly had different states of their own. Such was the case with the Congo Basin. This was claimed by King Leopold of the Belgians: he called it his 'share of the African cake'. And Leopold made good his claim, while knowing almost nothing about the Congo Basin, because the big powers, Britain and France and Germany, could not agree that any one of them should have this enormous piece of Africa. They preferred to give it to a little power, represented by King Leopold, and they let him draw a line around the Congo Basin, no matter what its African populations might think or want. When the Congo (now Zaïre) achieved its political independence in 1960, it was accordingly very difficult to form a united government. It has remained difficult.

Other parts of Africa had been divided into very small colonies, but for the same reason: it happened to suit the European powers that claimed them. So The Gambia took shape as a British colony, some 320 kilometres long, but only 20 to 30 kilometres broad, because the British did not want the French to control the Gambia river, which runs down the middle of those twenty or thirty kilometres. And the people of The Gambia, who for generations had lived in close trading and other relations with their neighbours, found themselves cut off from their historical community with neighbours, on either side of them, who were now in French-ruled Senegal.

Yet these lines on the map could not be simply wished away and replaced by more sensible and useful frontiers. In order to win their political independence, the Africans had to accept the colonial frontiers. They had to conduct their political struggles colony by colony. They had to take the frontiers as they were and they had to turn them, as well as they could, into the frontiers of separate nations-in-the-making.

The best of their leaders saw the disadvantages of having to do this. As long ago as the 1920s there were pioneers of African independence, in the four British colonies of West Africa – Nigeria, Gold Coast (Ghana), Sierra Leone, The Gambia – who called for the federal unity of all four countries. This idea was ahead of its time; besides that, it did not suit British interests. Nothing came of it.

There were other leaders in the French colonies who had the same idea. The French colonial system in West Africa consisted of eight separate colonies – Senegal, Mauretania, Guinea, Soudan, Ivory Coast, Niger, and (after 1948) Upper Volta – with the ex-German colony of Togo forming a ninth. But all these were ruled by a central colonial government in Dakar, capital of Senegal. During their struggles in the 1950s, some leaders of African opinion wanted all these

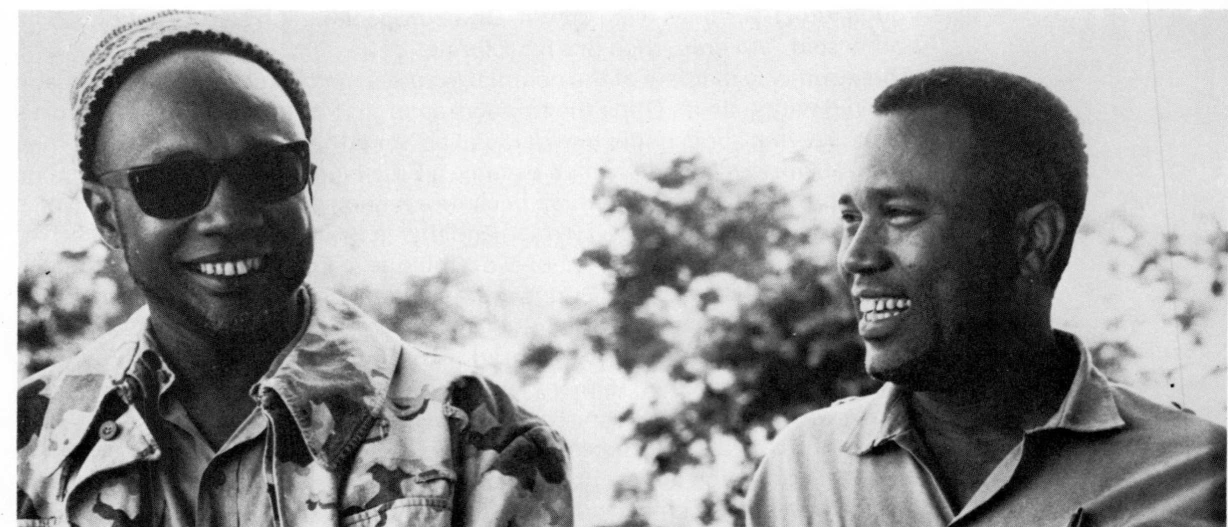

Amilcar Cabral (left), leader of the struggle for national liberation of Guinea-Bissau and Cape Verde against the Portuguese colonial system, with his younger brother, Luiz Cabral. The Africans won this struggle in 1974, but Amilcar was assassinated by agents of the Portuguese dictatorship in 1973. His brother Luiz is the president of independent Guinea-Bissau

The Africans of the Portuguese colonies had to struggle for many years to win their freedom. Women played a full part in those struggles. I took this photo of Teodora Gomes, a women's leader of Guinea-Bissau, during the liberation war which began there in 1963 and ended only in 1974

territories to stay together after independence. 'Let us,' they said, 'turn this colonial union into a federation of united states. In that way we shall be stronger and better able to make progress than if we divide up and go our separate ways.' This idea was not ahead of its time, and it might have worked. But it did not suit French interests, and, once again, nothing came of it.

Two things flowed from this; neither was good for progress. The first was that the frontiers stayed more or less exactly as the colonial powers had drawn them. Small colonies remained small, even though each had far too few people for any real economic advance to be possible. Secondly, there were many disputes or small wars about this or that frontier region. The OAU was able peacefully to end most of these conflicts, but the old frontiers remained. The great belief that Africans could best overcome their problems of development by uniting their strength in big federations, and by other ways of working closely together, overcoming the limits of nationalism, stayed largely a belief on paper.

Overcoming the heritage of the past

A third thing that flowed from the victory of African nationalism also held up progress. This was that the Africans, during the 1960s, began to follow the Europeans in building up, in each new nation, a privileged ruling group or 'boss class'. A few people got hold of a lot of money and political power, but most people stayed as poor and powerless as before. A big 'gap' began to widen between the few who ruled and the many who were ruled. People on different sides of this 'gap' began to look at each other with anger and distrust. This meant trouble, and it quickly came.

Making money in partnership with their 'big brothers' overseas, the new ruling groups tended to become corrupt, irresponsible, and dictatorial. The new situation became another sort of 'colonial situation'. There were many upheavals after about 1963, sometimes to the good, often to the worse. Ordinary people suffered much hardship. Many Asians settled in Africa were among these.

As we saw when reading about the old East African trade with the East, Asians have had an important place in African history. Often, lately, this has become a very hard place. In South Africa, which today has about 700,000 inhabitants of Asian origin (mainly from India), they suffer along with Africans from the racist oppression of South Africa's rulers. Many thousands of East African Asians have also suffered discrimination or expulsion at the hands of African ruling groups, though also because ordinary Africans have understandably resented Asian control of local trade. All this is another part of the colonial heritage, and a sad one.

The real dangers of this colonial heritage, and of a narrow-minded nationalism, began to be understood in some African political parties and governments during the late 1960s and early 1970s. These countries began to give a lead towards new forms of democratic freedom, and towards new methods of democratic control of government. Among these countries struggling for new solutions to the problems and troubles of the past and present were Guinea-Bissau, Mozambique, Angola, Tanzania, Somalia, and Algeria. These began to use their independence so as to battle against poverty and injustice.

All this forms the drama of today. In this book we have taken the long view of history. And in this view all these problems and troubles fall into place as part of Africa's process of change from old and out-of-date ways of community life to new and different ways. These problems are the cliffs and hills that Africa's peoples have to climb now. Some of them have begun the climb. Others have still to make a start. Like all other peoples, they face the challenge of summits of difficulty which have to become summits of success: stages in the long journey from an old civilisation to a better one.

Further reading

The following are books for further reading; material for teachers and pupils are listed separately.

We would wish to acknowledge the help of Margaret Killingray in compiling this list. A more detailed list is available from the School of Oriental and African Studies, University of London.

FOR TEACHERS

Amin, Samir *Neo-Colonialism in West Africa,* Penguin, 1973
Balandier, G. *Daily Life in the Kingdom of the Kongo,* Random House, 1968
Boahen, A. A. *Topics in West African History,* Longman, 1966
Clark, J. D. *The Prehistory of Africa,* Thames and Hudson, 1970
Davidson, B. *The Africans: an entry to cultural history,* Penguin, 1973
Davidson, B. *Africa in History: themes and outlines,* Paladin, 1974
Davidson, B. *In the Eye of the Storm, Angola's People,* Penguin, 1975
Davidson, B. *Old Africa Rediscovered,* rev. edn, Gollancz, 1959; Longman (paperback), 1970
Davidson, B. *Black mother: the African slave trade,* Gollancz 1961; Longman (paperback), 1965
Davidson, B. *The African Past: chronicles from antiquity to modern times,* Penguin, 1966
Fage, J. D. *West Africa: an introductory survey,* Cambridge University Press, 1969
Freeman Grenville, J. H. S. *A Modern Atlas of African History,* Rex Collings, 197
Hopkins, A. C. *An Economic History of West Africa,* Longman, 1973
Kiewiet, C. W. de *A History of South Africa,* Oxford University Press, 1950
Nkrumah, K. *Autobiography,* Nelson, 1957
Nyerere, J. K. *Freedom and Unity,* Oxford University Press, 1966
Oliver, R. and Fage, J. D. *A Short History of Africa,* Penguin, 1975
Shinnie, P. M. *Ancient African Kingdoms,* Edward Arnold, 1965

For those who want a handy series for narrative and reference within a general series for secondary schools:
The Growth of African Civilization in five volumes—

Omer Cooper, J. D. and others. *The Nineteenth Century to the Partition,* Longman, 1968
Ayendele E. A. and others. *The late Nineteenth Century to the Present Day,* Longman, 1971
Davidson, B. *East and Central Africa to the Late Nineteenth Century,* Longman, 1967
Davidson, B. *A History of West Africa to 1800,* Longman, 1965
Webster, J. B. and Boahen, A. A. *West Africa Since 1800,* Longman, 1967

FOR PUPILS

General books

African Encyclopaedia for Schools and Colleges, Oxford University Press, 1974
Chijioke, F. A. *Ancient Africa,* Longman, 1966
Curtis, A. *Africa,* Oxford Children's Reference Library, 1969
Davidson, B. *Guide to African History,* George Allen and Unwin, 1963
Encyclopaedia of Africa, Macdonald, 1976
Halladay, E. *The Emergent Continent: Africa in the nineteenth century,* Benn's World History, 1972
Killingray, D. *A Plague of Europeans: westerners in Africa since 1500,* Penguin, 1974
Lacy, L. A. *Black Africa on the Move*, Franklin Watts, 1972
Needham, D. E. *Iron Age to Independence,* Longman, 1974

There is also an African History journal produced by Longman for use in secondary schools called *Tarikh.*

Topic books

Elliott, K. *Benin,* Cambridge University Press, 1973
Fynn, J. A. *A Junior History of Ghana,* Longman, 1975
Killingray, D. *Samori Touré: Warrior King,* Hulton Educational, 1973
Killingray, D. *Olaudah Equiano and the Slave Trade,* Hulton Educational, 1974
McWilliam, H. O. A. *Muhammad and the World of Islam,* (Then and There Series), Longman, 1977
Sheppard, E. J. *Ancient Egypt,* (Then and There Series), Longman, 1960

There are some booklets on Africa for use at C.S.E. level and below in the *Making the Modern World Series*, Longman, 1972

Ripley, P. *Kenyatta*
Sanderson, F. *Nasser*
Williams, B. *South Africa*

There are three short booklets for the middle school years in the *World History Programme*, Harrap, 1974

Addison, J. *Traditional Africa*
Killingray, D. *Nyerere and Nkrumah*
Killingray, D. *The Slave Trade*

Heroes, stories, myths and legends

Arnott, K. *African Myths and Legends,* Oxford University Press, 1962
Mitchison, N. *African Heroes,* Bodley Head, 1968

Longman's *Makers of African History* series includes biographies of Shaka, King of the Zulu, and Queen Nzinga, a seventeenth century Angolan Queen.

Heinemann African historical biographies cover a wide range of subjects including Khama of Botswana, Menelik of Ethiopia, Nana of the Niger Delta and Mosheshwe of Lesotho.

Oxford University Press have a series which includes, Shaka, and Albert Luthuli as well as Khama and Mosheshwe.

For the more advanced reader the Heinemann *African Writers* series, numbering over 180 volumes, includes novels, poetry and autobiography.

Packs

African History Themes: a classroom pack, written for ILEA schools, with folders on food, work, family life, village and town; containing slides, photographs, worksheets and a tape. The folders can also be bought separately. For lower secondary use, Heinemann, 1974.

Schools Council Integrated Studies Project: *Living Together.* A pack containing number of sheets dealing with the history and culture of the Manding of West Africa. It includes work on Samori Touré, Sundiata and Mansa Musa, early Emperors of Mali, and a tape on which extracts from the oral history of Mali are told. A teacher's guide to the use of this pack and others in the same series is also available, Oxford University Press, 1974.

Index